Horace T. Ward

Desegregation of the University of Georgia,
Civil Rights Advocacy, and Jurisprudence

THE HONORABLE HORACE T. WARD

HORACE T. WARD

*Desegregation of The University of Georgia,
Civil Rights Advocacy, and Jurisprudence*

BY MAURICE C. DANIELS

Foreword by Horace T. Ward

CLARK ATLANTA UNIVERSITY PRESS
ATLANTA, GEORGIA • 2001

The contents of this publication were developed under a grant from the Department of Education. However, these contents do not necessarily represent the policy of the Department of Education, and you should not assume endorsement by the federal government.

The paper used in this publication meets the minimum requirements of American National Standard for Information Sciences-Permanence of Paper for Printed Library Materials, ANSI 239-48-1984.

Cover photograph of Horace T. Ward:
Courtesy of Elson Alexander, 7571 Altura Blvd., Buena Park, CA 90620.
Permission granted for publication only.

Frontispiece photograph of Horace T. Ward:
Courtesy of Gittings, 3500 Peachtree Rd., NE, Atlanta, GA 30326.
Permission granted for publication only.

Design and typography by True Designs, Atlanta, GA.

Library of Congress Control Number: 2001 131658

ISBN: 0-9668555-3-1

To my father, Eddie Daniels, Sr.

and to the memory of my mother, Maggie C. Daniels,
and my brother, La-Fronzo Daniels,

and to all the unsung persons
who fought for social justice

Contents

List of Illustrations

(Following page 128)

Foreword

By Horace T. Ward

D r. Maurice Daniels, while focusing on my life and career, deals with an important part of our history in a scholarly and comprehensive way. His book spans over fifty years, beginning with the struggle to desegregate the University of Georgia and related matters, continuing with the aftermath of the desegregation, a long process in which often I happen to have played a substantial role. Dr. Daniels treats both the general history of desegregation and civil rights efforts and the lives and careers of the principal players. The material in the book provided the basis for a television documentary that has been presented on public television in Georgia.

In interesting and thorough detail, the book outlines significant facts involving persons and events, many of which might have remained unknown except to the participants. In so doing, the lives and efforts of the persons who played key roles in the long and hard struggle are highlighted. I am pleased to have been included in that number.

The saga recounted in this book is only a segment of the ongoing civil rights movement by black citizens to secure equal rights and justice in this country. The Georgia segment began quietly in September 1950, when in search of a legal education, I applied for admission to the law school at the University of Georgia. Although I was determined and committed, the journey turned out to be much more difficult than I anticipated.

As the book reveals, conditions in 1950 were quite different from the present in Georgia, particularly regarding equal rights for black citizens. Herman Talmadge was the governor of Georgia and had been elected on a platform to maintain segregation in public education. Also, it was before the 1954 landmark decision of the United States Supreme Court in *Brown v. Board of Education*,[1] and the arrival of Dr. Martin Luther King, Jr., as the preeminent civil rights leader. Consequently, as Dr. Daniels's book shows, the legal efforts to desegregate higher public education in Georgia required more than ten years, beginning with my own, ultimately unsuccessful quest, and culminating in victory with the admission of Charlayne Hunter and Hamilton Holmes to the University of Georgia in 1961. The legal phase of this protracted struggle required the filing of three lawsuits in the federal courts—*Ward v. Regents* (1957), *Hunt v. Arnold* (1959), and *Holmes v. Danner* (1961).[2] Among the factors not commonly known are the tremendous amount of resources of time, energy, and money expended. Also, the emotional strain on the plaintiffs and their parents was staggering. These cases required three sets of courageous plaintiffs and skillful lawyers, together with dedicated parents and diligent supporters in the community.

The efforts of the plaintiffs and their supporters were met by determined opposition from state and university officials in terms of delays, new admission requirements, and legal defenses. Since state and university officials did not want to meet the issue of race head on, the plaintiffs' backgrounds and personal lives were investigated in an effort to find anything that might be used to disqualify them. A startling fact with respect to all of the black applicants was the insistent testimony in court by university officials that race was not a factor in the denial of admission. The irony of the situation was that plaintiffs' lawyers were required to go to great lengths to prove a fact that everyone already knew—that race was, of course, the primary factor. Dr. Benjamin E. Mays, for example, in his autobiography *Born to Rebel*,[3] stated that he was stunned and shocked to see high university officials testify in the *Ward* case that race was not a factor in the denial of my application.

Regarding my application, both sides were laboring under major misconceptions. I initially thought that I might be admitted to the law school without the necessity of court action based on my qualifications and the fact that the Supreme Court of the United States had struck down segregation at the University of Texas law school in the case of *Sweatt v. Painter* in June 1950.[4] The continued misconception of state and university officials was that I was not a bona fide candidate for admission to the law school, but was a "foot soldier" for the National Association for the Advancement of Colored People (NAACP) in its quest to break down segregation, and, moreover, was being paid for the job.

My optimism was short-lived as university officials formulated new guidelines and requirements, which led to the filing of the lawsuit contending that I had been denied admission on the basis of race and color. That lawsuit was eventually tried in federal court and dismissed on technical grounds, without reaching the merits of why I had not been admitted. Judge Frank Hooper stated that I had not exhausted administrative remedies and had abandoned my application. In my opinion, this was an erroneous decision, as the new requirements were adopted after I applied. Also, later case law held that state administrative remedies need not be exhausted in civil rights cases.[5] My long, drawn-out case, though unsuccessful, offered encouragement to other applicants and served as a foundation for later cases by pointing out pitfalls to be avoided. In the meantime I enrolled in the law school at Northwestern University from which I graduated with a J.D. degree in January 1959 (proving, at least, that I was a bona fide candidate and possessed the ability to successfully study law).

In addition to the efforts of the applicants and plaintiffs, this book ably describes the vital contributions of several courageous attorneys and community leaders. One prominent participant was the late Dr. William Madison Boyd, a professor of political science at Atlanta University and state president of the NAACP conference of Georgia. Dr. Boyd, who was my mentor and advisor, personally traveled the state seeking to raise money for legal expenses in my case.

The skillful black lawyers representing the plaintiffs in the Georgia cases included Thurgood Marshall, Robert Carter, Constance Baker Motley, A. T. Walden, E. E. Moore, and Donald Hollowell, with Hollowell and Motley litigating in all three. Both I and Vernon Jordan, now a prominent lawyer and investment banker, got our start in the law working on the *Holmes* case. It is clear from the record that these black lawyers were equal to the task; moreover, the same was true in various courtrooms of the South, where black lawyers won their cases, demonstrating that they matched white lawyers in intellect, education, and skills.

Also set forth in this book are the positions taken and the sacrifices made by a few white students at the University of Georgia, particularly the editors of the *Red and Black*, the student newspaper. They resigned their positions to avoid censorship for supporting my application and desegregation of the university. A similar fate awaited the one law professor at the university, James Lenoir, who opposed what he considered improper obstacles to my application— at the time a voice speaking in the wilderness and admirable for its integrity.

On a more positive note, Dr. Daniels's book points out that the plaintiffs became successful in their chosen fields. The late Hamilton Holmes graduated from the University of Georgia as a Phi Beta Kappa member, later finished Emory University medical school, and became a fine orthopedic surgeon. Charlayne Hunter, following her graduation, became an outstanding journalist, both in the press and on television, and is now the CNN bureau chief in South Africa. The first black graduate of the University of Georgia was Mary Frances Early. Following the court order in *Holmes v. Danner*, she subsequently joined Hamilton and Charlayne at the University of Georgia, and presently heads the music department at Clark Atlanta University. And, of course, I was privileged to move on to a long and rewarding career.

My career is covered in considerable detail in the book. Initially I joined the Hollowell law firm in Atlanta and participated in several leading civil rights cases. Thereafter, while continuing the practice of law, I was elected to the state senate of Georgia, as the second black senator since Reconstruction. My career, although not my societal and legal concerns, changed in 1974 when I was appointed by Governor Jimmy Carter to the Civil Court of Fulton County. Some two and a half years later I was promoted by Governor George Busbee to the Superior Court of Fulton County. In December 1979, by appointment of President Jimmy Carter and confirmation of the United States Senate, I was sworn in as a judge on the United States District Court. This book shows that as a federal judge, I have handled several notable cases, with the *Jan Kemp* case against the University of Georgia officials perhaps the best known.[6]

In October 2000 I was invited to the law school at the University of Georgia to deliver the John A. Sibley lecture and to spend a day meeting with faculty and students. Another salutary occasion was the fortieth anniversary celebration of the desegregation of the University of Georgia on January 9, 2001, at which Charlayne Hunter-Gault was the keynote speaker. During the celebration, university officials praised the desegregation effort by Holmes, Hunter, and others for creating a climate that has allowed the University of Georgia to become one of the top twenty research universities in the country. The highlight of the occasion was the renaming of the Academic Building on the university campus as the Holmes-Hunter Academic Building. Toward the end of his book, Dr. Daniels discusses the present level of desegregation at the University of Georgia and provides a critical evaluation based on current fact and circumstances.

An interesting sidelight of the protracted *Ward* case is that four of the persons involved in that litigation became federal judges, including three of my attorneys and myself. Thurgood Marshall was appointed a judge on the United States Court of Appeals for the Second Circuit and later a justice on the Supreme Court of the United States. Constance Baker Motley, Robert Carter, and I were appointed to the United States District Court. The other two lawyers representing me, A. T. Walden and Donald Hollowell, were equally qualified for similar appointments, and should have been so rewarded. Nonetheless, their courageous litigation for civil rights over several decades made its mark, and I am pleased their achievements are documented in this book.

I would like to think that I have followed in the footsteps and shared the journey of such great civil rights lawyers. I have certainly given my best efforts to this task, and if they have served to advance the yet unfinished struggle for equal justice for all, then I am amply rewarded.

ENDNOTES

[1] *Brown v. Board of Education*, 347 U.S. 483 (1954).

[2] *Ward v. Regents*, 191 F. Supp. 491 (N.D. Ga. 1957); *Hunt v. Arnold*, 172 F. Supp. 847 (N.D.Ga. 1959); *Holmes v. Danner*, 195 F. Supp. 394 (M.D. Ga. 1961).

[3] Benjamin E. Mays, *Born to Rebel* (New York: Charles Scribner's Sons, 1971).

[4] *Sweatt v. Painter*, 339 U.S. 629 (1950).

[5] *McNeese v. Board of Education*, 373 U.S. 688 (1963). This case held that when relief is sought in civil rights cases, it is not necessary that plaintiffs exhaust state administrative remedies, if such remedies are inadequate.

[6] *Kemp v. Ervin*, 651 F. Supp. 495 (N.D. Ga. 1986). In this case, Dr. Kemp, an English teacher, sued university officials, charging a violation of free speech rights. She was successful in winning a large monetary award and was reinstated in her position.

Preface and Acknowledgements

My interest in this research originated as a result of a conversation I had with eminent civil rights attorney Donald L. Hollowell and his wife Louise Hollowell, Professor of English (Emeritus) at Morris Brown College. I had the opportunity to escort the Hollowells on several occasions beginning in the early 1990s when they visited the University of Georgia (UGA) campus to attend the annual Holmes/Hunter lecture series, which commemorated the admission of the first two African American students at UGA— Hamilton Holmes and Charlayne Hunter. During these occasions, they shared information with me concerning some of their poignant experiences in the civil rights movement. One story related to the contributions of a relatively unrecognized trailblazer in the battle to desegregate colleges and universities in Georgia: Horace T. Ward.

Their revelations made such a forceful impression that I began to seek additional information concerning Horace Ward's contributions to the desegregation of the University of Georgia. As an aspiring civil rights scholar, I was embarrassed not to know more about this man who had helped pave the way for the desegregation of the flagship university in my home state and who later became a noted federal judge. I initially sought to locate library sources simply to educate myself about Horace Ward and found few that provided any detailed information on Ward. Colleagues I consulted had not heard of him or, if they had, knew little about his role in the movement for social justice.

Ward, despite his many accomplishments, remains a relatively unsung hero. Because of the richness and compelling nature of the story that Hollowell eagerly shared with me, and because I felt it was important for Ward's history to be told, I was inspired to research and write this book on this remarkable man who had fought to desegregate the university where I held a faculty position, and subsequently had gone on to a distinguished, history-making career as an attorney and jurist.

I am especially grateful to Federal Judge Horace Ward, who at Hollowell's request agreed to an initial interview with me in 1994. I interviewed Ward numerous times and he has reviewed draft chapters of this manuscript and provided important research materials; his cooperation, support, and constructive criticism were invaluable to me. Despite his suggested revisions, I appreciate the fact that he always insisted on my right to editorial freedom in developing the manuscript based on my assessment of the historical events. Nonetheless, although I tried to maintain strict objectivity in this process, I labored on this project with the realization that Judge Ward has the authority to dispatch federal marshals.

My first two interviews with Hollowell and Ward began a process that later resulted in interviews with Federal Judge Constance Baker Motley, Federal Judge William A. Bootle, Dr. Hamilton Holmes, Sr., Vernon Jordan, former U.S. Senator Herman Talmadge, former Governor Ernest Vandiver, and many other significant figures in the battle to desegregate Georgia's colleges and universities. I owe a great debt of gratitude to Donald and Louise Hollowell, who helped launch this study and introduced or guided me to many other civil rights veterans whom I interviewed. Equally important to telling this story were the interviews with persons who have not shared the limelight for their civil rights crusades and are not public figures, but played vital roles in the civil rights movement. These include Reverend Van J. Malone, Gene Britton, Chester Davenport, Jr., Priscilla Arnold Davis, Mary Frances Early, Myra Payne Elliott, Jesse

Hill, Alfred Killian, Archibald Killian, Walter Lundy, Betty Mapp, and several others who are identified in this book.

A special debt of gratitude is owed to Diane Miller for her skillful editiorial assistance and for supplying much practical advice. I am also indebted to Bryndis Roberts for her inspiration, wise counsel, and helpful criticism related to my analysis of the legal cases covered in this manuscript, and her perceptive editorial recommendations. Derrick Alridge's knowledge of educational history and policy helped me to broaden the scope of this manuscript; his friendship and scholarship made this work more enjoyable, challenging, and stimulating.

The initial interviews for this study were made possible by the Georgia Center for Continuing Education and the University of Georgia School of Social Work. I thank my friend and colleague, producer Janice Reaves, who encouraged this project from its inception. Her brilliant skills and work ethic helped to bring this project to fruition. After sharing my vision about a PBS television documentary on Horace Ward and the desegregation of the University of Georgia, Janice proposed the project to Georgia Center television services director Jim Shehane, who approved production services for the two-part documentary that has aired on Georgia Public Television several times. Thanks also to executive consultant Bryndis Roberts; co-producer George Rodrigues; scriptwriters Greg Morrison, La Geris Bell, and Valerie White; academic adviser Derrick Alridge; and narrator Julian Bond for their help in bringing this documentary to public television.

This study could not have been completed without the assistance of several research assistants: Victoria Seals, Kimberly Miller, Valerie D. White, Valencia Jackson, Kenneth Cooke, Geneva Wiggs, Sha-Rhonda Adams, Tracey Ford, Cherry Collier, and Andrea Heath; much appreciation also to Sharon Lane, Judge Ward's administrative assistant. I also must extend thanks to the archivists and librarians who supported my research: archivist Charles Freeney and other staff of the Atlanta University Center Robert Woodruff Library, and archivists Charles Reeves, National Archives-Southeast Region; Linda Tadic and Nancy Smallwood, University of Georgia Peabody Collection; Peter Roberts, Georgia State University Special Collections; and John Lovett, Oklahoma University Western History Collection. I also obtained valuable sources for this project from the Atlanta History Center, Auburn Avenue Research Library on African American Culture and History, Atlanta Bar Association, Columbus State University Simon Schwob Memorial Library, Emory University Robert Woodruff Library, Emory University School of Medicine Library, Georgia Department of Archives and History, NAACP Legal Defense and Educational Fund, Inc., University of Texas at Austin Center for American History, University of Georgia Libraries, and University System of Georgia Board of Regents.

In addition, Betty Boyd Mapp and William Boyd, Jr., have my thanks for the many original documents shared with me related to the civil rights efforts of William Madison Boyd. My sincere gratitude to Robert Lenoir and Katie Lenoir Knepper, who supplied voluminous research materials and photographs from the papers of their father, James J. Lenoir. I wish to thank also Walter Lundy for his "pack rat instinct" in saving scores of original documents related to the journalistic controversy surrounding Ward's admission. I thank him for loaning the original documents to me for research on this project. The Walter A. Lundy Collection has recently been donated to the University of Georgia Richard B. Russell Library for Political Research and Studies.

I am indebted to my University of Georgia colleagues who extended valuable support and insights to this project, especially Katheryn Davis, Letha See, Cheryl Davenport Dozier, Jeanelle Muckle, and Geraldine Jackson-White. Finally, I thank my wife Renee for her encouragement and understanding, and our children Carrin, Lauren, Nicole, and Maya, who inspired me in more ways than they will ever know. I also thank all the other family and special friends who inspired and supported me in this project.

Maurice C. Daniels
Athens, Georgia, May 2001

Introduction

The 1950s and 1960s were a turbulent time for this nation, and nowhere was this more apparent than in the battle over segregation in the South. In 1964, confronting a nation marred by dissension and racial turmoil, President Lyndon Johnson pushed the Civil Rights Act through Congress. On July 2, 1964, speaking in a nationally televised broadcast, Johnson declared that under the Civil Rights Act, "those who are equal before God shall now also be equal in the polling booths, in the classrooms, in the factories, and in hotels, restaurants, movie theaters, and other places that provide service to the public."[1] The act forbade discrimination in employment, public accommodations, public facilities, and federally assisted programs. In addition, the act conferred jurisdiction to the federal courts to provide injunctive relief against discrimination and authorized the U.S. Attorney General to initiate lawsuits to protect constitutional rights.[2]

Less than one year later, spurred by the bloody events surrounding the historic civil rights march from Selma to Montgomery, President Johnson proposed the Voting Rights Act to prohibit ongoing discrimination in voting. In his address to a joint session of Congress on March 15, 1965, Johnson proclaimed that: "with the outrage of Selma still fresh, I came down to this Capitol . . . and asked the Congress and the people for swift and for sweeping action to guarantee to every man and woman the right to vote."[3] An important feature of the Voting Rights Act required a federal court in Washington, D.C., to approve any changes in voting rules before they could be instituted at the state or local level. This feature of the act was targeted at Southern states and counties that regularly changed voting rules to deny black[4] citizens the right to vote.[5] On August 6, 1965, President Johnson signed the Voting Rights Act. Afterward, speaking from the President's Room off the Capitol Rotunda, Johnson stated that the act was:

> . . . one of the most monumental laws in the entire history of American freedom . . . It is nothing less than granting every American Negro his freedom to enter the mainstream of American life. . . . For centuries of oppression and hatred have already taken their toll. It can be seen throughout our land in men without skills, in children without fathers, in families that are imprisoned in slums and in poverty.[6]

Leading up to these watershed events, from 1954 to 1965, the civil rights movement in the United States gained momentum. Public colleges and universities in the Deep South became a major battlefront for blacks to assert their constitutional rights. In 1956 the courageous Autherine Lucy sought to enter the all-white University of Alabama but was driven from the campus by rioting whites. In 1962 James Meredith encountered a violent mob in his bid to enroll in the University of Mississippi. In 1963, in another bold challenge to break the bonds of segregation in Alabama, James Hood and Vivian Malone came face-to-face with segregationist Governor George C. Wallace. As television cameras recorded the confrontation, Wallace bodily blocked their entrance to the University of Alabama.

With equal fervor, blacks challenged segregation in primary and secondary schools. In 1958 the "Little Rock Nine" achieved an important milestone in the struggle against social injustice when they enrolled at Central High School in Little Rock, Arkansas. After being admitted under a U.S. Supreme Court order, the nine black students entered the school amid violent and hostile resistance.

Following a request from Little Rock's mayor for federal intervention, President Dwight Eisenhower federalized the Arkansas National Guard and ordered the Secretary of Defense to use whatever means necessary to prevent further obstruction of the Supreme Court order. As a result of President Eisenhower's order, units of the 101st Airborne intervened and established order around Central High School. Two years later, after a protracted court battle between Louisiana officials and the New York-based NAACP Legal Defense and Educational Fund (LDF),[7] federal marshals escorted four black girls into two public white elementary schools in New Orleans. Violence erupted and riotous demonstrations marred the enrollment of the black students in the formerly all-white Louisiana schools.[8]

The LDF filed dozens of legal cases challenging public officials' massive resistance to desegregating public schools and their refusal to enforce court-ordered desegregation. The turning point in the movement for equal educational opportunities in public schools, and the key case that bolstered the panoply of LDF cases, was the LDF's victory in the landmark 1954 *Brown v. Board of Education* decision. Thurgood Marshall, chief counsel to the LDF, who later became a Supreme Court justice, led the LDF legal team in the case, in which the Supreme Court overturned the historic 1896 *Plessy v. Ferguson* decision that legalized state-sanctioned segregation.[9] It was in this context that a young Baptist preacher, Martin Luther King, Jr., emerged as a national civil rights leader. King began to galvanize a crusade for social justice and human rights that ultimately gained worldwide support and altered the course of American history.[10]

King's mobilization of black Americans as well as white supporters helped the civil rights movement reach a pinnacle with the 1963 March on Washington, where more than two hundred and fifty thousand civil rights protesters rallied for social justice. While the March itself did not result in immediate social change, the triumphant event engendered a sense of hope that the nation was not blind to the blatant social injustice suffered by blacks. Moreover, the diverse mass of marchers, representing a multitude of different spheres of American society, showed the nation that the civil rights movement was firmly grounded and that there was no turning back on the road to a more just society. Civil rights veteran Bayard Rustin, who helped direct the planning of the March, remembered, "The March took place because the Negro needed allies . . . The March was not a Negro action. It was an action by Negroes and whites together. Not just the leaders of the Negro organizations, but leading Catholic, Protestant, and Jewish spokesmen called the people into the street. And Catholics, Protestants, and Jews, white and black, responded."[11]

The courage of these foot soldiers trumpeted in the national media, the NAACP's legal victories against segregation, and King's nonviolent revolution all played pivotal roles in securing the passage of the Civil Rights Act of 1964 and the Voting Rights Act of 1965. Yet, even before any of these nationally televised, historic events transpired, a lesser-known figure from La Grange, Georgia, Horace Taliaferro Ward, began his personal crusade for social justice. Ward's pioneering battle against racial segregation at a flagship university in the Deep South established crucial precedents and helped to lay the groundwork for subsequent victories in the struggle to defeat Jim Crow in Deep South colleges and universities. Ward's challenge to segregation occurred when the so-called "hard core states" of Alabama, Georgia, Mississippi, and South Carolina not only rejected desegregation in their tax-supported institutions, but moved generally toward increasingly rigid segregation through official actions and legislation.[12] By looking at the historical milestones that followed Ward's challenge to segregation, which began in 1950, we can appreciate the real significance of Ward's trail-blazing battle. Although his valiant contributions to the civil rights movement have not previously been chronicled, they are significant—the courageous deeds of an "unsung hero," —and his story is compelling.

Deep in Ward's character was a yearning for personal uplift and a desire to aid the causes of human rights and social justice. In 1979 President James Earl Carter appointed Ward to the United States District Court for the Northern District of Georgia. Ironically, this was the same federal district court in which, twenty-two years earlier, Ward was the plaintiff in *Ward v. Regents* to gain admission to the law school at the University of Georgia. After university officials rejected his application because of his race, Ward began a long and arduous struggle to break down racial barriers and enroll in the school, a struggle that in turn paved the way a decade later for the legal victory of desegregation of the University of Georgia. The untold story of his dream of becoming a lawyer and his fight to defeat segregation is of powerful intrinsic interest in the history of civil rights in the United States.

This study traces Ward's efforts to enter the all-white public law school; the panoply of legal and political maneuvers used by state and university officials to block his entrance; his lawsuit against the regents to seek admission to the law school; the influence of his advocacy, as a lawyer and state senator, on subsequent civil rights efforts; and his culminating career as a state and federal judge.

An extensive review of the literature reveals that no book has been published that records the contributions of Horace T. Ward or explores his impact on the civil rights movement. Moreover, although the desegregation of colleges and universities in Georgia preceded the highly publicized desegregation of universities in Alabama and Mississippi, no book has chronicled the history and legal cases related to the desegregation of colleges and universities in Georgia. This research study documents the contributions and influence of a pivotal figure in a landmark battle for civil rights.

In developing this study, I have used various historical documents that provide an original and substantive examination of the subject matter. These materials include various library and archival documents, the personal papers of many public officials who opposed desegregation of Georgia's colleges and universities, as well as the papers of prominent civil rights leaders who battled segregation in Georgia's educational system. Analysis of federal trial records secured from the National Archives provides detailed insight into the strategies and legal arguments on both sides of the historic debate on segregation in public higher education. The study also incorporates important information from a variety of newspaper sources.

Newspaper reports from major white-owned papers such as the *Atlanta Journal* and the *Atlanta Constitution* are certainly essential, but articles published in black-owned newspapers such as the *Atlanta Daily World* and the *Atlanta Inquirer* provide a more detailed view of events, and from a black perspective.[13]

Personal interviews with key individuals involved in this struggle enrich our understanding of the events leading to the desegregation of colleges and universities in Georgia. These interviews bring to life the struggle from the insiders' perspectives. The book includes insights from Federal Judge Horace T. Ward, based on several interviews conducted with him and on personal papers that he shared with the author. Persons interviewed also include leaders of the effort to sustain segregation and, conversely, legal experts and civil rights leaders who actively sought to dismantle segregation. Some of the notable persons who shared their insights include civil rights lawyer Donald Hollowell, who became chief counsel in the *Ward* and *Holmes* cases; Federal Judge Constance Baker Motley, who represented the New York-based NAACP Legal Defense and Educational Fund in Ward's and other desegregation cases; Federal Judge William Bootle, who presided over the historic *Holmes* case; the late Dr. Hamilton Holmes, who joined Charlayne Hunter as a complainant in the landmark case that resulted in the enrollment of the first two black students at the University of Georgia; Attorney Chester Davenport, Jr., the first black graduate of the University of Georgia Law School; Chief Justice Robert Benham of the Supreme Court of Georgia; business leader and civil rights activist Jesse Hill; Attorney Vernon Jordan, who clerked for the Hollowell law firm during the early 1960s; Attorney E. Freeman Leverett, a former associate state attorney general who defended state officials in *Ward* and other desegregation cases; newspaper columnist Bill Shipp, who as a student editor wrote a series of articles supporting desegregation for the University of Georgia's *Red and Black* and has gone on to professional journalistic distinction; and last, but not least, former Governors Herman Talmadge and Ernest Vandiver, both of whom ardently defended segregation during their terms of office.

In this study of Ward's saga and the surrounding events, Chapter 1 begins by discussing the origins of the NAACP as an organization dedicated to the fight against racial segregation and discrimination. As the NAACP evolved, it directed its focus not only toward challenging the whites-only barriers, but also toward developing campaigns against lynching and other forms of violence against blacks; however, its major focuses were on the achievement of civil and political rights for blacks and the eradication of segregation. In tracing the organization's development, this chapter discusses how the NAACP's victories in its legal challenges to Jim Crow propelled the organization to adopt legal redress as a major strategy in the battle for civil and political rights. Finally, the chapter examines the NAACP's strategies to defeat segregation and how public higher education became a focal point in the battle for social justice in states such as Maryland, Missouri, Oklahoma, and Texas.

In Chapter 2 I take up the story of Ward's early development and his upbringing in a segregated Southern community. Ward was the beneficiary of a family and community that pushed him to maximize his keen abilities. The chapter shows how various forces converged to influence his work ethic and willingness to take on social responsibility. Within the consortium of respected black colleges where Ward attended college and graduate school, he was exposed to great thinkers and civil rights leaders who provided him with a traditional liberal arts education, while also insisting that he and other students join in the struggle for social, economic, and political equality for blacks. These scholar/activists challenged their students to use their talents and abilities for racial uplift in a society marred by state-sanctioned oppression of blacks.

It soon became clear in this research process that the story of Ward's ambition to become a lawyer and his struggle for social justice is intertwined with the stories of many persevering, lesser-known persons who fought long, hard struggles against racial oppression. It is not possible to do justice to these persons in a work whose main subject is Horace Ward. However, in chronicling Ward's story, I have tried to shed some light on those unheralded persons who influenced Ward and made significant contributions to the civil rights movement. This consideration of largely unknown and often overlooked leaders and events in the civil rights movement reveals how social change is the coalescence of many activities, persons, groups, and communities.

Chapter 3 explores the intransigence of Georgia officials in their response to white students who supported Ward's admission to the UGA law school. The chapter especially focuses upon the efforts of the editors of the University of Georgia student newspaper, the *Red and Black*, who defended their right to free speech after raising the ire of major political forces in Georgia through editorials denouncing segregation and supporting Ward's enrollment. State officials' fury with the student editors over their support for desegregation prompted their resignations from the paper. Despite an outpouring of support from prominent newspaper editors and citizens throughout the country, opposition to the students came from the highest levels of state government, including the governor, the university president, and the university regents.

While obstructionist tactics continued to delay Ward's enrollment, on August 12, 1953, the U.S. Selective Service System ordered Ward to report for induction to the armed forces.[14] On September 9, 1953, just thirty days before his federal court case was scheduled to begin, the army inducted him, a "coincidence" questioned by Ward's attorneys and other supporters.[15] The federal judge in the case ordered the *Ward* trial removed from the court docket indefinitely. White officials expressed jubilance that Ward was, at least temporarily, no longer a threat to their cherished way of life.

While Ward served his country, including a tour of duty in Korea, the U.S. Supreme Court heard the *Brown v. Board of Education* case. On May 17, 1954, in a unanimous decision authored by Chief Justice Earl Warren, the Court declared racial segregation in schools unconstitutional. Despite this landmark ruling, resistance to segregation grew even stronger in Georgia. In fact, the *Brown* ruling led supporters of segregation in the South to galvanize massive resistance to any form of racial integration. Political leaders in the former

Confederate states denounced the *Brown* ruling and vowed to defy the Court decision. Chapter 3 also examines the *Brown* case, describes the resistance that this case engendered, and explores how the momentum generated by *Brown* impacted Ward's reactivated lawsuit against the regents after his military discharge.

On August 19, 1955, the U.S. Armed Forces granted Ward an honorable discharge from the army. In large part as a result of Ward's earlier assault on the all-white University of Georgia and the *Brown* declaration, Georgia's political leaders had adopted a multitude of state laws designed to thwart court-ordered integration. Despite such opposition, on August 25, 1955, Ward filed for the continuation of his legal case with the help of Georgia NAACP president William Madison Boyd, local civil rights attorney Austin Thomas Walden, and Thurgood Marshall in his renewed court action against the regents.

In response to Ward's renewal of his lawsuit, Georgia's attorney general, Eugene Cook, declared: "It's ripe for a showdown. If he wins, all he will do is close down the law school."[16] Cook's reference was to a new Georgia law that prohibited spending state funds on school units that contained racially "mixed classrooms."[17] As the state heightened its legal maneuvers to deter Ward, William Madison Boyd recruited emerging civil rights expert Donald L. Hollowell to assist Walden on the case. Hollowell devoted much of his time and law practice to civil rights matters; he was active in the Atlanta branch of the NAACP and served as its legal counsel.[18] Hollowell became chief local counsel for the *Ward* case and Thurgood Marshall, busy with the multitude of NAACP civil rights cases, assigned Constance Baker Motley to represent the LDF.[19]

In Chapter 4 I examine in detail the *Ward v. Regents* case, the first lawsuit in Georgia history to challenge the centuries-old practice of segregation at the University of Georgia, a relatively elitist public university founded in 1785 that prided itself on its academic traditions and its role as the path to economic and political success for generations of white Georgians. White leaders, ensconced in traditions that excluded blacks from the flagship school, lamented the challenge to the university's whites-only status. This chapter shows how Hollowell, Walden, and Motley, who represented Ward at the trial, exposed the dilatory tactics, contradictions, and legal maneuvering of university officials, regents, and state political leaders to sustain segregation at their most cherished institution. The trial record reflects how the brilliant legal strategizing of Hollowell, Walden, and Motley began to undermine many of the state's arguments. Indeed, Ward's case precipitated a series of events that would have far-reaching effects on the university, the regents, and the body politic of the state of Georgia. Through analysis of this landmark case, we can see how *Ward v. Regents* set the stage for the desegregation of colleges and universities in Georgia.

Chapters 5 and 6 examine the historic *Holmes v. Danner* case and its aftermath, which led to the dismantling of segregation in Georgia's public colleges and universities. Ward, with a recent degree from Northwestern University's School of Law, played a unique role as a lawyer assisting Donald L. Hollowell in this lawsuit, Ward's first major case as a practicing attorney. Importantly, issues that had surfaced in his own lawsuit became central to the outcome of this case that resulted in the enrollment of Hamilton Holmes and Charlayne Hunter at the University of Georgia in January 1961. Moreover, as Constance Baker Motley noted in her book, *Equal Justice under Law*, the struggle to end segregation at the University of Georgia—the struggle that began with Ward's legal challenge—also emboldened James Meredith to seek admission to the University of Mississippi in 1961.[20] And in Georgia, the aftermath of the trial included a progressive crumbling of segregation at all levels of public education.

Following his legal work on the historic *Holmes v. Danner* case, an auspicious start for a young lawyer, Ward achieved a distinguished record of public service and continued to forge his place in history. Chapter 7 details his continuing accomplishments as a lawyer and state senator, often challenging defiant segregationists in his persistent quest for racial and social justice. Overall, the contrast between his early rejection by the University of Georgia Law School and his subsequent success is richly ironic, reflecting a deeply satisfying outcome that might be characterized as poetic justice. In the 1950s, for example, senior university officials derided his character and said he did not have the mind to be a lawyer. Today, many judicial colleagues and lawyers regard him as one of the best judges in the federal system.

Starting in 1961, immediately after his work with the legal team in the *Holmes* case, Ward launched his practice in civil rights law by becoming a partner in Donald L. Hollowell's law firm. Ward established a successful practice as a civil rights lawyer, even joining chief counsel Hollowell in a 1960 case to secure the release of Dr. Martin Luther King, Jr., from the maximum security prison in Reidsville, Georgia. His prominence as a lawyer helped him to win election to the state Senate that earlier had adopted resolutions to keep him out of the state law school. In turn, as a senator, Ward became respected as a quietly effective champion of civil and human rights legislation. Subsequently, Ward became a state, then federal judge of singular distinction in the same state that had declared him unfit to attend its law school.

The final chapter of this study, Chapter 8, chronicles Ward's judicial career as first a civil, then superior court, and finally, a federal judge—each a historic first appointment of a black to such judicial positions in the state of Georgia. His federal judgeship from 1979 to the present is the longest and most significant appointment and the chapter highlights some of the key federal cases that he presided over and ruled upon, most notably the nationally celebrated 1986 *Kemp v. Ervin* free speech case. On May 16, 1994, Ward's pursuits culminated in a commemoration ceremony recognizing his senior status as a federal jurist, in which friends, lawyers, and fellow judges attested to his vision, intellect, and courage. Ironically, the ceremony took place in the same court where Ward fought the legal battle to become a law student at the University of Georgia.

While outlining Ward's significant impact on the desegregation of colleges and universities as a plaintiff and a lawyer, in itself a virtually untold story, this study also relates the phenomenal success of persons who supported Ward and continued the struggle to overcome racial injustice in colleges and universities. In addition to Ward, three of the attorneys who represented him also became federal judges, while Hamilton Holmes and Charlayne Hunter also achieved remarkable success in their professions. This study offers, then, a central paradigm of a historic struggle to achieve equality and justice. But especially, an examination of Ward's climb from humble beginnings to the impressive chambers of a United States federal judge offers a provocative, inspiring chronicle. The story of his remarkable achievements is exemplary for scholars, historians, and contemporary crusaders for justice.

INTRODUCTION NOTES

[1] *Radio and Television Remarks upon Signing the Civil Rights Bill*, July 2, 1964, National Archives and Records Administration, Lyndon B. Johnson Library and Museum, Austin, TX, 2.

[2] *U.S. Statutes at Large*, 78, Public Laws 24th Amendment to the Constitution, *Civil Rights Act of 1964*, July 2, 1964, Public Law 88-352, 78, Stat. 241.

[3] *Remarks in the Capitol Rotunda at the Signing of the Voting Rights Act*, August 6, 1965, National Archives and Records Administration, Lyndon B. Johnson Library and Museum, Austin, TX, 2.

[4] During most of the time period covered in this book, the general public used the term "Negro" or "colored" in reference to blacks. I generally use the term "black" or "African American" throughout this book instead of "Negro" or "colored" because these are the terms preferred today and this book is intended for a contemporary audience of scholars, educators, students, and the general public. Periodically, I use the term "Negro" in its historical context in reference to quoted material, to give the reader a better feel for the time period. For a discussion of the terms, see Mary Frances Berry and John Blassingame, *Long Memory: The Black Experience in America* (New York: Oxford University Press, 1982), 389-396.

[5] Jack Greenberg, *Crusaders in the Courts: How a Dedicated Band of Lawyers Fought for the Civil Rights Revolution* (New York: Basic Books, 1994), 300; *U.S. Statutes at Large*, 79, Public Laws, Public Law 89-110, *Voting Rights Act of 1965*, August 6, 1965.

[6] *Remarks in the Capitol Rotunda*, op. cit., 2, 4.

[7] The acronym LDF is commonly used by NAACP officials and scholars to refer to the NAACP Legal Defense and Educational Fund although it does not correspond exactly per letter with the full name of the NAACP Legal Defense and Educational

Fund, Inc. "Inc. Fund" is also often used to refer to the organization; I use the term LDF throughout this book.

[8]Tony Freyer, *The Little Rock Crisis* (Greenwich, CT: Greenwood Press, 1984), 87–114; Constance Baker Motley, *Equal Justice Under Law: An Autobiography of Constance Baker Motley* (New York: Farrar, Straus & Giroux, 1998), 129–130; Adam Fairclough, *Race and Democracy: The Civil Rights Struggle in Louisiana, 1915-1972* (Athens: University of Georgia Press, 1995), 243–244.

[9]*Brown v. Board of Education*, 347 U.S. 483, 74 S. Ct. 686 (1954). For a study of the brilliant legal work of Thurgood Marshall and the historic *Brown* decision, see Waldo E. Martin, Jr., *Brown v. Board of Education: A Brief History with Documents* (Boston: Bedford Books, 1998); Mark V. Tushnet, *Making Civil Rights Law: Thurgood Marshall and the Supreme Court, 1936-1961* (New York: Oxford University Press, 1994); Richard Kluger, *Simple Justice: The History of Brown v. Board of Education and Black America's Struggle for Equality* (New York: Alfred A. Knopf, 1976); Juan Williams, *Thurgood Marshall: American Revolutionary* (New York: Random House, 1998); Carl T. Rowan, *Dream Makers, Dream Breakers: The World of Justice Thurgood Marshall* (Boston: Little, Brown and Company, 1993); Papers of the NAACP, The Campaign for Educational Equality: Legal Department and Central Office Records, 1913-1950, 1951-1955. The Papers of the NAACP Collection are located at the Library of Congress, Washington, D.C. Reproduced copies of the 1913-1950 and 1951-1955 records are located in the University of Georgia Libraries. Reproduced copies of the 1956-1965 records, which are also cited in this book, are located at the Emory University Robert Woodruff Library.

[10]See Taylor Branch, *Parting the Waters: America in the King Years, 1954-1963* (New York: Simon and Schuster, 1988) and David J. Garrow, *Bearing the Cross: Martin Luther King, Jr., and the Southern Christian Leadership Conference 1955-1968* (New York: William Morrow and Company, 1986).

[11]Juan Williams, *Eyes on the Prize: America's Civil Rights Years, 1954-1965* (New York: Penguin Books, 1988), 201–202.

[12]William H. Robinson, "Desegregation in Higher Education in the South," *School and Society* 7 (May 1960): 238.

[13]William Alexander Scott II was the first black after the Civil War to publish a daily newspaper in the United States. On August 3, 1928, he published the first issue of the weekly *Atlanta World*, and in 1930 as a semiweekly. In 1932 the *Atlanta Daily World* became the first successful, black-owned daily newspaper. Recognizing the need in the segregated black community for an end to racism, editorials focused on an end to racial oppression. However, the newspaper also sought to inspire readers by reporting positive news about blacks. See Joseph P. McKerns, *Biographical Dictionary of American Journalism* (Greenwich, CT: Greenwood Press, 1989). Civil rights activists in the Atlanta movement, such as Moses Carl Holman, Jesse Hill, Jr., Clinton Warner, J. Lowell Ware, and William H. Strong, established a more activist black-

owned paper in July 1960, the *Atlanta Inquirer*. The weekly paper chronicled the civil rights movement in Atlanta and throughout the South. The *Atlanta Inquirer*'s staff included persons actively involved in the civil rights struggle, such as Julian Bond and Charlayne Hunter.

[14]"Order for Transferred Man to Report for Induction," Horace Taliaferro Ward, August 12, 1953, Local Board No. 49, Mobile, AL.

[15]George M. Coleman, "NAACP Attorneys Move Fast to Save School Bias Suit," *Atlanta Daily World*, September 22, 1953, 1; Donald Hollowell, interview with author, Atlanta, GA, July 27, 1993.

[16]Charles Pou, "Cook Gets Aid in Fight to Keep Schools Segregated: Negro to Renew Effort to Enter University Law Unit, He Learns," *Atlanta Journal*, July 8, 1955, 1, 10.

[17]General Appropriations Act, Secs. 8, 9, GA Laws 1951, 425. Similar provisions appear in the General Appropriations Act, Secs. 8, 9, GA Laws Jan.-Feb. Sess. 1953, 154 and General Appropriations Act, Secs. 8, 9, GA Laws 1956, 762.

[18]Louise Hollowell and Martin C. Lehfeldt, *The Sacred Call: A Tribute to Donald Hollowell: Civil Rights Champion* (Winter Park, FL: Four-G Publishers, 1997), 92-113.

[19]Constance Baker Motley, interview with author, New York, NY, March 30, 1995.

[20]Motley, *Equal Justice*, op. cit., 166. Mississippi governor Ross Barnett, the Mississippi legislature, and riotous mobs repeatedly blocked James Meredith's court-ordered admission to the University of Mississippi. Following the legal maneuvers and political jockeying between President Kennedy and Governor Barnett, twenty-three thousand soldiers safeguarded Meredith's entry in the University of Mississippi. See Branch, op. cit., 62; *Meredith v. Fair*, 306 F. 2d 374, (1962).

CHAPTER *1*

The NAACP's Formative Role:
A Crack In The Wall

In the early 1950s, bolstered by a series of state Jim Crow laws and a U.S. Supreme Court that had sanctioned segregation, Southern politicians were zealous in their segregationist actions and rhetoric. Georgia and other Deep South states sustained an apartheid system that relegated blacks to inferior segregated public schools and colleges. Georgia officials, led by segregationist governor Herman Talmadge, made clear their intentions to continue the practice. On June 5, 1950, during his reelection campaign for governor, Talmadge repeated his solemn promise to uphold segregation: "As long as I am your governor, Negroes will not be admitted to white schools."[1]

These acrimonious words of Governor Herman Talmadge and the segregationist sentiments behind them set the stage for a watershed event in higher education in Georgia. On September 30, 1950, despite Governor Talmadge's promise to maintain segregation, and in the face of legally sanctioned public opposition to integration, Horace T. Ward began the struggle to eliminate educational segregation in Georgia. Ward, a 1949 honors graduate of Morehouse College who received his M.A. in 1950 from Atlanta University, applied to enter the University of Georgia School of Law. Ward refused to accept the university's offer to pay his tuition to attend law school out of state—a practice then prevalent among Southern and regional universities seeking to maintain segregation.

1

With his application, Ward became the first black student in history to apply to an all-white college or university in Georgia. This historic and courageous action resulted from the confluence of Ward's desire to secure a law degree and practice law in his home state and the driving force of the ongoing battle of the National Association for the Advancement of Colored People (NAACP) against segregation in graduate and professional schools. This chapter examines the background of the NAACP, its legal program for equal justice, and the ways in which its actions to defeat segregation laid the groundwork for Ward's battle to enter the University of Georgia. The following chapter will continue with the story of Ward and how it intersects with NAACP efforts.

To appreciate the force that helped propel the first challenge to desegregate the University of Georgia, it is necessary to recall the NAACP's longstanding struggle against social injustice in America and the ways in which public higher education became a focal point in its battle against racial inequities. In the early 1900s, blacks struggled against a wall of pervasive racial oppression underpinned by centuries-old ideas about the inferiority of people of African descent. While unjust laws and statutes buttressed some indignities, time-honored customs and traditions also constituted sufficient justification for whites to manifest violence and unfair treatment toward blacks, no matter the legality of those actions. In the first year of the new century 100 blacks were lynched, and by the start of World War I, more than 1100. Meanwhile, more subtle forms of brutality also evolved. In addition to recorded lynchings, many, if not more, blacks were the victims of "legal lynching" (sham court trials followed by quick executions) and private white violence, murdered by a variety of means in isolated rural areas and dumped into rivers or creeks.[2] In addition to such outright racial violence, governmental and private entities denied blacks equal access to education, transportation, legal redress, and voting rights. Even when the white power structure extended so-called rights to blacks, such as participation in the armed services, blacks invariably were regarded as second-class citizens and encountered grossly inferior treatment.

In June of 1905, in response to the continuing unfair treatment and societal inequities that post-Reconstruction blacks endured, the Niagara Movement (born in Niagara Falls, Canada, an important terminus of the Underground Railroad) was founded, led by the legendary W. E. B. Du Bois. Its principles included the abolition of all caste distinctions based on race or color, advocacy for voting rights, and demands for social justice.[3] Despite the relative success of the organization in reviving the spirit of abolitionism, and despite its progressive platform recognizing the principles of human brotherhood, the organization never gained a membership of more than four hundred predominantly black, upper-class college graduates and possessed only meager financial resources.[4] A meeting in Oberlin in 1908 was the last formal meeting of the Movement; most of its leadership merged with a new and enveloping organization in which Du Bois played a key role: the National Association for the Advancement of Colored People (NAACP).[5]

In 1909, a riot and lynching in Springfield, Illinois, was the major impetus that led Du Bois, several other members of the Niagara Movement, and a group of white liberal leaders to organize the NAACP. The occurrence of such an atrocity in the historic homeplace of "the Great Emancipator" shocked many white liberals and propelled them to call for a revival in the "spirit of abolitionists."[6] The organization's key principles also included fighting segregation and other forms of discrimination. Among the organizers were social scientists, philanthropists, social workers, and victims of racial oppression continuing the struggle for human liberation.[7]

Du Bois's preoccupation with the NAACP—including his editorship of *The Crisis*, the NAACP's official organ, which he founded in 1910; his service as NAACP Director of Publications and Research; and other lofty human liberation ventures—led him to cancel the 1911 annual meeting of the Niagara Movement to devote his energies to building the NAACP. Du Bois urged the Niagara Movement members to join the NAACP, which had greater resources. Most of them did so, leading the Niagara Movement to disband officially in the summer of 1911.[8]

In the midst of the rising white hostility toward blacks, white liberals, including Mary White Ovington, Oswald Garrison Villard, and Charles Edward Russell, helped organize the NAACP. Because they were all descended from abolitionists, it was natural for them to embrace social justice for black Americans. Villard, for example, was the grandson of the famous abolitionist, William Lloyd Garrison. Other whites in the group were descended from very different backgrounds. For example, founder William English Walling was a Southerner and the descendant of a slave-owning family.[9]

Joel Spingarn, another NAACP founder, possessed neither an abolitionist nor a slave-owning ancestry. Spingarn, whose parents were Jewish immigrants, grew up in New York City. Spingarn earned undergraduate and doctoral degrees from Columbia College, where he majored in literature, later teaching at Columbia and developing a reputation as a brilliant literary scholar. However, Spingarn possessed maverick ideas and his willingness to confront the status quo often provoked strong opposition from the mainstream white establishment. Spingarn would become the foremost white liberal leader to influence the NAACP over the next two decades. By 1914 his exceptional leadership and courage in NAACP battles led to his election as chairman of the NAACP board.[10] The program that NAACP leaders advanced emphasized the attainment of full civil and political rights for blacks; its 1911 mission statement declared its intention "to uplift the colored men and women of this country by securing to them the full enjoyment of their rights as citizens, justice in all courts, and equality of opportunity everywhere."[11]

During its formative years the NAACP decided to use legal redress whenever possible, as the most pragmatic means to the desired end. When legal redress was not possible the organization relied on peaceful agitation and protest by local branches, including appeals to public conscience through the written and spoken word. In 1915, Moorfield Storey, the first president of the NAACP, filed a *amicus curiae* on behalf of the NAACP in the *Guinn v. United States* case, which challenged some states' practices that prohibited a person from voting unless an ancestor had been eligible to vote prior to

January 1, 1866. The NAACP won a momentous decision in the case when the U.S. Supreme Court ruled against "grandfather clauses" in state constitutions. In 1917, in *Buchanan v. Warley*, the NAACP won a protracted struggle against residential segregation that invariably restricted blacks to the least desirable and healthful areas when the Court ruled against the practice.[12] These and other legal victories led the organization to use legal redress as a primary tactic in battling Jim Crow. The fact that the organization included members with exceptional legal talent, and the fact that it had experienced several failures trying to organize mass protests also made legal redress a more viable alternative.

Du Bois, who quickly became the major voice of the NAACP as a result of his cogent articles in *The Crisis* and his scholarly authority on race matters, played a powerful role in developing from the outset the association's strategy of legal redress, and indeed its overall mission. But from the beginning, he also was something of a phenomenon, an autonomous, visionary African American leader in an organization dominated by white executives—a fact which surely rankled Du Bois. Until 1916, he was the NAACP's only black executive officer, when James Weldon Johnson was appointed field secretary and national organizer.[13] As early as the preceding year, Du Bois had insisted in a *Crisis* editorial that blacks not only should control such organizations but "hold them unswervingly to our aims and ideals."[14] For Du Bois, those aims and ideals included more than civil rights advocacy and litigation. His *Crisis* editorials urged the NAACP to adopt racial uplift and economic development programs, goals that became increasingly important to his personal philosophy during the ensuing decade. However, the preponderance of NAACP leaders were at the time emphatically committed to the NAACP's mission in advocating and litigating for civil rights.[15]

During the 1920s also, white dominance within the organization's leadership declined as more black executives were appointed and James Weldon Johnson's influence increased; by the 1930s, the NAACP's board consisted of a critical mass of black members.[16] Du Bois, however, continued to criticize the NAACP's policies, noting with particular disapproval that even the new preponderance of black board members chose to maintain that the pursuit of civil rights should take precedence over any program of black cultural and economic uplift.[17] Distancing himself even further from the NAACP's central agenda, he even advocated the principle of "voluntary segregation" as a pragmatic means for blacks to work together for their own advancement. In a 1934 *Crisis* editorial, Du Bois asserted his broadened, and controversial, vision of the NAACP's historic mission in this way:

> The thinking colored people of the United States must stop being stampeded by the word *segregation*. The opposition to racial segregation is not or should not be any distaste or unwillingness of colored people to work with each other, to cooperate with each other, to live with each other. The opposition to segregation is an opposition to discrimination. . . . It is the race conscious black man co-operating together in his own institutions and movements who will eventually emancipate the colored race.[18]

Du Bois's continued emphasis in his *Crisis* editorials on the validity of "voluntary segregation" and programmatic emphasis on racial economic uplift alienated and even alarmed the majority of NAACP leaders.[19] Joel Spingarn, still an influential voice in the NAACP, together with many of the new black NAACP leaders insisted that the organization maintain its central focus on desegregation and the legislation of civil and political rights for African Americans. Spingarn thus spoke for many, if not indeed the majority of NAACP leaders, when he asserted in a 1934 *Crisis* symposium of viewpoints that "We have always believed that even voluntary segregation is an evil, though perhaps a necessary evil."[20] Atlanta University graduate Walter White, who succeeded James Weldon Johnson as NAACP executive secretary, went even further in challenging Du Bois's position:

> To accept the status of separateness, which almost invariably in the case of submerged, exploited and marginal groups means inferior accommodations and a distinctly inferior position in the

national and communal life, means spiritual atrophy for the group segregated.[21]

The controversy that Du Bois had initiated soon led, by the spring of 1934, to an irreconcilable opposition between his stance and that maintained by other NAACP leaders. Louis T. Wright, who succeeded Spingarn in 1934, becoming the first black NAACP board chairperson, argued that any form of racial segregation was undesirable and unacceptable.[22] Subsequently, the board formally adopted a position that opposed "the principle and practice of enforced segregation of human beings on the basis of race and color" and refused to endorse Du Bois's advocacy of an NAACP program to help develop the cultural and economic status of black Americans generally.[23] The board, moreover, passed a resolution banning criticism of the NAACP or its leaders in *The Crisis*. The consequence of the board's actions was virtually inevitable: W. E. B. Du Bois resigned his editorship of *The Crisis* and his membership in the NAACP in July 1934.[24]

The resignation of this towering intellectual and activist left a void in the NAACP, but one that was filled by the echo of his words. Despite the NAACP's opposition to his views, which reached a climax during the spring and early summer of 1934, those views had made an impact that was, if anything, magnified by his departure. Ironically, the NAACP began a serious effort, shortly after Du Bois's resignation, to address some of the very reforms that he had proposed. In September 1934, a board committee drafted a "Future Plan and Program" that challenged the NAACP's lack of a strong economic component for black uplift. The new plan and program also included other changes that Du Bois had advocated, such as involving rank and file members of the NAACP in policy decisions.[25]

In 1935 an extremely significant outcome of the "Future Plan and Program" committee's deliberations, and at the urging of NAACP secretary Walter White, was the selection of Charles Hamilton Houston as the first full-time director to coordinate the NAACP's legal work. Early in the 1920s, Du Bois had clearly articulated the need for what would become the focal point of the NAACP's legal program, as developed by Houston: "To secure justice for Negro[es]in the schools of the nation . . . [t]here must be a way to bring their cases before both state and federal courts."[26]

Houston, a brilliant and passionate advocate for racial justice, became the first black to direct the NAACP's legal program. The only child of William Houston (a Howard Law graduate) and Mary Hamilton Houston, Houston graduated as the valedictorian of one of the leading black high schools in Washington, D.C., and graduated from Amherst College in 1915, where he was elected to Phi Beta Kappa. The next year, he joined the army and completed a tour of duty in France. The segregation of and double standard for blacks in the armed services during World War I influenced his decision to pursue law as a tool to fight for social justice. Houston recalled, "I made up in my mind that I would never get caught again without knowing something about my rights; that if luck was with me, and I got through this war, I would study law and use my time fighting for men who could not strike back."[27]

After his return from military service, Houston entered Harvard Law School. Although Harvard had welcomed black students for decades (most notably, W. E. B. Du Bois in the 1890s), Houston was the first black to be elected editor of the prestigious *Harvard Law Review*. He graduated from Harvard Law School in 1922, well prepared to apply his highly developed skills in the fight against social injustice. Houston began his law practice in Washington, D.C., with his father while teaching part-time at the Howard University law school, becoming dean of the school in 1929. In the next six years he transformed it from a law school with a part-time faculty and student body into an accredited institution that became a "West Point of civil rights," producing an annual graduating class of lawyers rigorously trained to do battle for equal justice.[28] Under Houston's guidance, Howard's law school became a training ground for the legal struggle to win civil rights for disenfranchised blacks.[29]

Houston, who became the chief architect for the NAACP's legal program to end segregation and discrimination, fashioned the

8

strategy of using the Fourteenth Amendment as the basis for legal action to challenge segregation, under its provision that "no state shall deny to any person . . . the equal protection of the laws."[30] As the first full-time lawyer, and the first black, to head the legal department of the NAACP, Houston held a position from which he designed a strategic framework for the NAACP's legal thrusts.[31] His strategy to defeat Jim Crow began with efforts to win the entrance of blacks into graduate and professional schools. Higher education provided the best chance of legal success because the disparity between educational opportunities for blacks and whites was most apparent in postbaccalaureate programs.[32] While the Jim Crow states of the South provided marginal educational opportunities for black students at the secondary school and undergraduate levels, graduate and professional educational opportunities for blacks were almost nonexistent.

Houston's approach was to start with the rights of blacks to pursue a legal education in states where segregationist laws banned their enrollment. He reasoned that judges might be receptive to a young man's desire to get a good legal education in his home state. Furthermore, since most law students were males, he hoped to sidestep the philosophical idiocy of many segregationists who were first and foremost concerned about keeping black men and white women apart.[33] Finally, Houston thought that pursuing an end to segregation in professional or graduate schools would not result in the kind of massive resistance that Southern politicians regularly threatened in their impassioned speeches.[34]

In the mid-1930s, with Houston directing its legal program, the NAACP began a step-by-step battle that focused on eliminating segregation in graduate and professional schools. Thurgood Marshall, Houston's star pupil, was one of the first to enlist in the battle. The University of Maryland Law School, in Marshall's home state, denied him admission. Fortuitously, Marshall subsequently graduated from Howard University Law School in 1935, where he studied under Houston. Marshall became a protégé of Houston, and Howard University's civil rights training ground prepared him to join in the battle for equal justice.

Later in 1935, after Marshall graduated from Howard, he and Houston brought a lawsuit before Judge Eugene O'Dunne of the Baltimore City Court on behalf of Donald G. Murray against the same school that had rejected Marshall's application apparently due to race. Murray, a native Marylander and Amherst graduate, sued on the grounds that the all-white University of Maryland Law School did not admit him because he was black. During the trial, responding reluctantly to Houston's penetrating questions, University President Raymond Pearson agreed that all racial groups except Negroes would be admitted to the University of Maryland. Houston and Marshall were successful in gaining Murray's admission to the law school in 1936. Judge O'Dunne, whose decision was later affirmed by the Maryland Court of Appeals, agreed with their argument that if the state did not have a separate law school for Negroes, it had to admit Murray to the only state law school in Maryland.[35] Murray successfully completed his law degree there and after graduation set up a successful law practice in Maryland.

However, in *Gaines v. Canada*, two years later, Houston and Marshall were not as successful. Lloyd Gaines, a twenty-five-year-old black man, sought to enter the University of Missouri to study law. The State of Missouri offered Gaines a scholarship to attend a school outside the state, a common practice in several states during that period.[36] The Jim Crow states of the South often offered blacks the trivial "favor" of limited financial aid to attend graduate or professional schools outside the state, in order to maintain their all-white institutions and avoid the cost associated with establishing black professional schools. Many black students took advantage of the out-of-state aid because it offered them their only opportunity to pursue graduate or professional education, and because it gave them the opportunity to attend some of the nation's most prestigious institutions. However, Gaines refused to accept the out-of-state aid offer, and with the assistance of the NAACP, he sued the University of Missouri.

When the case reached the Supreme Court, the Court ruled that the State of Missouri could not free itself of its Fourteenth Amendment obligation by sending its black students out of state.

Holding that a state could only provide equal protection within its own borders and jurisdiction, the Court ruled that the state must either supply a law school for blacks substantially equal to the white law school, or admit blacks to the all-white University of Missouri.[37] However, the Supreme Court did not order the admission of Gaines to the all-white law school, as the Baltimore City Court had done in the *Murray* case, thereby sidestepping the issue of the unconstitutionality of segregation. Nonetheless, it was an important victory because states would either have to spend thousands of dollars creating black professional schools within their own borders or agree to open the doors of the exclusive institutions reserved for whites only.

In response to the Court's decision, the State of Missouri chose the first of these options, appropriating more than half a million dollars to establish a separate law school for blacks at the all-black Lincoln University. NAACP officials attempted to find Gaines in the ensuing years, but he had vanished from sight and his disappearance has been shrouded in mystery ever since.[38]

While a few states maintaining separate and unequal systems, such as Maryland, Missouri, and Oklahoma, began minimal efforts at compliance with the Court, the Court mandate did little to deter the hard-line segregationist states, such as Georgia. The hardliners not only refused to open white institutions to blacks, they also refused to allocate funds for establishing black professional schools. When Clennon W. King, Jr., a black Georgia resident, requested an application to enter the University of Georgia School of Law in 1940, the registrar forwarded King's letter to Chancellor S. V. Sanford in the regents' office. Sanford stated in an April 15, 1940, letter to King that "there is no provision for aiding negroes in graduate or professional study"; three days later, King wrote a letter to NAACP secretary Walter White asking for help: "I'm just another Negro trying to get an education, and in my attempts I have tried to apply for admission to my own state (Georgia) university and have been politely refused."[39]

Although Sanford refused King, he later expressed concern about the lack of educational opportunities for blacks. Sanford, whom biographer Charles Stephen Gurr described as "merely a moderate racist," recommended to the regents that "the same educational opportunities should be provided for the negro as for the white, and that the sum of five thousand dollars should be allocated to equalize these opportunities."[40] Despite the absurdity and obvious inequity of the recommendation, Regent Sandy Beaver stressed that this action would convince Negroes that the regents were their friends and were trying to provide them equal educational opportunities as rapidly as possible.

The provisions that the Georgia regents adopted for Negroes in 1943 offer a further, dramatic example of how segregationists evaded legal precedent that declared a state must either admit blacks to its all-white schools or supply a substantially equal black school within its borders. In response, Georgia's regents established an *out-of-state* scholarship program for blacks to attend out-of-state graduate or professional schools where they might be accepted.[41]

Because the NAACP did not qualify under its original charter as a tax exempt organization, by 1940 some contributors, including John D. Rockefeller, Jr., refused to renew their contributions. Therefore, in that year the NAACP created the NAACP Legal Defense and Educational Fund, Inc. (LDF) as a separate charitable, tax-exempt organization. Because the new organization would do the legal work of the association, it needed a charter approved by the Supreme Court of New York County to practice law as a corporation. On March 20, 1940, the LDF charter was created and subsequently approved by the court.[42]

In 1940, when Houston retired from the NAACP, he tapped his close associate Thurgood Marshall to replace him and to carry on the plan for abolishing legal segregation.[43] Houston, exhausted from the overwhelming pace of trying cases, had begun to develop health problems, and returned to work at his father's law practice. However, Houston maintained a strong association with the NAACP and continued to fight against racial segregation as a private lawyer.

When World War II began for the United States in 1941, the NAACP suspended its attack on racial discrimination in education.

The sentiment of the NAACP board was that it would be embarrassing to the national government to pursue a frontal attack on racial discrimination while the country was fighting a war for democracy in Europe and yet denying equal rights to its own citizens.[44] But the unfair treatment of blacks during the war, including segregated facilities on military posts and preferences for white soldiers in transportation and accommodations, contributed to black servicemen joining the NAACP in unprecedented numbers. Black servicemen were also concerned about mistreatment in the armed services with respect to the harsh sentences they received for minor infractions, and the frequency with which they were court-martialed. These servicemen often turned to the NAACP to take their cases. The NAACP thus became involved in trying to eliminate a patently racist double standard of justice in the military.[45] Fighting against inhumane aggression in foreign lands emboldened black servicemen to oppose racial inequities within their own military ranks. Moreover, upon their return as veterans of a war fought ostensibly for world freedom, black servicemen pursued their aspirations for full citizenship at home. The momentum that the NAACP built among black servicemen during World War II spurred its leadership to take a firmer stand against segregation in other arenas after the war. Accordingly, rather than filing cases within the "separate but equal" context of the historic *Plessy v. Ferguson* decision, the NAACP determined that future cases would make a direct assault on segregation.[46]

Thurgood Marshall, now the NAACP's new special counsel, boldly led the NAACP's legal attack on segregation. Marshall traveled extensively to handle NAACP litigation and was also in high demand as an eloquent, persuasive speaker; Marshall frequently spoke at mass meetings sponsored by NAACP local branches, rousing audiences to enthusiastic support. Because of the increasing demands of litigation and his exhausting travel schedule, Marshall expanded the NAACP legal staff for assistance in legal research, brief writing, and other legal and organizational work. In 1944, Marshall hired Robert L. Carter, who like Marshall himself was a graduate of Lincoln University and also the Howard University Law School, Charles

Hamilton Houston's now well-established civil rights training ground. The hard-working, knowledgeable Carter quickly became Marshall's primary assistant, and played a key role in the NAACP's legal battles.[47]

At the end of World War II, Marshall and Carter reignited the fight against segregation in graduate and professional schools with Oklahoma as the first battleground. In 1946, Marshall and Carter undertook the representation of Ada Lois Sipuel, an honor graduate from the State College for Negroes at Langston, Oklahoma, who applied to the law school at the University of Oklahoma (the only state law school in Oklahoma). The school denied her admission because of her race. Marshall, Carter, and other LDF lawyers sued the all-white law school to admit her. Two years later, in a unanimous decision, the Supreme Court held that the state was constitutionally obligated to provide Sipuel with an equal education, based upon the 1938 *Gaines v. Canada* decision which declared that states could not free themselves of the obligation to provide equal education by sending their black students out of state. The Court declared that the state must provide a legal education to Sipuel, pursuant to the equal protection clause of the Fourteenth Amendment.[48] The Oklahoma regents, seeking to evade the court order no matter how ludicrous their actions, roped off a space in the state capitol building as a law school for Sipuel and other blacks, assigning three teachers to the makeshift school. Sipuel refused to attend the so-called law school and appealed the regents' action. However, despite the obvious gross inequities, the appellate court refused to intervene.[49]

Shortly after the *Sipuel* case began, the LDF filed a case against the University of Texas on behalf of Heman Marion Sweatt. Sweatt, a black mail carrier and veteran of World War II, sought to enter the University of Texas Law School. The school denied Sweatt admission and, with the assistance of the NAACP, Sweatt filed a lawsuit. The Court found that Sweatt possessed the credentials for admission and that the law school had denied him admission solely because of his race. However, the Court stayed the decision for six months to allow the state time to set up a separate law school for blacks. Texas officials, taking a cue from Oklahoma, set up a law school for Negroes in the basement of a building in Austin; Sweatt, however, refused to enter the grossly inferior facility and appealed the case.[50]

On June 5, 1950, in a unanimous decision, the Supreme Court held that the "special" black law school that Texas had hastily set up for Sweatt in the basement was in no way equal to the law school at the University of Texas, noting obvious inequalities such as library facilities, reputation of the faculty, and opportunity to exchange ideas with fellow law students. The Court opined that students should not have to study in an academic vacuum.[51] The Court also took a bolder step forward in eliminating segregation: Besides finding the so-called black law school unequal, the Court ordered the admission of Sweatt to the University of Texas.[52] Although the *Plessy v. Ferguson* decision was not specifically overruled, Marshall noted that its effectiveness in maintaining segregated graduate and professional education had been fatally undermined. He predicted that the end of legal segregation loomed on the horizon and vowed that the NAACP would continue its legal battles to overturn segregation.[53]

Following the unsatisfactory resolution of the *Sipuel* case, G. W. McLaurin, a black citizen of Oklahoma who possessed a master's degree, continued the court battle to end segregation in graduate and professional schools in Oklahoma. After Oklahoma officials rejected his application to seek a doctorate degree in education, he filed a lawsuit to enter the all-white University of Oklahoma's graduate school. After several LDF triumphs in the lower courts, the University of Oklahoma admitted McLaurin into the graduate school. However, once again, the school provided separate, but hardly equal treatment, requiring McLaurin to sit in a special seat in a broom closet (called an anteroom) outside the main classroom. McLaurin also had to sit at a special table in the library, use a separate toilet, and dine in an area segregated from other students in the cafeteria. After an LDF appeal, the Supreme Court ruled—on the same day as the *Sweatt* decision—that once university officials admitted McLaurin to the graduate school, they could not segregate him within the school.[54] The Court declared that separate treatment impaired or inhibited his ability to study and to engage in the free exchange of views with other students, and thus hindered him from learning his profession. Furthermore, the Court concluded that separate dining facilities, bathrooms, classrooms, and housing facilities on the University of Oklahoma campus were unconstitutional.[55]

The *Sweatt* and *McLaurin* decisions represented major victories for the LDF lawyers, resulting in severe cracks in the pervasive wall of legal segregation maintained by the *Plessy v. Ferguson* precedent. These victories encouraged the direct assault on racial segregation that Houston had envisioned. Sadly, Houston died a few weeks before the pivotal rulings in the *Sweatt* and *McLaurin* cases. Marshall and the LDF lawyers knew that they had lost a giant; however, Houston had prepared them well and he had engineered a powerful plan to defeat segregation that would move forward even in his absence. William H. Hastie, Houston's close friend, former pupil, and comrade in the civil rights movement, who also served as an advisor to President Roosevelt and became the first black judge appointed to the federal bench, provided the following apt and eloquent tribute:

> He guided us through the legal wilderness of second class citizenship. He was truly the Moses of that journey. He lived to see us close to the promised land of full equality under the law, closer than even he dared hope when we set out on that journey and so much closer than would have been possible without his genius and leadership.[56]

CHAPTER 1 NOTES

[1]"Henderson, Sweatt, McLaurin Rulings Hailed by Leaders," *Atlanta Daily World*, June 6, 1950, 1; "Talmadge Vows Segregation Will Remain in State," *Athens Banner Herald*, November 17, 1953, 1.

Herman Eugene Talmadge, the son of Governor Eugene Talmadge, represented the fourth generation of Talmadges to attend the University of Georgia, receiving his LL.B. degree in 1936. After his father died while governor, Talmadge was elected governor in 1948 and served until 1955. Talmadge was an effective administrator and led several significant and progressive improvements in state services during his tenure. However, his recalcitrant approach to racial equality marred his record as governor. During his governorship, Talmadge initiated several legislative resolutions enacted by the General Assembly to preserve segregation. After six years as governor, he was elected to the U.S. Senate, where he served for four terms (1956-1980). See James F. Cook, *The Governors of Georgia, 1754-1995* (Macon, GA: Mercer University Press, 1995); Herman Talmadge, *You and Segregation* (Birmingham, AL: Vulcan Press, 1955).

[2]John Hope Franklin and Alfred Moss, Jr., *From Slavery to Freedom: A History of Negro Americans* (New York: McGraw Hill, 1988), 282; Leon F. Litwack, *Trouble in Mind: Black Southerners in the Age of Jim Crow* (New York: Alfred A. Knopf, 1998), 284; Robert L. Zangrando, *The NAACP Crusade Against Lynching, 1909-1950* (Philadelphia: Temple University Press), 4. Also see *Thirty Years of Lynching in the United States, 1889-1918* (New York: National Association for the Advancement of Colored People, 1919).

[3]William Edward Du Bois, *The Autobiography of W. E. B. Du Bois: A Soliloquy on Viewing My Life from the Decade of Its First Century* (New York: International Publishers, 1968), 249-251. Besides the avowed purpose of the Niagara Movement's organizing meeting, political scientist Robert Brisbane noted that the meeting was called "to assemble the most capable and outstanding opponents of Booker T. Washington and to plan methods of counteracting his doctrines." Following the organizing meeting in Niagara Falls in 1905, the organization met in Harper's Ferry, the scene of John Brown's martyrdom, in 1906; in Boston, the center of Eastern Abolitionists, in 1907; and in Oberlin, Ohio, a hotbed of Western Abolitionists, in 1908. See Robert H. Brisbane, *The Black Vanguard: Origins of the Negro Social Revolution, 1900-1960* (Valley Forge: Judson Press, 1970), 39-41; Franklin and Moss, op. cit., 286-287.

[4]Francis L. Broderick and August Meier, *Negro Protest Thought in the Twentieth Century* (Indianapolis: Bobbs-Merrill Company, 1965), 48-49.

[5]Du Bois, op. cit., 254.

[6]Franklin and Moss, op. cit., 287. While Lincoln is known as the "Great Emancipator," largely for the Emancipation Proclamation of January 1, 1863, to free slaves, except those in states or parts of states not in rebellion against the United States, scholars have debated Lincoln's stance on social, economic, and political equality for blacks. See Lerone Bennett, Jr., *Forced into Glory: Abraham Lincoln's White Dream* (Chicago: Johnson Publishing Company, 1999); Richard Kluger, *Simple Justice: The History of Brown v. Board of Education and Black America's Struggle for Equality* (New York: Alfred A. Knopf, 1976), 41-43.

[7]Jack Greenberg, *Crusaders in the Courts: How a Dedicated Band of Lawyers Fought for the Civil Rights Revolution* (New York: Basic Books, 1994), 14.

[8]David L. Lewis, *W. E. B. Du Bois: Biography of a Race, 1868-1919* (New York: Henry Holt and Company, 1993), 439; Brisbane, op. cit., 35-47; Du Bois, op. cit., 254. While the majority of the Niagara Movement members joined the NAACP, William Monroe Trotter, a clear voice of black militancy and distrustful of the NAACP's white

leadership, refused to join the new organization. For more information on Trotter, see Lewis, op. cit.; Brisbane, op. cit.

[9]Constance Baker Motley, *Equal Justice under Law: An Autobiography of Constance Baker Motley* (New York: Farrar, Straus & Giroux, 1998), 97; Barbara Joyce Ross, *J. E. Spingarn and the Rise of the NAACP, 1911-1939* (New York: Athenum, 1972), 18.

[10]Ross, op. cit., 4-11.

[11]NAACP First Annual Report (New York: NAACP, 1911), 4.

[12]Du Bois, *Autobiography*, op. cit., 260; Walter White, *A Man Called White: The Autobiography of Walter White* (New York: Viking Press, 1948), 72, 84-85; *Buchanan v. Warley*, 245 U.S. 60; *Guinn v. United States*, 238 U.S. 347. In addition to the *Guinn* and *Buchanan* victories, two significant victories in the 1920s also bolstered the NAACP's legal program, the *Moore v. Dempsey* ruling in 1923 against mob dominance in the courtroom, and the 1927 *Nixon v. Herndon* ruling against the exclusion of blacks from participation in the Democratic primaries.

[13]James Weldon Johnson, immortalized as the author of "Lift Every Voice and Sing" (commonly referred to as "the Negro National Anthem") was born in Jacksonville, Florida, in 1871 and lived until 1938. An 1894 graduate of Atlanta University, he became highly regarded as a folklorist, creative writer, and literary scholar; some of his most important publications include *The Autobiography of an Ex-Colored Man* (1912), *The Book of American Negro Spirituals* (1925), and *God's Trombones* (1927). Widely regarded as a race leader for his fifteen years of service to the NAACP (1916-1930) as field secretary and national organizer, his defining moment in that career was his successful lobbying of the U.S. House of Representatives to pass the Dyer Anti-lynching Bill (1921), defining lynching as a federal capital felony. Although the bill did not pass the Senate (largely due to a Southern-coalition filibuster), it served as the spearhead effort of the NAACP's protracted struggle over the ensuing years to vehemently oppose the practice of "lynch law" in the South through numerous legal suits, protest campaigns, and constant adversarial publicity of such outrages of human rights.

[14]Quoted in Elliott Rudwick, *W. E. B. Du Bois: A Study in Minority Group Leadership* (Philadelphia: University of Pennsylvania Press, 1960), 171.

[15]Ibid., 195-196.

[16]Ross, op. cit., 80, 110-111.

[17]Ibid., 172; also for an analysis of Du Bois's theory of economic cooperation, see Joseph DeMarco, "The Rationale and Foundation of Du Bois's Theory of Economic Cooperation," *Phylon* 35 (March 1974): 5-15.

[18]William Edward Du Bois, "Post script by W. E. B. Du Bois," *The Crisis*, January 1934, 20.

[19]Ross, op. cit., 193. For a more complete discussion on Du Bois's perspective on voluntary segregation, see William Edward Du Bois, "Does the Negro Need Separate Schools?" *Journal of Negro Education* 4 (July 1935): 328.

[20]J. E. Spingarn, David H. Pierce, Walter White, and others, "Segregation—A Symposium: J. E. Spingarn, David H. Pierce, Leslie Pinckney Hill, and Others," *The Crisis*, March 1934, 79.

[21]Ibid., 80. W. E. B. Du Bois and James Weldon Johnson recommended White as NAACP assistant secretary in 1917. White accepted the position in 1918 and became the organization's chief executive in 1931. White, who occasionally "passed" for white to personally investigate white mob lynchings and race riots, boldly led the organization from 1931 until his death in 1955, working closely with Charles Hamilton Houston, Thurgood Marshall, Roy Wilkins, and other civil rights leaders to eradicate racial injustice in America. For a study of Walter White, see Walter White, *A Man Called White: The Autobiography of Walter White* (New York: Viking Press, 1948).

[22]Ross, op. cit., 80, 193.

[23]Ibid., 196.

[24]The board's passage of the 1934 resolution banning criticisms of the NAACP and its officials in *The Crisis* was central among Du Bois's reasons for resigning from the NAACP. Du Bois's resignation was preceded by correspondence with the board, reaffirming his position; see for example his "Letter[s] to the Board of Directors of the NAACP," June 11, 1934, and June 26, 1934, in *The Correspondence of W. E. B. Du Bois: Vol. I Selections, 1877-1934*, ed. Herbert Aptheker (Amherst: University of Massachusetts Press, 1973-78), 478-481.

[25]Ross, op. cit., 217.

[26]Mark V. Tushnet, *The NAACP's Legal Strategy Against Segregated Education, 1925-1950* (Chapel Hill: University of North Carolina Press, 1987), 6.

[27]Juan Williams, *Eyes on the Prize: America's Civil Rights Years, 1954-1965* (New York: Penguin Books, 1988), 4.

[28]Greenberg, op. cit., 5.

[29]Vernon Jordan, interview with author, Washington, D.C., February 28, 1997; Mark V. Tushnet, *Making Civil Rights Law: Thurgood Marshall and the Supreme Court, 1936-1961* (New York: Oxford University Press, 1994), 6-7.

[30]Jordan, interview, op. cit.; Greenberg, op. cit., 56.

[31]White, op. cit., 142. The NAACP had begun to develop a plan for the coordination of litigation as early as 1925. James Weldon Johnson proposed to the American Fund for Public Service (also known as the Garland Fund) to finance a legal program "to give the Southern Negro his constitutional rights." The Fund offered the NAACP $100,000 for a litigation campaign in 1930. With an endorsement from Charles Hamilton Houston, Harvard Law graduate Nathan Margold began to devise a litigation strategy. For a review of the Garland Fund's impact on the development of the NAACP's legal program, see Tushnet, *The NAACP's Legal Strategy*, op. cit., 1-20.

[32]Sally Seawright, "Desegregation at Maryland: The NAACP and the Murray Case in the 1930s," *Maryland Historian* 1 (spring 1970): 59; Constance Baker Motley, interview with author, New York, NY, March 30, 1995; Williams, op. cit., 10-11.

[33]Greenberg, op. cit., 5-6.

[34]Motley, interview, op. cit.

[35]*Pearson et al. v. Murray*, 182 A. 590, 592 (Md. App. 1936); Sally Seawright, op. cit., 66-71. Also see Edward J. Kuebler, "The Desegregation of the University of Maryland," *Maryland Historical Magazine* 71 (spring 1976): 37-49.

[36]Leon Higginbotham, Jr., *Shades of Freedom: Racial Politics and Presumptions of the American Legal Process* (New York: Oxford University Press, 1996), 164-165.

[37]*Gaines v. Canada*, 305 U.S. 337, 352, 59 S. Ct. 232, 238 (1938).

[38]White, op. cit., 162; Brisbane, op. cit., 191.

[39]Steadman Vincent Sanford, letter to Clennon W. King, April 15, 1940; Clennon W. King, letter to Walter White, April 18, 1940, Papers of the NAACP, The Campaign for Educational Equality: Legal Department and Central Office Records, 1913-1950. Series B: 1940-1950, NAACP Archives, Library of Congress, Washington, D.C.

[40]Charles S. Gurr, *The Personal Equation: A Biography of Steadman Vincent Sanford* (Athens: University of Georgia Press, 1999), 159; University System of Georgia Board of Regents Minutes, April 23, 1943, Archives, Office of the Board of Regents, Atlanta, GA.

[41]University System of Georgia Board of Regents Minutes, August 11, 1943; June 4 and 5, 1944; and November 8, 1944, Archives, Office of the Board of Regents, Atlanta, GA. The regents adopted a resolution on August 11, 1943, that established scholarships for Negroes. According to the November 8, 1944, minutes, the board had made available out-of-state scholarships totaling $2,398.26 to twelve Negro students. At the height of the out-of-state scholarship program during the mid-1950s, the regents provided almost $300,000 per year in state money to more than twenty-seven hundred black students. Also see Roger M. Williams, *The Bonds: An American Family* (New York: Atheneum, 1971), 139.

[42]Motley, *Equal Justice*, op. cit., 99; Greenberg, op. cit., 19.

[43]Carl T. Rowan, *Dream Makers, Dream Breakers: The World of Justice Thurgood Marshall* (Boston: Little, Brown and Company, 1993), 75-76.

[44]Motley, interview, op. cit.

[45]Franklin and Moss, Jr., op. cit., 396; Motley, interview, op. cit.

[46]*Plessy v. Ferguson*, 163 U.S. 537 (1896). Also see Papers of the NAACP, The Campaign for Educational Equality: Legal Department and Central Office Records, Legal File 1946: Special Lawyers Conference, NAACP Archives, Library of Congress, Washington, D.C. At an April 27-28, 1946, NAACP Special Lawyers Conference, officials generally agreed that the NAACP would not pursue actions to establish or equalize colored schools, but would encourage plaintiffs to apply to all-white schools.

[47]Kluger, *Simple Justice*, op. cit., 272-273; Mark V. Tushnet, *Making Civil Rights Law: Thurgood Marshall and the Supreme Court, 1936-1961* (New York: Oxford University Press, 1994), 35.

[48]*Sipuel v. Board of Regents of University of Oklahoma*, 332 U.S. 631, 68 S. Ct. 299 (1948).

[49]In June 1949, as the LDF increased its attack on segregation in other states, the Oklahoma legislature amended its laws to permit blacks to attend graduate and professional programs in all-white colleges and universities on a segregated basis only, and only where the state did not offer such programs in black schools. Subsequently, the University of Oklahoma admitted Sipuel under the new law. White, op. cit., 146; Greenberg, op. cit., 66-67.

[50]Motley, interview, op. cit.; White, op. cit., 149.

[51]*Sweatt v. Painter*, 339 U.S. 629 (1950).

[52]Ibid.

[53]"End of Jim Crow seen by NAACP Counsel Marshall: Conference of Lawyers to Implement Decisions," *Atlanta Daily World*, June 11, 1950, 1.

[54]Alvis V. Adair, *Desegregation: The Illusion of Black Progress* (New York: University Press of America, 1984), 29.

[55]*McLaurin v. Oklahoma*, 339 U.S. 637-642 (1950).

[56]Quoted in Greenberg, op. cit., 3.

CHAPTER *2*

Horace Ward's Ambition:
Widening the Crack in the Wall

Not surprisingly, despite the Supreme Court rulings resulting from cases in Texas and Oklahoma (and related cases in Maryland, Missouri, and other states), segregationists in the Deep South either openly defied the Court orders or devised legal evasions. During the first half of the twentieth century, little had been done to break down the legal mantle of segregation in the Deep South, either in education, voting, housing, or employment. One notable exception was the landmark case of a little-known but courageous black country preacher, Primus E. King from Muscogee County, Georgia, in 1945. The state Democratic party had denied black Georgia residents the right to vote in the all-white Democratic primary. Undeterred by threats on his life, bombs exploding on his doorstep, and other terrorist acts, King sued in federal court, asserting his right to vote.[1] With the assistance of Thurgood Marshall and the LDF, King won his argument before the district court in the Middle District of Georgia on October 12, 1945. The United States Court of Appeals for the Fifth Circuit upheld the verdict on March 6, 1946. King's successful lawsuit opened primary elections to blacks in Georgia.[2] King recalled:

> People were afraid to associate with me during those days . . . Man come up to me one day and said, "You the nigger cause so much disturbance in the white primary? You must want to be put

23

in the river." I told him, "You throw so many in for nothing, I don't mind being thrown in for something."[3]

It was against this historical backdrop that the quiet, unassuming, but ambitious Horace T. Ward sought to enter the all-white University of Georgia School of Law. Ward, a lifelong resident of Georgia, grew up in La Grange. He was the only child of Minnie Ward, a young mother who, after his birth, worked away from home as a maid for a white family. During this time Ward lived with his maternal grandparents, who were hardworking people, and he developed a strong work ethic. After entering school at age nine, he lived with his mother and his stepfather, Richard Harrison, a laundry worker. Ward recalled that the state of Georgia did not enforce school attendance age requirements when he entered school and that it was not uncommon for students to start school at age eight or nine. Ward also said that his grandparents, who did not attain a formal education, may not have fully appreciated the value of starting school early.[4]

Ward's first heroes were his grandfather, who was a deacon and superintendent of the Sunday School at a local Baptist church, and his uncle, who was the first member of his family to earn a high school diploma. Ward developed an interest in reading early in his life. Although his family did not own any books, his mother and other women who worked as maids or cooks for rich white families often brought home magazines that he read. Ward's interest in history grew out of his reading stories as a child in magazines such as *National Geographic, Look,* and *Life.*[5]

Church leaders and teachers nurtured Ward and strongly influenced his aspirations. Reverend Phale Hale, a former teacher and minister in La Grange, described Ward as brilliant and destined for success. Hale remembered Ward as a quiet young man who was industrious and conscientious about learning, working hard in his studies, and preferring reading over recess.[6] His work ethic impressed his fourth grade teacher, Mrs. D. B. Davis, who encouraged him to read further and checked out books from the school library for him. Ward's high achievement and enthusiasm for learning led her to recommend to the principal that he skip fifth grade.[7] The principal approved, and Ward continued his successful educational progress.

At an early age Ward had an opportunity to hear the preeminent attorney Austin Thomas Walden, one of a handful of black attorneys in Georgia, speak to an assembly in his hometown. Ward has said he did not even know that black lawyers existed before his exposure to the charismatic Walden.[8] Walden, the son of former slaves, grew up in Fort Valley, Georgia. He earned an A. B. degree from Atlanta University in 1907 and a law degree from the University of Michigan in 1911. He became one of the first blacks to practice law in Georgia.

Walden had provided legal assistance to Primus King and the LDF and helped King win the right for blacks to vote in the Democratic primary.[9] Capitalizing on this newfound freedom for black Georgians, Walden was very active in voter education and voter registration throughout Georgia and used his influence to mobilize the black vote. Walden's influence in increasing black voter turnout led the white political leadership to seek his counsel when dealing with issues in the black community. Constance Baker Motley remembered that Walden was part of what was called the "old guard" or the "black cabinet," and that white officials had a practice of meeting with black leaders such as Walden on important matters related to the black community.[10]

For a black man during the 1940s and 1950s, Walden had an unusual entree into the white power structure, and he used it effectively to try to uplift the black community. He was involved in several history-making legal cases, including cases against the Ku Klux Klan, a case to desegregate the public golf courses in Atlanta, and a case involving equal pay for black public school teachers, which he won after a six-year court battle. Though he faced threats on his life, Walden continued his struggle to overcome racial injustice all his life, undaunted by such attempts at intimidation.[11]

Walden inspired several generations of blacks to become lawyers and to fight segregation. Vernon Jordan, future Director of the Urban League, was another young man who heeded Walden's call,

becoming a prominent lawyer and civil rights leader. Jordan recalled
Walden's impact:

> The reason I'm sitting here in this law firm as a senior partner is
> not unrelated to the incredible influence of A. T. Walden, who
> was the first black lawyer I ever saw. Mr. Walden was so impres-
> sive, and I liked the way he talked. I liked the way he stood straight
> and tall. I liked the way he articulated his views, and I can hear
> him saying about segregation, "I'll be glad when you're dead, you
> rascal you." He was so moving, so articulate. He had a huge influ-
> ence on me as a kid. I wanted to be a lawyer like A. T. Walden. I
> wanted to walk like him and talk like him and hang out my
> shingle on Auburn Avenue just like Walden.[12]

Walden made a similarly dynamic impression on the young
Ward, and in part because of the force of that impression, Ward began to consider practicing law as a means of taking on social responsibility. High school principal and former Morehouse instructor C.
E. Warner was among the black community leaders who noted Ward's
ambition and encouraged him to continue to excel. Ward's academic
success in high school, where he was senior class valedictorian and
president of the student body, led to his acceptance at the prestigious Morehouse College in 1946, encouraged by Warner and
Morehouse graduate Phale Hale.

At Morehouse Ward was influenced by great thinkers and activists in the civil rights movement. Continuing with the interest in
history he had developed as a child reading hand-me-down magazines, he majored in history and earned his bachelor's degree in 1949.
Ward graduated from Morehouse one year after Martin Luther King,
Jr., and recalls that King and other upperclassmen, who very often
could be found discussing the social and political issues of the day,
heightened his social awareness. Ward remembered being impressed
not only by King's scholarship, but also by his seriousness of purpose
and persuasiveness as a speaker on social issues.[13] Ward's exposure to
King and other students concerned about social conditions reinforced the ideas that his high school mentors had shared with him
regarding the importance of community uplift and social responsi-

bility. This reinforcement, combined with the early influences that encouraged him to take on social responsibility, influenced his decision to pursue a graduate degree in political science. He subsequently earned his M.A. in political science from Atlanta University in 1950.

While Ward was a student at Morehouse and Atlanta University, Harvard Ph.D. graduate and political scientist Robert Brisbane and other noted scholars persuaded him to pursue his interest in law.[14] These scholars promoted a legal education not only as an opportunity for professional advancement, but also as a tool for the advancement of civil rights for black people. Morehouse College, under the leadership of the internationally renowned Benjamin E. Mays (president from 1940 to 1967), was strongly committed to the pre-professional training of black men. Mays encouraged many Morehouse graduates to pursue medicine, dentistry, law, and other professions. Brisbane recalled:

> I was recruited by Dr. Mays to come to Morehouse to teach political science. I taught a class on the U.S. government that had a registration of about thirty-five students, and I learned that thirteen of the students were men who hoped to study law, including Horace Ward. At that time Morehouse had not developed a pre-law program, so I got busy trying to figure out what I could do to help these men get into law school and to help them succeed once they got there. Horace Ward was a quiet young man but soon demonstrated that he was the smartest man in that class. Ward established himself as a solid student who was really interested in moving ahead in the practice of law.[15]

In an interview with the author, Ward noted that Mays was uncompromising in his insistence that Morehouse students accept their duty to help uplift their communities from the forces of racial oppression and bigotry.[16] Mays regularly challenged Morehouse students to oppose the segregationist system, and he set a tone within the Morehouse walls that encouraged students to take on social responsibility. Ward recalled that Mays even admonished Morehouse students for attending segregated theaters and other establishments that relegated blacks to an inferior status. "Benjamin Mays preached that you don't do anything to segregate yourself, except out of necessity. For instance, if you couldn't afford a car, you had to ride the segregated bus. But you didn't go to theaters where you had to sit in the balcony because that's not a necessity of life."[17] Dr. Hugh Gloster, who succeeded Mays as Morehouse president in 1967, noted how Morehouse students and faculty embraced Mays's ideas and accepted the responsibility of fighting against social injustice. Gloster pointed out that it was not accidental that so many Morehouse graduates strongly opposed segregation and contributed so much to the elimination of the practice. Ward has noted the profound influence that Mays had on him, furthering the commitment to social responsibility that he had first learned from Walden and his early mentors in La Grange.[18]

William Madison Boyd, who chaired the department of political science at Atlanta University, also had a profound effect on Ward's pursuits. Boyd, with master's and doctorate degrees from the University of Michigan, was a prolific writer, lecturer, and news analyst. Boyd's leadership and service with the American Friends Service Committee, the Institute on International Relations, and the American Political Science Association earned him international stature. In 1947 the Carnegie Foundation awarded Boyd a grant to study the social and economic conditions in England, France, Holland, Denmark, Sweden, and Poland; despite such international acclaim, however, Boyd's foremost passion was for the racial uplift of his people. Because of his desire to serve and elevate blacks from second-class citizenship, Boyd, like others of his time, was not satisfied with an academic role alone. Instead, he applied his scholarship to community development aimed at achieving first-class citizenship for black Americans. Boyd used the air waves of WERD in Atlanta, the nation's first black-owned radio station, to address a large black audience with a weekly community forum analyzing socioeconomic issues and urging blacks to join in the struggle against social injustice.[19]

Boyd also served as the president of the NAACP Georgia State Conference of Branches (Georgia's NAACP chapters) and often ventured into hostile territory, investigating civil rights violations and pursuing voter rights for blacks. His perseverance in the civil rights struggle had a major impact beyond his own state of Georgia, as he played a key advisory role to Thurgood Marshall and Walter White in the wider civil rights spectrum. In speaking of the NAACP and civil rights efforts in the late 1940s and early 1950s in Georgia, civil rights leader Constance Baker Motley recalled Boyd as a fearless leader who often carried the NAACP on his back. Political scientist Robert Brisbane described Boyd as the "big NAACP man in the southeast."[20] Betty Mapp, Boyd's widow, said:

> Way back in the 1940s when it was dangerous to be talking about first-class citizenship and civil rights, that was during Eugene Talmadge's time, Bill never bit his tongue. He said whatever he wanted to say. He first got involved with the NAACP when he organized the student chapter at Fort Valley State College. And when we moved to Atlanta, he became president of all of the branches for the state. He worked very closely with Walter White, who at that time was executive secretary of the NAACP. They had a campaign to register blacks to vote, and I remember Bill would go out to all these little towns in Georgia, talking to churches and trying to get people to register. I was really afraid, and many nights I lay awake waiting for him to come home.[21]

Speaking before the NAACP Conference of Lawyers meeting in June 1950, Thurgood Marshall strongly urged blacks wanting a graduate or professional education to apply to their state universities for admission.[22] Ready for the challenge, Marshall realized the struggle was not only against institutionalized oppression, but also the slothful attitude of blacks content with the status quo. Marshall stressed the fact that the NAACP could move no faster than its constituency would move in the fight to defeat segregation. For several years, Marshall and NAACP officials had fervently advocated the need to attack segregation in the South, and they needed someone to answer the rallying call.[23] Boyd answered that call and sought blacks for admission into all-white colleges and universities, daring to travel throughout the segregationist state seeking students to pursue graduate or professional education.

Ward learned of Boyd's support for prospective black applicants to Georgia's segregated institutions while studying at Atlanta
University. Ward reminisced:

> Dr. Boyd was actively seeking to get black persons to apply to the
> graduate and professional schools in Georgia, and I came to know
> about that. So I went to see Dr. Boyd and told him that I was
> interested in studying law and that I might as well file an applica-
> tion to the University of Georgia Law School. He told me if you
> make up your mind to do so, come to see me and I'll assist you
> and give you all the support that I can.[24]

Ward's interest was good news for the NAACP officials who had
orchestrated the campaign to combat segregation in graduate and
professional education. On April 17, 1951, at an NAACP membership mass meeting in Atlanta, NAACP chief Roy Wilkins predicted
that the University of Georgia would enroll a black student by 1952.[25]

Betty Mapp specifically remembered her husband's efforts to
identify candidates interested in pursuing law school, the NAACP's
first line of attack in desegregation efforts. She said Boyd first interviewed Martin Luther King, Jr., who was a Morehouse student at
the time, about studying law at UGA, but King was interested in
pursuing a degree in the ministry. Mapp recounted that Boyd later
interviewed Ward about applying to the law school and considered
him the perfect candidate, possessing intellectual ability, the credentials needed to pursue the study of law, and the steady determination to fight for social justice. Political scientist Brisbane noted that
Ward was not a loud demonstrator and was not attracted to the more
dramatic phase of protest, but rather, strong inside, with heart and
soul behind his efforts.[26]

Thus, against the massive opposition to mixing races in schools,
but with Boyd's urging, on September 30, 1950, Ward applied to
enter the University of Georgia. Besides Boyd's influence, that of his
family, teachers and preachers in La Grange, A. T. Walden, Benjamin
E. Mays, and his Morehouse experience in general converged to
effect this momentous decision in his life.[27]

Although Ward possessed impressive credentials, graduating with honors from Morehouse College and Atlanta University, the entrenched forces of segregation did not retreat. Governor Herman Talmadge made it clear that he was elected governor on a pledge to preserve segregation, and he ardently reaffirmed his campaign promise: "As long as I am your governor, Negroes will not be admitted to white schools."[28] Acting on that promise, he became personally involved in trying to block Ward from entering the University of Georgia, deputizing his personal attorney, B. D. Murphy, to work with the state attorney general to that purpose.

During an interview with the author, Talmadge insisted that his actions to bar Ward and other blacks from the University of Georgia were not related to his personal feelings about blacks. Talmadge said:

> I grew up with blacks on the farm. We went fishing together, swimming in the nude. Some of the best friends I had were black. And then when it got time to where I attended school, our paths were divergent. I had no animosity toward any color whatsoever. In fact, I've seen many blacks that I admire very much.[29]

Despite such recent protestations, Talmadge was unequivocal in the 1950s in carrying out his campaign promise to sustain segregation, asserting that desegregation of public schools or colleges would create societal chaos and mayhem. Talmadge has defended his past policies by asserting that segregation was a way of life in the South and politicians had to subscribe to this culture to sustain their political life:

> We had had several hundred years of segregation. It was the mores and custom. Not only with people, but it was written in the constitution, and laws. Any political figure that dared to defy that wouldn't have carried a county in the state. Any Southern leader who would have had different views from mine would have been run out of office.[30]

Journalist Bill Shipp, who was a University of Georgia student during the 1950s, described the Talmadge administration's staunch defiance of desegregation:

Although it did several good things, the overriding issue of that administration was first and foremost maintaining a segregated society. All of their literature, all of their campaign rallies were filled with racial hatred. In retrospect it was a terrible era to live in. It is almost ironic that it came after World War II, which was ostensibly a war to free everyone—to grant liberty throughout the world. And yet in this state at that time and in this region you still had governors preaching racial tyranny.[31]

Talmadge, affirming that the mood of the state at the time overwhelmingly favored segregation, vowed to enforce Georgia's segregation laws against all hazards.[32] Although the U.S. Supreme Court had banned discrimination and had forced graduate and professional schools in other states to admit blacks, Southern politicians bragged that no black had been admitted to a college or university in the Deep South. Leading officials minced no words in vowing to maintain the status quo in their Jim Crow states. University regents in Georgia clamored for new strategies to discourage black applicants and declared that they would use all of their legal resources to fight the admission of Ward or other blacks.[33]

Ward's application therefore was not considered for admission. Instead, the admissions office passed the application on to L. R. Siebert, executive secretary of the Board of Regents, to offer Ward out-of-state aid, the customary practice that the regents had adopted since 1944 for dealing with black applicants. Between 1944 and 1949, the regents awarded twenty black students scholarships to attend out-of-state law schools, paying the costs of tuition as well as a room and board allowance.[34]

Some University of Georgia students supported the discriminatory policy of sending black students out of state. An editorial in the University of Georgia student newspaper the *Red and Black*, shortly after Ward had applied, described the sentiments behind Georgia's insistence on the odious racial practice:

> Negroes have nothing to gain by forcing open segregated schools with court action. Equal education is already available to them.

The state is now spending upwards of $70,000 a year to assure them comparable facilities in other states. What they might gain in eliminating segregated education would be toppled over and smothered by a revolution of prejudice and hatred which does not now exist. Fires of discord among the races that long ago burned to embers would be rekindled and fanned to frightening proportions. Retardation of progress could be measured in terms of years. It is not discrimination to bar a Negro student from the University when he can get a comparable education in another state where he is accepted gladly. On the other hand it would be harsh to allow admittance. He would find himself in the middle of a hostile group—where a deep-rooted tradition of the Southern way of life had been over-run. He'd be alone here. And he wouldn't have equal opportunities, for he'd feel the terrible loneliness that only a man alone in the world can feel. He could enjoy the same physical plant as his fellow students, but that wouldn't open the door of comradeship to him. *You can't legislate good will.*[35] [Emphasis added]

In addition to such discouragement of Ward's attempt to enter UGA, segregationists also used more covert tactics to hinder his efforts. White business leaders approached prominent blacks such as Benjamin Mays and Atlanta Urban League president Grace Hamilton to encourage them to convince Ward to end his attempt to enter UGA and opt for the out-of-state scholarship. One well-known, distinguished white leader even promised Mays that Atlanta University could get money to build a law school for Negroes. The business leaders claimed they were not necessarily opposed to desegregation, but that Ward's insistence on entering UGA could cause disturbances and that perhaps the time was not yet right for such a move in Georgia. But Mays and Hamilton refused to discourage Ward; on the contrary, they strongly urged him to pursue his ambitions. Mays recalled, "I promised the gentlemen who came to see me that . . . I saw no honorable way I could persuade Mr. Ward to withdraw his application and accept out-of-state aid . . . and that it had long been my hope that the University of Georgia would open its doors to Negroes without federal mandate."[36]

However, Ward recalled that some blacks expressed their opposition to his quest and encouraged him to proceed more moderately. Segregation in Georgia and other Deep South states was so firmly entrenched during this period in the early 1950s that many black Americans did not actively oppose segregation, and many tended to regard it simply as a way of life without open hostilities between blacks and whites. Many blacks felt that Ward's challenge to the status quo would antagonize whites and create a hostile environment. Ward remembered that many black people just thought that "segregation was the way to go" and were "afraid that something might happen" if there was a serious effort to try to desegregate any of the public schools in Georgia.[37] Conservative blacks perceived what they saw as the radical efforts of Ward and the NAACP as a threat to their modest gains. For some it was a basic bread-and-butter issue in that their survival was largely dependent on whites who controlled the economy. Many blacks justifiably feared violent consequences for openly confronting the oppressive system, since those who did were often harassed and their lives threatened; others were primarily concerned for their social standing. Political scientist Robert Brisbane discussed the attitudes of conservative blacks in a 1995 interview with the author:

> There is the assumption that all blacks were unified in support of Horace Ward; that is an erroneous assumption. I just got through showing this film to my class on *Brown v. Board of Education* and some of the toughest opposition Thurgood Marshall encountered was from some conservative blacks who felt that he was pushing too fast. It is also true that when Horace Ward sought entrance to the University of Georgia, there were some who felt he was doing too much too fast and that he should be content and take the out-of-state aid and be satisfied. They felt he was just making too many waves.[38]

Despite white segregationist sentiments and the apprehensions of those blacks who asserted that he was moving too fast, Ward declined the out-of-state aid and appealed to regents officials to consider him as an applicant for admission to the law school rather than an applicant for out-of-state aid. Benjamin Mays noted Ward's courage in his book *Born to Rebel*. Observing that it was physically and professionally dangerous for a Negro to apply to enter a white Georgia school in 1950, Mays asserted, "Horace Ward was one of the few Negroes willing to put his career on the line and suffer the harassment."[39]

Ward wrote to the regents and stated that as a citizen of the state he felt entitled to the same opportunities available to whites. Shortly afterwards, on November 8, 1950, the regents adopted a uniquely elaborate appeals process incorporating new procedures, including the appointment of a special committee to interview any applicant and make a recommendation to the president of the university. After a series of protracted delays, the regents returned Ward's application to admissions director Walter Danner, who subsequently denied the application on June 7, 1951, nine months after it was submitted. In denying Ward's application, Danner gave no reasons for his decision.[40]

In yet another move to safeguard Georgia's all-white schools and colleges, in 1951 the Georgia General Assembly passed an appropriations bill that declared that any school or college that mixed the races would lose all state funds. In addition to enlisting his personal attorney and the state attorney general to thwart Ward, Talmadge had now galvanized the legislature to create more obstacles. Nevertheless, Ward appealed the denial to university president O. C. Aderhold. Aderhold created a special committee to interview Ward and determine his eligibility for admission as required by the newly constituted appeals procedures. The committee interviewed Ward and expressed concerns about his character and ability to study law. On September 14, 1951, based on the special committee's recommendation, Aderhold upheld Danner's rejection of Ward's application for admission.[41]

Ward appealed Aderhold's decision to Chancellor Harmon Caldwell. In a September 20, 1951, letter to Caldwell, Ward contended that he had met all lawful requirements for admission to the law school and plainly stated that officials had rejected him due to his race. Ward said that "the only possible reason for the refusal to admit me, a Negro, to the Law School of the University of Georgia is my race and color."[42] Despite Ward's accusation that officials had acted in a racist manner, Caldwell upheld Aderhold's rejection of Ward for admission to the law school.

Ward continued further administrative appeals, but the regents' office employed numerous delaying tactics to stall his efforts. The state adopted additional, devious provisions designed to bar blacks from entering white schools and the regents hastily passed a resolution on February 13, 1952, requesting the law school to develop entrance examinations and make new recommendations to the regents regarding admissions requirements for students seeking admission to the law school. Ward received notice from the regents that they would act upon his application based upon the outcome of this resolution.

When Thurgood Marshall and NAACP officials learned of the resolution, they questioned the regents' motives. The NAACP legal staff expressed in a February 1952 legal department report that the action of the regents was undoubtedly an attempt to further delay action on Ward's application and to devise a means for eliminating Ward as a qualified applicant.[43]

On July 19, 1952, the regents adopted recommendations from the law school faculty that prospective students must pass entrance examinations and submit "certificates of good moral character" from law school alumni in order to be admitted to the law school.[44] Ward declined to take the examinations and insisted that his application be considered based on the admissions requirements in place when he filed his original application. Maintaining that the regents had devised the entrance examinations as a stumbling block to halt Ward's admission, Thurgood Marshall claimed, "Ward cannot be required to do anything that was not required when he applied—anything else is unreasonable."[45] Regents officials declared that not requiring Ward to meet the new admissions standards would be unfair to other applicants. Outrageously enough, the institution that for 165 years had excluded blacks argued that excusing Ward from the tests would result in discrimination against white applicants.

The law school faculty's decision to create the new entrance requirements was among the most reprehensible of the actions taken to keep Ward out of the law school. The mere fact that the faculty of the state's flagship institution colluded with the regents in establishing policies to thwart black enrollment was abominable, contradicting any pretense of academic integrity. This collusion would have been an unprofessional action by the faculty of any educational institution, but it was most egregious for a law faculty, which presumably should have had a higher respect for legal principles.

The silence of the tenured law faculty, in particular, was appalling. However, one lone member of the law faculty, native Mississippian James J. Lenoir, vehemently opposed the underhanded action of the law school. Lenoir was an eminent legal scholar who held a law degree from Columbia University and a Ph.D. from the University of Illinois. Lenoir could not reconcile the treatment of Ward with either his moral or his legal ethics. In a letter from Lenoir to Dean Hosch, Lenoir documented the questions he raised in an April 30, 1952, law faculty meeting. His comments deserve consideration at length:

> Although I have not been given an opportunity to examine the directive or resolution of the Board of Regents, there are some questions in regard to it which seriously disturb me. They are as follows and I shall appreciate it if the Dean will enlighten me:
>
> 1) Is it one of the purposes of the Board of Regents to have the faculty devise a system of tests which will be a means of keeping negroes out of our law school?
>
> 2) Is it the purpose of the Board of Regents to have the faculty devise a method by which the type of students admitted to the law school will meet a higher educational standard, thereby improving the quality of our students?
>
> 3) Is it the opinion of the Board of Regents that we are accepting students whose qualifications are lower than those exacted by Emory or Mercer, or by other law schools? If the answer is Yes, what is the basis for this conclusion?
>
> 4) In the light of the newspaper history and reports of the Ward case, should we not hesitate to make a recommendation unless we have a clarification of the purposes behind this direc-

tive of the Board of Regents which would either affirm or deny that the proposal we are asked to make is an effort to get around the decisions of the Supreme Court of the United States with respect to segregation in law school?

5) Should we not avoid subterfuges and, as a group of lawyers, face the issue squarely, whatever it may be?

6) I am perfectly cognizant of the Georgia appropriation statute and the terms in which it is written; but it seems to me that, as a group of lawyers, we should not let that act blind us to actual facts or lead us to participate in any kind of subterfuge by which we would become parties or accessories to a method of discrimination because of race or religion. For my part I cannot see how, legally, we can get around the Supreme Court decisions. Certainly our sister states of Virginia, North Carolina, Tennessee, Louisiana, Kentucky, Arkansas, and Texas have apparently adjusted themselves to these decisions without any great difficulty, and they are as much Southern as we are. If it is one of the purposes of the Board of Regents to devise a system by which negroes may be excluded from the law school, should we not as a law faculty, examine more carefully the legal problems concerned?

You will recall that you refused to answer these questions, saying that you did not know the answers. Thereupon I asked you if you could obtain answers from the Board of Regents, and you said that you would not. You further said that I could try to get the answers from the Board of Regents. Thereupon I moved that the faculty ask the Board of Regents for a clarification of the matter. The motion died for want of a second.[46]

Although Lenoir cogently and diplomatically posed essential, pertinent questions to the law faculty, Lenoir, Hosch, and their law colleagues well knew that these examinations were designed specifically to block Ward. The law faculty also had to know that Hosch had been colluding with the regents to stall Ward's admission.[47] Lenoir's letter to Hosch no doubt represented the views of some of the other law faculty as well. However, aside from Lenoir, neither morality, legality, nor fairness compelled the faculty to speak out for Ward and possibly face severe sanctions.

The fact that Lenoir stood alone in openly defying the regents may have been related to the ouster of a dean for his liberal views some ten years earlier. In 1941 Governor Eugene Talmadge (Herman Talmadge's father) forced the regents to fire a dean for allegedly supporting racial coeducation. Talmadge charged that Walter Dewey Cocking, dean of the College of Education, advocated social equality and had worked and planned for the day when black and white children would be educated together in Georgia. Talmadge targeted Cocking and vowed that he would remove any person in the university system advocating communism or racial equality.[48] Although the law faculty was derelict in not recognizing the regents' motives, which must have appeared obvious to the most naive person, the faculty's fears of retaliation if they openly opposed segregation were real.

On August 18, 1953, Lenoir resigned from the law school in protest of the regents' actions. Lenoir expressed the following sentiments in his resignation letter to Aderhold:

> In the Spring of 1952 I was seriously disturbed by the Regents' action in seeking recommendations from the law faculty for aptitude and character tests to be given to all applicants for admission to the law school. In view of the Ward case it seemed to me that the faculty were entitled to an explanation of the motive behind the Regents' resolution, and had the moral responsibility of meeting, without subterfuge, whatever was the true issue.
>
> It now appears that in April 1953 the Board of Regents took further action, now effective, requiring character tests for all who apply for admission to any unit of the University system, apparently basing this action on the precedent set by the law school.
>
> Although I am entirely in favor of a faculty adopting educational tests in an honest endeavor to raise educational standards, I am opposed to the prostitution of educational standards by the setting up of educational tests which are in reality a subterfuge to attain some other end. This is the stand which I took in the law faculty meetings on the Regents' resolution.[49]

Without answering Lenoir's charges, Aderhold accepted the resignation the following day and merely commented in a letter to Lenoir:

> I am indeed sorry that you have become disturbed by certain actions of the Board of Regents. In all cases I believe the members of the Board of Regents make judgments in terms of what they believe to be of the best interest of the people of the state and University.[50]

In a satirical article published by the *Mercer Law Review* in spring 1954 and widely circulated throughout the nation, Lenoir expressed his outrage with the law faculty's action and with the institution he had grown to love during his eight-year faculty tenure:

> What I cannot understand was the apparent unquestioning compliance of the law faculty. The subterfuge which the Regents had in mind was clearly discernible from the newspaper publicity. I would think that a self-respecting educational institution would not care to have anything to do with a subterfuge, that it has a responsibility to not only know the law but to respect it.[51]

Lenoir received volumes of letters from prominent leaders in Georgia and other states. Several law faculty and attorneys from prominent law firms expressed agreement with Lenoir's viewpoint. However, Lenoir noted that those in agreement with him expressed their support only in personal letters, and nowhere did his article receive any public comment.

On June 23, 1952, (shortly before the Regents adopted new entrance examinations), Ward, convinced that the state and regents would continue their legal chicanery to keep him out of the law school, filed a civil suit in the United States District Court, Northern District of Georgia. Ward's suit named the Regents of the University System of Georgia; Dr. Harmon W. Caldwell, chancellor; Dr. O. C. Aderhold, president of the university; Walter N. Danner, registrar of the university; and Dr. J. Alton Hosch, dean of the law school. A. T. Walden filed the action, along with Thurgood Marshall and

Robert L. Carter of the LDF. Walden was Ward's local attorney but he, along with Boyd, had been instrumental in gaining the assistance of Marshall and the LDF. Marshall and NAACP officials had previously investigated the possibility of filing two cases against the University of Georgia to gain the entrance of Clennon W. King and Annie Louise Brown to the University of Georgia School of Law, but these efforts did not come to fruition.[52] Marshall also had particular interest in winning such cases in the Deep South.

The *Ward* complaint contended that regents and university officials denied Ward admission solely because of his race, while at the same time the university had admitted white applicants of equal or lesser qualifications. The complaint further alleged that the university provided legal training and facilities to white citizens, paid for with public funds, while refusing to provide such facilities to Ward and other Negro citizens solely on account of their color. Marshall said in the complaint that these actions constituted unlawful discrimination and a denial of the right of Ward and other Negroes to the equal protection of the law according to the Fourteenth Amendment.[53]

In 1952, Governor Talmadge announced that he would throw the full resources of the state government into the defense of the state's segregation laws and would provide Attorney General Eugene Cook with the assistance to fight the case through "every court in the land."[54] The state tried to have the suit dismissed and used a variety of obstructive legal maneuvers that delayed the scheduling of the case for trial until October 9, 1953.[55]

While the case was pending, the armed services deferred Ward from the military draft for medical reasons. However, after corrective surgery, the selective service reclassified him, and shortly thereafter the Atlanta draft board called him for military duty during the Korean War draft. Ironically, Ward's call to duty to defend the rights of persons overseas preempted his challenge to segregation at home. Cancelling the scheduled court hearing, the judge continued Ward's case indefinitely when Marshall and Walden advised the court that the draft board had ordered Ward to duty on September 9, 1953, only thirty days before his case was scheduled for trial. For two years the defendants would be free from Ward's efforts to enter the University of Georgia.[56]

The draft board action frustrated for the time being Ward's ambition to be a lawyer and delayed the NAACP's efforts to dismantle segregation in Georgia. But NAACP leader William Boyd quickly pointed out that "Georgia has won this round, but it has not won the battle by any means."[57] Boyd, Marshall, and other NAACP officials regarded the matter as only a temporary setback and vowed to continue their efforts once Ward completed his tour of duty.[58]

The state had employed a variety of tactics to halt Ward, ranging from laws to close schools in the event of court-ordered desegregation to requiring white alumni certifications for admission. Before the court could rule on the constitutionality of these matters, the judge postponed the suit due to his induction. Ward was off to the army, but his quest to get a legal education at the all-white law school in his home state had rekindled the flames of the struggle for equitable education for black Americans.

CHAPTER 2 NOTES

[1]Jeff Denberg, "Tough Old Primus King—A Man to Be Remembered," *Atlanta Journal*, October 27, 1980, B-1; Primus King, interview with Paul A. Davis, Columbus, GA, July 16, 1979. King interview and other materials regarding Primus King can be found in the Columbus State University Simon Schwob Memorial Library, Columbus, GA.

[2]*King v. Chapman*, 62 F. Supp. 639 (M.D. Ga. 1945); *King v. Chapman*, 154 F. 2d 460 (5th Cir. 1946). Two years before the Court of Appeals ruled on the *King* case, William Hastie and Thurgood Marshall won a U.S. Supreme Court decision nullifying Texas white primary practices. See *Smith v. Allwright*, 321 U.S. 665 (1944); Robert H. Brisbane, *The Black Vanguard: Origins of the Negro Social Revolution, 1900-1960* (Valley Forge: Judson Press, 1970), 192-193.

[3]Denberg, op. cit., B-1; King, interview, op. cit.

[4]Horace Ward, interview with author, Atlanta, GA, May 28, 1999.

[5]Ibid.

[6]Reverend Phale Hale, interview with author, Atlanta, GA, January 19, 1995.

[7]Ward, interview, op. cit.; Margaret Shannon, "Justice at Last for Horace Ward," *Atlanta Journal and Constitution Magazine*, March 13, 1977, 9.

[8]Horace Ward, interview with author, Atlanta, GA, June 29, 1994.

[9]Vernon Jordan, interview with author, Washington, D.C., February 28, 1997.

[10]Constance Baker Motley, interview with author, New York, NY, March 30, 1995.

[11]"Atlanta Bar Group Hears A. T. Walden," *Atlanta Daily World*, April 29, 1950, 1. Austin T. Walden, an unheralded pioneer in the civil rights movement, served as attorney for movement leaders including "Daddy" King and Ralph David Abernathy, Sr. He waged a six-year court fight that won equal pay for black public school teachers, served as chief negotiator when blacks integrated Atlanta lunch counters in 1961, and defended the Freedom Riders at the height of the Civil Rights movement. The Georgia State Democratic Executive Committee selected Walden as one of its first two black members in 1963. His appointment in 1964 by Mayor Ivan Allen as an alternate judge of the Municipal Court of Atlanta was the first such appointment in Georgia and the South since Reconstruction. Walden was chief counsel for Horace T. Ward in his lawsuit against the University of Georgia Law School and championed civil rights efforts for several decades. Personal papers chronicling the achievements of Walden are held in the Atlanta University Robert W. Woodruff Library and the Atlanta History Center.

[12]Jordan, interview, op. cit.

[13]Renee Turner, "Remembering the Young King," *Ebony*, January 1988, 42.

[14]Robert Brisbane, interview with author, Atlanta, GA, January 19, 1995. In 1948, Dr. Benjamin Mays recruited Brisbane to join the faculty at Morehouse College. Brisbane founded the political science department at Morehouse College and worked for nearly fifty years inspiring students to become community leaders and civil rights activists. Brisbane established a brilliant scholarly record and trained civic leaders and civil rights activists, including Julian Bond, *Ebony* editor Lerone Bennett, and Georgia's first black senator, Leroy Johnson. The Morehouse College Brisbane Institute was founded in 1984 to further Dr. Brisbane's goals in education. See Georgia House of Representatives HR1013, (1998), A resolution honoring the life of Robert H. Brisbane, Ph.D., State of Georgia Government Documents, Atlanta.

[15]Ibid.; also see Benjamin E. Mays, *Benjamin E. Mays: Born to Rebel—An Autobiography* (New York: Charles Scribner's Sons, 1971), 205-207.

[16]Horace Ward, telephone interview with author, November 3, 1995.

[17]Sam Heys, "Horace Ward and the University: Irony Goes to Court," *Atlanta Constitution*, May 2, 1986, C-4.

[18]Hugh Gloster, interview with author, Atlanta, GA, January 19, 1995; Horace Ward, interview with author, Atlanta, GA, June 29, 1994.

[19]Sandra Adell, *Dictionary of Twentieth Century Culture: African American Culture* (Detroit, MI: Gale Research, 1996), 435. Prominent Atlanta black businessman Jessie B. Blayton, Sr., purchased WERD, a 900-watt AM station on October 4, 1949. For an interesting analysis of the role of radio in racial politics prior to the 1950s, see Barbara Dianne Savage, *Broadcasting Freedom: Radio War and the Politics of Race, 1938-1948* (Chapel Hill: University of North Carolina Press, 1999).

43

[20]Brisbane, interview, op. cit.

[21]Betty Mapp, interview with author, Atlanta, GA, December 17, 1996.

[22]"End of Jim Crow Seen by NAACP Counsel Marshall: Conference of Lawyers to Implement Decisions," *Atlanta Daily World*, June 11, 1950, 1.

[23]Marshall wrote Roscoe Dungee, president of the Oklahoma Conference of NAACP Branches, on April 16, 1946, expressing the importance of an NAACP lawyers' meeting scheduled to take place in Atlanta. Marshall said that "we will be able to exchange ideas and at the same time let the South know that we mean business and did not stand off some place, but came to the middle of the South and made arrangements to blast their discriminatory practices sky high." See Papers of the NAACP, The Campaign for Educational Equality: Legal Department and Central Office Records, 1913-1950. Series B: 1940-1950; "End of Jim Crow Seen by NAACP Counsel Marshall," op. cit.

[24]Horace Ward, interview with author, Atlanta, GA, August 22, 1994.

[25]"Attainment of Full Equality Goal of NAACP, Wilkins Says: Sees Negro in State Grad School by '52," *Atlanta Daily World*, April 18, 1951, 1.

[26]Mapp, interview, op. cit.; Brisbane, interview, op. cit.

[27]Horace Ward, interviews with author, Atlanta, GA, May 28, 1999, and June 29, 1994.

[28]"Henderson, Sweatt, McLaurin, Rulings Hailed by Leaders," *Atlanta Daily World*, June 5, 1950, 1.

[29]Herman Talmadge, interview with author, Hampton, GA, January 23, 1995.

[30]Ibid.

[31]Bill Shipp, interview with author, Atlanta, GA, January 23, 1995.

[32]Talmadge, interview, op. cit.; "Thompson Predicts Talmadge's Defeat," *Atlanta Daily World*, May 9, 1950, 1.

[33]"Out of State Tuition Offer Refused by Negro Law School Applicant: Regents Promise Legal Fight as Admission Threat Looms," *Red and Black*, October 20, 1950, 1.

[34]University System of Georgia, Board of Regents Minutes, July 12, 1950, 20, Archives, Board of Regents Office, Atlanta, GA; Gwen Y. Wood, *A Unique and Fortuitous Combination: An Administrative History of the University of Georgia School of Law* (Athens: University of Georgia Press, 1998), 101.

[35]"Fires of Discord," *Red and Black*, October 20, 1950, 4.

[36]Ward, interview, June 29, 1994, op. cit.; Mays, *Born to Rebel*, op. cit.

[37]Ward, interview, ibid.

[38]Robert Brisbane, interview with author, Atlanta, GA, January 19, 1995.

[39]Mays, op. cit., 206.

[40]Horace T. Ward, letter to L. R. Siebert, October 17, 1950, and Walter N. Danner, letter to Horace T. Ward, June 7, 1951, Hargrett Rare Book and Manuscript Library/University of Georgia Libraries, Walter N. Danner Subject File; "Negroes Will Be Rejected at University, Caldwell Warns," *Atlanta Daily World*, June 12, 1951, 1; *Horace T. Ward v. Regents of the University System of Georgia*, Civil Action No. 4355, no.

11, Federal Records Center, East Point, GA (1956), 41.

[41]General Appropriations Act, Secs. 8, 9, GA Laws (1951), 425. Similar provisions appear in the General Appropriations Act, Secs. 8, 9, GA Laws Jan.-Feb. Sess. (1953), 154 and General Appropriations Act, Secs. 8, 9, GA Laws (1956), 762. For a report of the faculty committee that interviewed Ward, see Report of the University of Georgia Faculty Committee on the Appeal of Horace T. Ward, September 13, 1951, Hargrett Rare Book and Manuscript Library/University of Georgia Libraries, J. Alton Hosch Papers, Folder: Horace T. Ward case.

[42]Horace T. Ward, letter to Harmon Caldwell, September 20, 1951, Hargrett Rare Book and Manuscript Library/University of Georgia Libraries, Walter N. Danner Subject File.

[43]Papers of the NAACP, The Campaign for Educational Equality: Legal Department and Central Office Records, Supplement to Part 1, 1951-1955. Legal Department Monthly Report, February 1952, NAACP Archives, Library of Congress, Washington, D.C.

[44]University System of Georgia Board of Regents Minutes, April 10, 1957, 290, Archives, Board of Regents Office, Atlanta, GA.

[45]Lerone Bennett, Jr., "Federal Judge Refuses to Dismiss Horace Ward Suit," *Atlanta Daily World*, December 16, 1952, 1, 6; Anne Gowen, "University Application Suit Delayed," *Atlanta Constitution*, December 16, 1952, 7.

[46]Robert L. Lenoir of Tucson, Arizona, and Katie Lenoir Knepper of Sparks, Nevada, son and daughter of James J. Lenoir and Lora Deere Lenoir, supplied the author with copies of the personal papers of James J. Lenoir. The papers include personal letters and other documents related to Mr. Lenoir's courageous stand against segregation and the actions of the regents, university, and law school to halt the admission of Horace T. Ward. James and Lora Lenoir wrote a short fictionalized portrayal of the efforts of Ward to enter the law school and the various maneuvers of the state and university to keep him out. The *Mercer Law Review* published the story and the Lenoirs received widespread communications and acclaim from legal scholars, law practitioners, and grassroots persons throughout the nation, and even Supreme Court Justice Hugo Black. The Lenoir papers also include a collection of letters from prominent legal scholars and attorneys expressing their views on segregation.

[47]Regent Robert O. Arnold to J. Alton Hosch, Horace T. Ward Case Folder, Hargrett Rare Book and Manuscript Library/University of Georgia Libraries, J. Alton Hosch Papers, February 25, 1952. In a January 10 letter to Professor Elliott Cheatham at the Columbia University Law School, Lenoir said, "Alton [Hosch] is working with the Board of Regents to throw the responsibility on his law school for the subterfuge adopted to keep the negro Ward out of the law school (at the same time, in the faculty meeting, professing ignorance of any motive except to raise educational standards)." Personal papers of James J. Lenoir.

[48]For a review of the events leading to the firing of Walter Dewey Cocking and the

responses of University of Georgia students and faculty and the Georgia electorate, see "Georgia Students 'Burn' Their Governor in Protest of His Academic Meddling," *Life*, October 27, 1941, 43; Thomas Dyer, *The University of Georgia: A Bicentennial History, 1785-1985* (Athens: University of Georgia Press, 1985), 224-240; Charles S. Gurr, *The Personal Equation: A Biography of Steadman Vincent Sanford* (Athens: University of Georgia Press, 1999), 182-187.

[49]James J. Lenoir, personal communication to President O. C. Aderhold, August 18, 1953, Lenoir papers, op. cit.

A. T. Walden and Thurgood Marshall addressed the *new* procedures the regents had adopted in the *Ward v. Regents* complaint. The attorneys asked the court to issue an injunction to restrain defendants from "unlawful attempts to govern his [Ward's] application by new rules and procedures not in force at the time he applied and not then made applicable to white students of equal or less qualifications." *Ward v. Regents*, op. cit.

[50]O. C. Aderhold, personal communication to James J. Lenoir, August 19, 1953, Lenoir papers, op. cit.

[51]Lora D. Lenoir and James Lenoir, "Compulsory Legal Segregation in the Public Schools with Special Reference to Georgia," *Mercer Law Review* 5 (1954): 234-236.

[52]Papers of the NAACP, Series B: 1940-1950, Legal File: University of Georgia, 1940-46, NAACP Archives, Library of Congress, Washington, D.C. Marshall expressed to Clennon W. King in an April 24, 1940, letter that the NAACP was investigating his attempt to register at the University of Georgia School of Law. On September 20, 1946, special counsel Robert L. Carter corresponded with Attorney Austin T. Walden concerning the attempts of Annie Louise Brown to apply to the University of Georgia School of Law. The author has been unable to confirm whether Annie Louise Brown continued her professional education. In the case of Clennon W. King, it is known that he applied for admission to the University of Mississippi in Oxford in 1958. Governor James P. Coleman met King when he appeared on the university campus and directed policemen to shuttle him to a mental institution. King's younger brother, civil rights attorney Chevenne Bowers (C. B.) King, secured Clennon's release from Whitfield Asylum in Mississippi. Clennon, C. B., and other activist members of the King family of Albany, Georgia, became noted civil rights advocates, and C. B. became the first black candidate to seek the governorship of Georgia. See Fred Powledge, *Free At Last? The Civil Rights Movement and the People Who Made It* (Boston: Little, Brown and Company, 1991); Taylor Branch, *Parting the Waters: America in the King Years, 1954-1963* (New York: Simon and Schuster, 1988).

[53]*Ward v. Regents*, op. cit., 7.

[54]"Segregation at Georgia University in U.S. Suit," *Atlanta Constitution*, June 24, 1952, 1.

[55]In September 1952 the defendants filed a motion to dismiss that was heard in December 1952, at which time the court ordered the defendants to pass on Ward's application. The defendants later passed on his application and specifically denied

him admission on the ground that he had not taken the qualifying examination. The court finally ruled on the motion to dismiss in May 1953, denying the motion and ordering a trial on the issue of whether university officials were acting in good faith by requiring that applicants to the university law school must submit to a qualifying examination. Papers of the NAACP, The Campaign for Educational Equality: Legal Department and Central Office Records, Supplement to Part 1, 1951-1955. Legal Department Monthly Report, NAACP Archives, Library of Congress, Washington, D.C.

[56]Ibid.

[57]George M. Coleman, "NAACP Attorneys Move Fast to Save School Bias Suit: Horace Ward in Army—NAACP Lawyers Win Postponement," *Atlanta Daily World,* September 22, 1953, 1.

[58]Ibid.

CHAPTER *3*

Ward's University of Georgia Application: The Journalistic Controversy

Georgia officials expressed relief at Ward's induction into the army just as his battle to enter the university law school was about to reach its climax. At the same time, segregationists continued to mount barriers to protect the cherished tradition of racial segregation. Three months after the postponement of Ward's lawsuit, the legislature even created a special commission of political leaders, Regents, and State Board of Education officials to thwart desegregation efforts at taxpayers' expense.[1]

Ward's foremost mentor, Georgia's NAACP chief William Madison Boyd, declared that although Ward's drafting was an unexpected setback, the NAACP would persist in its efforts to crack the walls of segregation in schools of higher learning.[2] With the dismantling of legal segregation in other states underway and the prospect of forced desegregation of Georgia's flagship university on the horizon, segregationists rallied throughout the state. Major newspapers ran advertisements urging citizens to resist any threats to the time-honored traditions of segregation. For example, the Democratic Party of Georgia had sponsored a full-page ad in the *Atlanta Constitution* on November 2, 1952, exhorting Georgians to resist mixed schools: "This is your last chance to help defend yourself and uphold the heritage and traditions of Georgia. The threat to our schools and colleges is now. Shall we . . . elect a governor and other state officials who will sit idly by, while our traditional pattern of segregation is swept aside?" (The advertisement also included a photocopy of the cover page of the *Ward* lawsuit.)[3]

Georgia's leading proponent of segregation was, without doubt, Roy Harris of Augusta, Georgia. A 1919 graduate of the UGA School of Law, and a life-long career lawyer, Harris was also an extremely effective state politician. Harris was first elected to the Georgia House of Representatives in 1921, serving there for more than twenty years, including two terms as Speaker of the House. Harris was also effective as a "kingmaker," managing three successful gubernatorial campaigns. An avowed segregationist, Harris, more than any other individual, influenced the resistance to integration in Georgia for more than forty years.[4] Judge Albert Pickett, Harris's former law partner, portrayed him as follows:

> Roy was a practical and effective politician, one of the greatest political strategists this state has ever known. A behind-the-scenes, smoke-filled room guy. He was the planner. He had contacts all over the state, back in the Talmadge days. He could get on the phone and talk to somebody in every county. He had an incredible knack and ability, honed over the years, and a network of contacts and friends that was vast.[5]

E. Freeman Leverett, a prominent assistant attorney general during the 1950s and 1960s, also recognized Harris's powerful and perennial influence on politics in Georgia:

> Roy Harris undoubtedly influenced the governors of Georgia from Herman Talmadge to Marvin Griffin to Ernest Vandiver because he was a political kingmaker. He had been Speaker of the House. He was a person who had a lot of personal magnetism and he could influence people and he had this newspaper [*Augusta Courier*] that was really scurrilous in its presentations. He had a section printed in red, and he made all these claims that this was going to happen or that was going to happen as a result of desegregation.[6]

Indeed, Harris successfully popularized his racist ideas through vitriolic editorials in his personal newspaper, the *Augusta Courier*. During a 1964 interview, Harris bluntly asserted that he founded the red-lettered, right-wing weekly paper in 1947 "so I could say what I damn well pleased."[7] As editor and publisher, Harris freely espoused his separatist political views. An October 2, 1950, column by Harris typifies his style of appeal to the racial prejudice of many Georgia citizens:

> If the negroes have sense enough to work with us in the con-
> struction and the advancement of separate but equal school fa-
> cilities, then we should go ahead with rapid progress to finance a
> real system of education for both the whites and the negroes. The
> negroes have made greater progress in this country than any other
> place on this earth. Were it not for the efforts of the white people
> and for what the white man had done for the negro, the negro
> would still be a naked savage in the jungles of Africa.[8]

Although black citizens typically considered Harris's views and scurrilous statements outrageous, many whites regarded them as colorful commonsense, and Harris as a hero for standing up to "outside agitators" and "putting blacks in their place." Segregationists hailed Harris for his wit and insight in political matters, and took quite seriously his predictions of doom to the state and destruction to the races if segregation ended—as in this October 9, 1950, editorial warning:

> And then there is another thing the negroes ought to con-
> sider, if they have any sense at all. When the time comes for the
> white and negro children to attend the same schools there is go-
> ing to be a lot of people killed in this state. If that day ever comes
> we will have bloodshed, race riots, a race war and the most ter-
> rible time this state has ever known.
> The negroes cannot hope to gain anything by this thing hap-
> pening. The negroes will be the losers in the long run. If this ever
> happens there are going to be a lot of negroes hurt and hurt bad
> in Georgia.[9]

Interestingly, and paradoxically, Harris maintained congenial relationships with some blacks in his hometown. Roy McCracken, Harris's former law partner, asserted that people who really knew

Harris took most of what he said as segregationist rhetoric, and reported that half of Harris's law clients were black. McCracken said, "I think black people knew him as a man of power, they respected him and they knew that if he served as their attorney that he could get results."[10] Judge Albert Pickett, another associate of Harris, recalled, "The popular notion of Roy Harris was akin to a caricature, with horns and a tail."[11] Pickett also confirmed McCracken's assertion that some of Harris's most faithful clients were black, including the prominent black-owned Pilgrim Life Insurance Company.

Another irony was Harris's later relationship with Ed McIntyre, a Morehouse graduate, civil rights activist, and the first black mayor of Augusta, Georgia. McIntyre appointed Harris to the position of city attorney, stating that Harris provided sound advice and financial support during his political campaigns. McIntyre recalls the first advice Harris gave him in his campaign:

> "Eddie," he said, "I've just been riding around town and I see you got these big billboards with your picture all over them; don't you know that's a waste? Why don't you just use [your name] Ed McIntyre; the voters are so stupid they won't even know you are black unless you put your picture up there; that's a big mistake you made."[12]

McIntyre also contends that Harris wanted to try to soften his racist image in his sunset days so he would not go down in history for being purely a segregationist, but would be remembered as a man who could support and work with African Americans. From his discussions with Harris about race, McIntyre concluded that Harris was not quite the rabid segregationist that detractors portrayed him to be, although he did retain his opposition to mixed marriages:[13]

> He may not have been the true segregationist he portrayed. Georgia politics in the early days was based on race and I think if you were going to get elected, the politicians who could holler "nigger" the loudest and vowed to keep down black folks in this state were the persons who would maintain their political

positions. I think that maybe I was just that individual, that tool, that person that Roy Harris found in the sunset of his years that maybe could somehow soften some of the things he said and some of the wrongs he had done to African Americans throughout the state.[14]

Despite his faults, Harris perhaps justifiably lambasted white liberals who attacked him as a racial extremist, yet themselves insisted on all-white churches and country clubs and sent their children to private schools. Harris pilloried them as hypocrites who would tolerate integration only if it did not personally affect them. He noted in a 1969 interview that "the fight today is not between segregationists and Negroes, but between hypocritical whites who favor integration until it affects them, and people like me."[15]

Harris also antagonized Ralph McGill, the prominent liberal editor of the *Atlanta Constitution.* McGill's political identity and views on race relations were antithetical to Harris's; his editorials in the *Atlanta Constitution* often criticized Harris and his supporters, while Harris routinely excoriated McGill and the Atlanta newspapers for their more liberal views. Ironically, in a state that overwhelmingly supported segregation, McGill was very popular despite his liberal views concerning racial equality. Earnest Brookins, a law student at the University of Georgia when Ward applied and who opposed Ward's admission, recalled McGill's love-hate relationship with white Georgians:

I remember we used to cuss ole Ralph McGill for his progressive racial perspectives to begin with. What he wrote sold papers, because people would grab his paper and start growling about what he had written because it was so foreign to the general population. He made us feel bad. Then we made him our hero. You talk about a pioneer. Ralph McGill was a pioneer. He took the fairness doctrine to heart and wrote about it every day, and took the abuse of the white population on a daily basis. I mean 80 percent of the people didn't like him to begin with. In the end I guess all except a fringe group loved him. He was a liberal, but a good writer.[16]

More succinctly, but in the same vein, a *Time* magazine article described McGill's relationship with readers as follows: "For four decades his daily column caressed the South with his love, lashed it for its faults, served as its conscience. Surveys repeatedly rated him as both the region's best liked and least liked writer—but always the most read."[17]

Contrary to their heated public debates and despite his emphatic and public disagreement with Harris's actions, McGill (like others) claimed that he liked Harris personally and respected him as an effective politician.[18] However, McGill's and Harris's mutual antagonism on civil rights issues escalated dramatically when the University of Georgia's student newspaper, the *Red and Black*, began to take up the cause for Horace Ward's entry into the law school.

While the *Atlanta Constitution* promulgated its appeal for moderation on racial issues and Ralph McGill became known as the "Conscience of the South," the quest for equal rights also dawned as an issue among the more liberal students at the all-white University of Georgia, including most significantly a group of editors for the *Red and Black*.[19] With the student newspaper as their platform, editor Walter A. Lundy, managing editor Bill Shipp, news editor Priscilla Arnold, and assistant news editor Gene Britton launched in 1953 a series of editorials condemning the administration of Governor Herman Talmadge for thwarting Ward's application for admission. The editorials, with Bill Shipp as the main voice, were unequivocal in asking why the state was denying not only Ward but a large segment of society the right to attend the university. One of Shipp's editorials that particularly aroused the ire of the segregationist establishment included the following harsh, and courageous, criticism of Georgia's governor:

"Created Equal"

Herman Talmadge has again shown the Mr. Hyde side of his political personality. He has condemned judicial efforts to give the Negro a chance to get education equal to the white man's as "the most fool-hardy sociological calamity in our national history."

In a speech at the Southern Governor's Conference, Georgia's chief executive said erasing segregation in schools is "a step toward national suicide."

We have commended Talmadge in the past for his good work in getting Georgia on the highway of progress. But we cannot commend him for wanting to deny a segment of mankind its right to an equal education.

The governor says we are spending millions to give Negroes equal education in segregated schools. Even a schoolboy economist should realize that it is impossible for taxpayers to support two "separate but equal" school systems. With communism knocking at the Negroes' back door, we cannot afford to let educational segregation barriers stand. It is as plain as the Red flag in Russia that continued segregation and suppression can and will cause the death of democracy by the hands of its own leader.[20]

The *Red and Black* editorial elucidated a major dilemma for Southern politicians. By the early 1950s, court decisions in border states, such as the *Sweatt* decision in Texas, had resulted in the admission of blacks to all-white schools. To deter such court actions, Deep South states began to spend more tax dollars for the education of blacks. In addition to the increased state revenues, philanthropists such as Julius Rosenwald, president of Sears, Roebuck and Company for many years, had been principal benefactors of Negro education in the United States during the first half of the twentieth century. For example, the Julius Rosenwald Fund had provided generous funding for the building of Negro schools between 1912 and 1931, helping to build more than five thousand Negro schools.[21]

Despite such historic philanthropic support and the increased state revenues to improve Negro schools, the amount of money spent per pupil remained grossly inadequate and inequitable as compared with the amount spent per pupil in white schools; the disparity was so enormous and pervasive that it would have taken generations to bring about any semblance of equity.[22] Though Southern states taxed blacks at the same rate as whites, in 1952 the average Southern state was spending $164.83 per white pupil, compared to $115.08 per black pupil.[23] Moreover, in order to equalize underfunded and neglected black schools, the spending ratio for black pupils would have needed to far exceed the rate for whites. It was commonplace for blacks to receive outdated, used books discarded by white schools, as well as other hand-me-down resources and equipment such as used buses (that is, when black schools had buses at all). School systems often bused black students to remote locations in the school district or even to other counties, even though schools for whites were near black students' homes. The often rundown, dilapidated facilities and disproportionately low teacher salaries at black schools only served to emphasize the gross inequities of these schools. Additionally, in more costly and specialized areas of study such as law, dentistry, and medicine, state schools for Negroes were virtually nonexistent. Shipp's editorial quoted above had correctly pointed out that even from an economic (much less a moral) vantage point, supporting two "separate but equal" systems was simply not viable.

In one of the first of such editorials, Bill Shipp expressly supported the admission of Horace Ward to the University of Georgia. Shipp challenged the absurdity of the segregationist system, even implying that Ward may have been drafted by the armed services to keep him out of the all-white university. The editorial, reprinted below in its entirety, also derided university officials for excluding blacks from the university.

"The Color is Black"

Horace Ward became a casualty the day he was drafted. The Atlanta Negro who has sued for admission to the free, white University of Georgia suddenly found himself facing two years in the not-so-free, non-segregated Army. Whether some string-pulling "friend" of the University gave Ward a gentle shove toward the militia or whether Fate, nobody's friend, caught up with him remains to be seen.

Nevertheless, Ward can be checked off as temporarily missing in action from the Many Years War of White versus Black.

He attempted to establish a beachhead on the vanishing white frontier. He failed. Others will try. Some won't fail.

Like it or not, "that old, black nigger" who sweeps your floors, shines your shoes and picks your cotton is out to stand on equal footing with you.

He figures the white man climbs into his trousers the same way the Negro does—one leg after the other. He's right, there's no denying it.

There is absolutely no logic in excluding the Negro from the white man's way of life, especially at a university. Yesterday I strolled across campus, spoke to a Chink I knew, bummed a cigarette from a Jew and ate supper with a Kraut.

And I thought what a miserable system it is when a university allows students of every race, creed and color—except black—to roam its campus and mix with us Anglo-Saxon Protestants while the Southern Negro, a born U.S. citizen, is placed in a separated group as if he were a leper.[24]

Despite the logic and passion of such editorials, Georgia's highest ranking officials severely chastised the *Red and Black*'s editors for denouncing segregation and supporting Ward; not even the fact that some were from prominent and affluent families could shield them from retribution. Much of the admonishment was directed at editor Walter Lundy, who approved the editorials, as well as Shipp, the main editorial writer and vocal supporter of Ward's admission. For example, President Aderhold told Lundy, now a retired U.S. foreign service officer, that he should have had better judgment than to take a stand contrary to that of the regents and the people who controlled the purse strings of the university.[25]

Roy Harris, recently appointed by Governor Talmadge to the Georgia Board of Regents, used his newspaper freely to denounce the student editors. In one editorial, after describing the editors as a "little handful of sissy, misguided squirts," he went on:

Every time I see one of these little sissy boys hanging around some college, the more I think every one of them ought to be made to play football. What we need today is more he-men and fewer sissies . . . we have never had an editor crazy enough to flaunt the Constitution of Georgia and advocate the mixing and mingling of the races in this state.[26]

A few weeks after Shipp's editorial "The Color is Black" was published, Shipp and news editor Gene Britton interviewed Harris after a regents' meeting. Harris threatened Shipp and Britton, warning that the regents would cut funding for the *Red and Black* if they printed any more editorials attacking segregation.[27] Rather than intimidating the students, however, Harris's threat had the opposite effect, prompting them to run a story recounting how Harris tried to intimidate them. Harris denied their claims, stating:

> I tried to explain to them that in their juvenile damn foolery they were hurting the University and the cause of education in this state . . . I didn't threaten them, I just told them what was going to happen. I frankly told them that the money for the operation of the *Red and Black* would be discontinued unless they could do a better job than they were doing.[28]

In recalling these past events, Bill Shipp, whose syndicated columns now appear in major newspapers, still expresses outrage about the university's racial discrimination against Ward. Shipp passionately stated:

> I think it was outrageous, and as a matter of fact, the more I talk about this with you, the more furious I get! I remember how angry we were back then. That the state of Georgia would tell another human being because of the color of his skin that he didn't have the right attitude; that he did not possess certain character qualities. That is an outrage that in the last half of the twentieth century that we were practicing that kind of segregation in this state![29]

To prevent any future editorials attacking segregation, the university established a policy requiring direct faculty supervision of the *Red and Black* staff—essentially a censorship structure, requiring a faculty Board of Control's approval of all proposed newspaper content to prevent publication of material that might be considered prejudicial to the university. Shipp described his response to the censorship:

John Drewry, Dean of the College of Journalism, and Dr. O. C. Aderhold, who was then the president, decided in the best interest of the university that a faculty supervisor take over to review all *Red and Black* editorials before they were printed, apparently to stop any further drive and any further editorial efforts in gaining Horace Ward entry into the law school. I decided we could not operate under those circumstances, so I resigned; so did several other staff members.[30]

The actions of Regent Harris, which precipitated the resignations of Shipp and other editors, were antithetical to the concept of a free press. Especially dismaying was the fact that the paper was censored with the approval of the dean of the College of Journalism, a reputable journalism school that supposedly stood for high journalistic ideals. Dean Drewry and the journalism faculty sacrificed the principles of free speech in order to squelch the *Red and Black* editorials supporting Ward's admission to the university.

Despite the powerful regents and university officials who muzzled the students' freedom to express their views, some university alumni publicly expressed their dismay over the situation. George C. Doss, Jr., a university alumnus and staff member with the *Macon Telegraph/Macon News*, published his support for the student editors and his disappointment with the university's administration and faculty in an editorial letter to Lundy, one of the editors who subsequently resigned from the *Red and Black*.

> Dear Walter,
>
> Ever since the controversy you and the other *Red and Black* leaders had with Roy Harris broke into the news several weeks ago I have wanted to write you and tell you how much I, as a University alumnus, admire and appreciate the firm but dignified stand you have taken throughout. The stand you took on the segregation issue and Talmadge's stand on it was not, of course, the question at issue with Harris, as you pointed out, but I do personally quite agree with you.
>
> I am greatly disturbed, however, over the lack of leadership from the administration and faculty in the struggle against politi-

cal interferences. In fact, it appears that there is a general spirit of knuckling under from the chancellor on down.[31]

The *Red and Black* named Priscilla Arnold and Gene Britton as editors to replace those who had resigned. However, the abridging of their rights to freely express their ideas was also a bitter pill for the new editors. The matter especially pained Priscilla Arnold, as she later recalled:

> I very much wanted to be the first woman editor of the *Red and Black* since the war. That would give me a leg up in the professional world after I graduated. After a good deal of soul searching and agonizing, wanting to stay and trying to find a way to stay with a clear conscience, I just could not do it. I remember that Gene Britton and I went to a prayer service at the Methodist Church and prayed about it. We talked and talked trying to decide whether or not we were going to stay or leave. Finally, he went to his dorm and I went to my sorority house. The next morning we got together and discovered that we had made the same decision. We went ahead with the issue of the *Red and Black* that we were putting out and resigned effective upon its publication.[32]

Harris's virulent comments about the student editors, the assault on freedom of the press, and the muzzling of students advocating racial justice combined to bring this story to the attention of the national media. In addition to the *Atlanta Constitution*, the *New York Times, Time* magazine, and various other media outlets covered the story, many expressing fervent support for the students and deriding Harris for his behavior and segregationist politics.[33] Numerous university and college newspapers, as well as business and professional leaders, civil rights advocates, university students, and everyday citizens also came to the support of the editors. Two students from Swarthmore College in Pennsylvania, outraged by the actions prompted by Harris, wrote the following letter to the *Red and Black*.

Dear Editors:
    My roommate and I were so incensed at the attitude of Roy V. Harris toward your intelligent stand on educational segrega-

tion that we have to let you know how we feel. We support you to the fullest extent. We wish to encourage you in your battle for both freedom of expression and enlightened attitude towards segregation.[34]

Several students who sent letters of support to the editors expressed concern about how the suppression of democratic ideas would affect the standing of the United States in the free world. A letter from a Canadian student at the University of Toronto is especially noteworthy:

Dear Sir:
   In the December 7/53 issue of *Time* news magazine (the Canadian issue) I was quite interested and flabbergasted by an article "The Juvenile Damn Foolery." The fragment of your editorial which was reprinted in *Time* represents an archaic problem which should have been solved many years ago. It is quite possible that it would have been if men like this Roy V. Harris had not interfered. . . .
   The United States of America, as one of the major powers in the democratic world, suffers a certain loss of respect when bullies such as Roy V. Harris take it upon themselves to dictate their foolish and thoughtless edicts. I sincerely hope that you will not be intimidated by this Goliath, but that you will take upon yourselves the role of David and stand firm.[35]

In contrast to widespread support from outside the university, the editors had little support from fellow UGA students. The general attitude of the student body overwhelmingly favored segregation. For example, former UGA law student Earnest Brookins stated that he could not remember a single classmate supporting Horace Ward's admission to the law school. Although they did not generally express their opposition actively, Brookins said many students regarded the student editors as "crazy, foolish, and liberal beyond belief."[36] Bill Shipp also recalled that many UGA students at that time were apathetic and did not take Ward's challenge seriously. Shipp noted that most UGA students at that time were from affluent families, immersed in fraternity or sorority culture, and "living the good life."[37] Shipp's characterization reflects the general mood of college campuses in the 1950s—a generation of college students who were far less likely to be involved in social issues than students in the 1960s and 1970s, when civil rights and Vietnam protests by students often set the tone for the nation at large. Consequently, desegregation, and Ward's application in particular, were not seen as realistic threats, and thus were not major issues for the largely affluent, politically apathetic UGA student body.

However, some UGA students did respond to the threat to freedom of the press prompted by Ward's application, the ensuing editorials, and consequent censorship of the Red and Black. One University of Georgia student pledged his support to the editors in a letter to Walter Lundy:

> Dear Walter,
> I am a student at the University of Georgia, and in that capacity, would like to express my CONGRATULATIONS to you and your staff for your opposition against anyone or anything that tries to take OUR freedom to express our views and ideals away from us.
> I am behind you folks one hundred per cent, and will be glad to do anything I can to help as long as you maintain your present policy of TRUE INTEGRITY. I am a veteran of World War TWO and the Korean War and therefore believe I have a right to write you this Letter of Congratulations.[38]

Even with such meager support for the newspaper from UGA students, Harris was determined to squelch any challenge to the cherished way of life in the South, and he persisted with his attacks on the student editors. His condemnation of the Red and Black's editors revived his battle with McGill. In a scathing editorial deriding Harris for his interference with the student editors, McGill compared Harris's actions to the thought control methods of Hitler, Mussolini, and Stalin. McGill's editorial also accused Harris of practicing dictatorial politics that stifled youthful idealism, integrity, and honesty. McGill wrote:

The editors of the university newspaper commented in the most general terms on the Supreme Court case dealing with racial segregation and called for calmness and a rational attitude, rather than one of harsh and unreasoning criticism likely to bring on violence.

This led to Roy Harris, most influential of the university Board of Regents, and for twenty years a legislative figure and the nearest thing to a state political boss the state has had, moving into action. Regent Harris apparently thinks the white race is so lacking in racial pride and integrity it soon would be reduced to a mulatto status if segregation is lifted, and he moved in against the student editors in his own publication.

Writing in the cultured, courteous manner the most powerful regent of a great university system would be expected to use in addressing students of his alma mater, Mr. Harris wrote of the editors as a "little handful of sissy, misguided squirts."

But what irritated Regent Harris was conformity. Or lack of it. It apparently annoyed him that any students of the state should not think as he did and so he ordered them into line as follows:

"The state of Georgia pays a big price to educate its college students. If the state is willing to spend this money it has the right to control what is taught and what is done at the university."

This was a plain warning to the faculty and students to hurry to the educational fount and wash their brains free of anything which doesn't conform to Regent Harris' policies or, as they say, else.[39]

Despite McGill's editorial, which crystallized the absurdity of the most powerful Regent's views and threats, state leaders did not defend the rights of the students to express their views freely. The silence of state officials reflected Harris's powerful influence and dramatized the strength of the general support of segregation; state leaders all too willingly sacrificed the principles of protecting academic integrity and freedom of speech. In fact, the state legislature deliberated a resolution requesting the resignation of the editorial staff of the *Red and Black* and condemned the student editors on the floor of the Georgia House for supporting Horace Ward's admission to the university.[40]

Following the public condemnations of the student editors, McGill penned a personal support letter to Walter Lundy's parents:

> Dear Mr. Lundy:
>
> I hope you and Mrs. Lundy are not perturbed by what I imagine has happened—critical comments from a few fanatics and, perhaps, an abusive anonymous letter or two. There are always those kind of people in any controversy, religious, political or whatever the issue may be. Some of the most bitter can be in the field of religious disputes.
>
> I have had my windows broken on one occasion, my wife is frequently abused and insulted by anonymous callers, and my own mail carries a rather consistent percentage of abuse. We just have to live through these things and be content with a little progress at a time.
>
> Your son sounds like a fine young man, and the stand he took at the University follows out of his training and background.[41]

Many journalists expressed disdain at the regents' attempts to censor the press and intimidate the students. Several letters praised the students for their courage and willingness to stand up to Roy Harris. Freedom of the press and Harris's unethical tactics became the major issues raised by the students' supporters. Excerpts from a few of the letters that reveal the wide spectrum of media support for the editors follows.

A staff member from the *Atlanta Journal* wrote:

> Dear Bucky, Bill, Priscilla and Gene:
>
> I'm proud of you!
>
> My only regret is that I wasn't right there with you to be a part of it all.
>
> It takes a bunch of idealistic people like you—who aren't afraid or embarrassed to state their ideals—to clear the air of the stifling stupidity and stuffiness imposed in the public by even more stupid and stuffy politicians. I certainly do hate to see the *Red and Black* deprived of such a fearless staff.[42]

The director of the *Virginia Press* wrote:

Dear Mr. Lundy:

I may say that (unofficially) the students, faculty, and administrative staff of the University of Virginia are in complete accord with the position which you and Mr. Shipp have taken. I am continually amazed to realize how many unintelligent, incompetent politicians have been placed in positions of responsibility where it is possible for them to do unmeasurable damage to institutions of higher learning . . . Personally, I'm happy you two had the intestinal fortitude to stand up to that imbecile.[43]

The editors also received strong support from student newspapers. The editor of the *Gamecock* at the University of South Carolina shared his views about the limits placed on the *Red and Black*:

Dear Walt:

Being from Aiken, only fifteen miles from Augusta, home of Roy Harris, I appreciate the role he plays in Georgia politics and also the narrowness of his political views. You may not harm him much in the battle but you expose a little more of that narrowness . . . I admire your standing up to Harris and the university. If you would like to work for a free paper, how about transferring to old U.S.C.?[44]

Similarly, a staff member from the *Miami Hurricane* at the University of Miami expressed his dismay with Harris's actions:

Dear Walter:

I have been meaning to write you since last December when the famous *Red and Black* case, as I like to call it, exploded onto the national scene. I don't have to tell you how mad the *Hurricane* staff was about the control measures toward your paper taken by the University of Georgia administration. And who could forget that great American patriot, the honorable Roy Harris, champion of a vanishing cause.

Two things have shocked me about the situation. First, I never expected a deep Southern college newspaper to come out with a definite stand against segregation, and with such vigorous statements. Secondly, I didn't dream there could ever be another man like Huey Long, and much worse at that.[45]

Talmadge, Harris, and other Southern politicians gave the impression that all white Southerners concurred with their intolerance and with the suppression of ideas that advocated racial equality. However, the multitude of letters the editors received revealed that some white Southerners had strong ideas to the contrary. And not only college students; an excerpt of a personal letter from a Texan read as follows:

> Dear Editors of the Crimson and Black,
> Segregation is real fuel for Commie propaganda, and its continuance will certainly endanger the very existence of our country. . . .
> God bless you "sissy, misguided squirts . . . ," and grant me the strength to emulate you.
> Incidentally, I'm white and from Texas. I'll understand if you fellows don't make All-American football players next year.[46]

Segregationists often labeled civil rights activists as communist or communist-influenced and used this tactic to help galvanize opponents against the civil rights movement and its leaders. Later on, this tactic was commonplace among civil rights opposition leaders who sought to besmirch the image of Dr. Martin Luther King, Jr.[47] Harris used the tactic in condemning the student editors and accused them of submitting to communist influences. Ironically, the authors of several letters, including the letter from Texas, attacked segregation itself as a practice that fueled communist propaganda. Many others who wrote letters of support also accused Harris of practicing the tactics of communist dictators.

In addition to agreeing that Harris was playing into the hands of communists, letters from Southerners focused on the importance of mobilizing people to dismantle segregation. White Southerners, who perhaps had not publicly expressed their moderate or liberal views previously, took the *Red and Black* crisis as the occasion to express them. This letter from a prominent UGA alumnus who opposed segregation, for example, urged fellow citizens not to vote for politicians who based their campaign platforms on racial segregation:

> Dear Sirs,
>
> By now you probably know that hundreds of Georgia alumni agree with your stand against segregation and that thousands of them protest the denial of your right to speak out.
>
> The sacrifice of the great liberal tradition of education to political realism by the school authorities, however unfortunate, is understandable. Where, then, does the blame lie? Who appointed a man like Roy Harris to the Board of Regents? Who elected Talmadge governor? Will the people of Georgia elect in 1954 another governor whose campaign is based on race hatred?
>
> Perhaps the furor raised by your editorial will make all of us think more clearly before we vote.[48]

The majority of black Americans were not involved actively in the civil rights movement during the early 1950s. However, as the decade progressed, blacks became increasingly impatient with the intransigence of opponents to racial equality and bolder in opposing segregation and its proponents.[49] In addition to the insistence of Ward and his supporters on the need for racial equality, other victims of racial oppression also became involved. A few blacks expressed strong support for the *Red and Black*'s stance against racial oppression. While blacks generally supported the courage of the editors in standing up to Harris, in contrast to the writing of white supporters, their letters centered much more than those from white supporters on racial equality than on freedom of the press. Letters from black individuals and predominantly black organizations came from both inside and outside Georgia. A Morehouse staff member wrote:

> Dear Mr. Shipp and Mr. Lundy,
>
> I realize the great courage and individuality that it took to defy those social pressures that Mr. Harris and others sought to exact upon you.
>
> I am only one person but I feel that I express the sentiments of those who know of your courageous actions when I say that I am proud to know that there are men like you who still exemplify

the fortitude and principles upon which this country was founded
and by which its freedom from bigotry will be sustained.[50]

The Jamaica, New York, Branch of the NAACP wrote:

Dear Mr. Lundy:
Some time ago at a meeting of the Jamaica Branch of the
NAACP, Mr. Guy Brewer, officer and member of the Association,
brought to our attention the fact that your campus paper had
taken an editorial stand on segregation that had merited for you
the disapproval of many persons in high places in Georgia.
We have since learned via *Newsweek* magazine that you have
resigned rather than alter your democratic stand. Please convey to
those who share your belief our commendation for your high
ideals.[51]

Harris's opposition to the students continued for several months
even after the university implemented its censorship of the *Red and
Black*. In a December 14, 1953, column in his *Augusta Courier*, Harris
criticized Emory University students who were leading the movement among college students to abolish segregation in Georgia. Harris denounced Ralph McGill as the culprit who had planted
integrationist ideas among Emory students, and alleged that McGill
was encouraging University of Georgia students to fight segregation
as well. Harris's article was accompanied by a political cartoon of
McGill mixing black and white persons in a big pot. The caption of
this caricature read "Mixed Schools—The Devil's Brew for Georgia."[52]

The explosion that emanated from Ward's application and the
Red and Black articles promoting racial equality produced a flurry of
discussion, pro and con, for several months. The editors championed
noble ideas—equality, justice, and freedom of the press. They lost
coveted positions with the paper, but they left with their dignity and
principles intact. However, Shipp, whom Harris called the ringleader
among the student editors, experienced other forms of harassment.
Shipp recalled:

My mother's porch was filled with garbage. Graffiti was written
on the side of my house in Marietta calling me all kinds of names.

It distressed my mother a great deal. She was not in good health.
I got virtually no support from the state or state officials.[53]

Shipp also confided that a journalism professor suggested that
everyone would be a lot more comfortable if he left school, so he
left and joined the army. Lundy, Davis, and Britton, the other editors
who resigned, continued in school and later graduated from the university. Despite the strong support for the student editors in newspapers, magazines, and letters, the university had prevailed in silencing
the controversy surrounding the *Red and Black*, with the Board of
Control continuing to monitor all copy and editorial content.

While Ward completed his army service and the *Red and Black*
controversy subsided, the NAACP's LDF filed several cases with the
Supreme Court to gain entrance for blacks into public schools. The
Supreme Court's unequivocal stand against racial inequality in the
Sweatt v. Painter and *McLaurin v. Oklahoma* cases encouraged blacks
and the LDF to challenge segregation in the public secondary
schools. In response, Southern political leaders warned that they
would never surrender and permit race mixing in the public
schools—especially after the 1954 landmark *Brown v. Board of Education* decision. This historic suit involved five legal cases filed in four
states—Kansas, South Carolina, Virginia, and Delaware—and the
District of Columbia. Although the cases involved different Negro
plaintiffs and varying local conditions, they all stemmed from a common legal question related to the inferior educational opportunities
available to blacks. Accordingly, they were consolidated under the
name of the first case (*Brown*). In contrast to many previous LDF
cases, the plaintiffs did not seek equalization of school facilities, but
the banning of segregation and the admission to the public schools
of their community on a nonsegregated basis. Thurgood Marshall
and Robert L. Carter, now a top-ranking member of the LDF legal
staff, assembled more than twenty-five legal scholars, constitutional
historians, and social scientists to provide expert testimony on the
effects of segregation. The legal arguments ranged from states' violation of the Fourteenth Amendment by separation of the races, to the
tragic consequences of the inferior educational system for blacks, to

the detrimental impact of segregation on the self-esteem of black children.[54] Thurgood Marshall argued to the Supreme Court that the plain purpose and effect of segregated education was to perpetuate the inferior status of blacks that was "America's sorry heritage from slavery."[55] In his argument, Thurgood Marshall asked: "Why of all the multitudinous groups of people in this country [do] you have to single out Negroes and give them this separate treatment?"[56]

On May 17, 1954, in a unanimous decision, the Supreme Court outlawed segregation and declared that the separate but equal doctrine established by *Plessy v. Ferguson* in 1896 was inherently unequal and therefore had no place in public education. Chief Justice Earl Warren lobbied his fellow justices for the unanimous decision. Warren knew if there was any dissent among the justices, the argument for segregation would continue and Southern resistance would become even more defiant. He believed, therefore, that the Supreme Court needed to convey a clear and powerful message to the South that the country could no longer uphold a policy segregating blacks.[57]

The legal triumph was a credit to the legal strategizing and brilliance of Marshall and other LDF lawyers. The *Brown* decision represented a turning point for blacks, raising hopes of relief from a legally sustained, oppressive system. But while the decision changed the law, the attitudes that underpinned racial discrimination continued to exist. Civil rights leaders realized that *Brown* was a great victory, but that much work lay ahead in the battle to enforce the landmark ruling. Roy Wilkins, in an address delivered at the Forty-Sixth Annual NAACP Convention in 1955, observed:

> Most of us knew that the victory was sweet, not because it immediately desegregated Jim Crow Schools, but because it gave us the prize we had been seeking for fifty-eight years: the declaration by the nation's highest court that segregation was now unlawful. . . . Just as the old order did not pass without prayer and struggle and sacrifice—even unto death—so the new order will not come into being unless we accomplish it by our own efforts. This is a time for action, not for resting.[58]

As civil rights leaders hailed the declaration and admonished their supporters to continue social action efforts, bedlam broke loose among opponents, with blatant suggestions of violence. Despite the Court's unanimous decision, Southern leaders retorted with open defiance. Governor Herman Talmadge declared, "No amount of judicial brainwashing is going to change Georgia customs . . . It would take several divisions of troops down here to police every school building in Georgia and then they wouldn't be able to enforce it."[59] Senator James O. Eastland of Mississippi was equally frank: "The South will not abide by nor obey this legislative decision by a political court."[60] The *Morgan County News* in Madison, Georgia, printed a typically virulent editorial:

> We believe that it would be best for the personal safety and liberty of both the white race and the negro race that every town and county in our state and every other state ought to organize a strong and well armed Ku Klux Klan. When the Yankees invaded the South before, our grandparents found that necessary to maintain law and order and keep their personal freedom.[61]

State political leaders in Alabama, Florida, Georgia, Louisiana, Mississippi, South Carolina, Virginia, and Arkansas adopted resolutions condemning the *Brown* decision as an attempt by the Court to usurp the power belonging solely to the states. A new organization, the White Citizens Council, was formed in the South to sustain its racist practices in defiance of the Supreme Court.[62]

On the other hand, civil rights stalwart and Georgia NAACP President Dr. William Madison Boyd countered in a radio address on WERD (Atlanta's only black-created and -owned radio station at the time):

> Politicians in Georgia, Texas, Mississippi, Alabama, South Carolina, Virginia, North Carolina, and the other Southern states may, in the words of a famous Georgia politician, kick, snort, and paw, and say what will not happen, but even they cannot obliterate the psychological effects of knowing that an era is dying. Negroes will not be deterred from their course of action by what verbose

politicians throughout the South may say. The chief concern is not politicians, but whether Negroes have the intestinal fortitude to stand up and fight in a democratic manner through the courts for their rights.[63]

One black man with the intestinal fortitude to stand up and fight for his rights returned from his tour of duty in Korea in the summer of 1955.[64] Ward's return from his army tour was especially timely for continuing his legal case, because the LDF was reactivating several desegregation cases that had been put on hold while the Supreme Court deliberated the *Brown* case. After the *Brown* decision, the Ford Foundation and other contributors, including the Rockefeller and Carnegie Foundations, made large donations to the LDF, placing it in a much stronger position to finance the legal cases. Prior to *Brown*, the LDF had operated on a shoestring budget and lived from paycheck to paycheck. Constance Baker Motley recalled that before the *Brown* case, the LDF relied primarily on small contributions from NAACP members and branches.[65]

With the LDF's new momentum and support, Ward immediately renewed his pursuit to enter the all-white law school at the University of Georgia. After his honorable discharge and while he waited for a court date, Ward taught political science at Alabama State College in Mobile, Alabama. While teaching there, he dated Ruth LeFlore Johnson, an assistant librarian at Alabama State. A graduate of St. Augustine College, she was also the mother of a young son, Theodore, by her previous marriage. On June 9, 1956, Ward married Ruth at the Good Shepherd Episcopal Church in Mobile, Alabama, and later adopted her son.[66]

Ruth LeFlore Ward was the daughter of John and Teah LeFlore. Her father was an NAACP official and a prominent civil rights leader in Mobile. Growing up in a family that actively supported civil rights, Ruth had a keen understanding of social justice issues and thoroughly endorsed Ward's quest to enter the University of Georgia Law School. Ward would need her strong support, because the state resumed its legal maneuvering to prevent his entry. The stage was thereby set for an enduring court battle, framed by the obstructionists' legal tactics to forestall Ward's admission and the strategies of civil rights lawyers who, building now on previous LDF successes, sought to dismantle segregation in Georgia's colleges and universities with Ward's case as a spearhead.

CHAPTER 3 NOTES

[1]General Acts and Resolutions, vol. 1, Georgia Laws 1953, Nov.–Dec. Sess., no. 97 (House Resolution 232-743r).

[2]George M. Coleman, "NAACP Attorneys Move Fast to Save School Bias Suit: Horace Ward in Army—NAACP Lawyers Win Postponement," *Atlanta Daily World*, September 22, 1953, 1.

[3]"A Full-page Advertisement Sponsored by the Democratic Party of Georgia," *Atlanta Constitution*, November 2, 1952, B-7.

[4]Roger N. Pajari, "Herman E. Talmadge and the Politics of Power," *Georgia Governors in an Age of Change*, ed. Harry P. Henderson and Gary L. Roberts (Athens: University of Georgia Press, 1988), 77; Tom Bennett, "Ex-Rep. Roy Harris Dies of Cancer," *Atlanta Constitution*, January 16, 1985, A-1, A-6. Harris directed the successful gubernatorial campaigns for Ellis Arnall, 1942; Eugene Talmadge, 1946; and Herman Talmadge, 1948. Harris also served variously as president of the States' Rights Council of Georgia and president of the [White] Citizens' Councils of America. Harris wielded political power not only as a legislator but as an influential member of the Board of Regents of the University System of Georgia almost continuously for over twenty years (1951-1958, 1960-1974).

[5]Judge Albert Pickett, interview with author, Augusta, GA, January 13, 1997.

[6]E. Freeman Leverett, interview with author, Elberton, GA, December 8, 1995.

[7]Reese Cleghorn, "The Segs: Perez, Harris, Shelton, Maddox, Simmons: The Five Most Influential Men in the Southern Resistance Tell You Exactly What They Think," *Esquire*, January 1964, 133; Harold Paulk Henderson, *The Politics of Change in Georgia: A Political Biography of Ellis Arnall* (Athens: University of Georgia Press, 1991), xii.

[8]Roy Harris, "Strictly Personal," *Augusta Courier*, October 2, 1950, 4.

[9]_____, "Strictly Personal," *Augusta Courier*, October 9, 1950, 4. Roy V. Harris's personal papers can be found at the Richard B. Russell Library for Political Research and Studies/University of Georgia Libraries, as well as Harris's *Augusta Courier* on microfiche. In the *Augusta Courier* editorials reviewed by the author, it is noteworthy that Harris never capitalized the word "Negro."

[10]William McCracken, interview with author, Augusta, GA, January 13, 1997.

[11]Albert Pickett, interview with author, Augusta, GA, January 13, 1997.

[12]Edward McIntyre, interview with author, Augusta, GA, January 13, 1997.

[13]Ibid.

[14]Ibid.

[15]"A Conversation with Roy Harris and Julian Bond," *Atlanta Magazine*, April 1969, 50.

[16]Earnest Brookins, interview with author, Atlanta, GA, May 15, 1995.

[17]Quoted in Calvin McLeod Logue, *Ralph McGill: Editor and Publisher*, 2 vols. (Durham, NC: Moore Publishing Company, 1969), vol. 1, 1.

[18]Ibid., 64.

[19]Zell Miller, *Great Georgians* (Franklin Springs, GA: Advocate Press, 1983), 141.

[20]Bill Shipp, "Created Equal," *Red and Black*, November 5, 1953, 4.

[21]Roger M. Williams, *The Bonds: An American Family* (New York: Atheneum, 1971), 97. For an extensive examination of the Rosenwald Fund and philanthropy for black schools, see James D. Anderson, *The Education of Blacks in the South, 1860-1935* (Chapel Hill: University of North Carolina Press, 1988); Eric Anderson and Alfred A. Moss, Jr., *Dangerous Donations: Northern Philanthropy and Southern Black Education, 1902-1930* (Columbia, MO: University of Missouri Press, 1999).

[22]John Hope Franklin and Alfred A. Moss, Jr., *From Slavery to Freedom: A History of Negro Americans* (New York: McGraw-Hill, 1988), 360-366.

[23]Samuel L. Meyers, Sr., *Desegregation in Higher Education* (New York: University Press of America, 1989), 3; Jack Greenberg, *Crusaders in the Courts: How a Dedicated Band of Lawyers Fought for the Civil Rights Revolution* (New York: Basic Books, 1994), 116.

[24]"The Color is Black," *Red and Black*, October 8, 1953, 4.

[25]Walter Lundy, interview with author, Atlanta, GA, September 1, 1995.

[26]Roy V. Harris, "Strictly Personal," *Augusta Courier*, November 23, 1953, A-4.

[27]Walter Lundy, interview with author, Atlanta, GA, September 1, 1995; *Red and Black*, November 12, 1953, 1.

[28]Harris, op. cit., November 23, 1953, 3.

[29]Bill Shipp, interview with author, Atlanta, GA, January 23, 1995.

[30]Ibid.

[31]George C. Doss, Jr., "Letter to Walter Lundy," *Macon Telegraph/Macon News*, December 9, 1953, 7. On September 1, 1995, together with Georgia Center Television producer/director Janice Reaves and production manager William J. Evelyn, I interviewed Lundy in the regents' office in Atlanta. I requested that Lundy bring copies of any documents or artifacts related to the Ward matter; he brought scores of original letters, newspaper clippings, and other documents that greatly enhanced this research effort. Lundy wrote in a September 13, 1995, letter to Evelyn, "I am glad to hear you think the material I brought will be useful . . . The whole point in saving the letters and clippings was for someone to use, should there ever be any historical interest in what happened back then. For once, my pack rat instincts proved worthwhile." The Lundy collection contains several documents of historical interest that

researchers have not previously used.

[32]Priscilla Arnold Davis, interview with author, Atlanta, GA, May 11, 1995.

[33]"Juvenile Damn Foolery," *Time*, December 7, 1953, 56; John N. Popham, "Bias Dispute Stirs Georgia University," *New York Times*, November 27, 1953, 29, 36; Ralph McGill, "Wash Brains or Else!" *Atlanta Constitution*, December 5, 1953, 1.

[34]Mary White and Beth Wood, Swathmore College students, letter to Walter Lundy, December 4, 1953.

[35]Paul W. Ormrod, University of Toronto student, letter to Walter Lundy, December 6, 1953.

[36]Earnest Brookins, interview with author, Atlanta, GA, May 15, 1995.

[37]Shipp, interview, op.cit.

[38]William Wyatt Bibb, University of Georgia student, letter to Walter Lundy, December 13, 1953.

[39]McGill, "Wash Brains or Else!", op. cit.

[40]Shipp, interview, op. cit.; *Journal of the House of Representatives of the State of Georgia*, January 12, 1953-December 16, 1953, 1242. By a vote of seventy ayes to fifty-three nays, the House tabled the resolution; however, by then the university had already implemented its censorship of the *Red and Black*.

[41]Ralph McGill, letter to Walter Lundy's parents, December 8, 1953.

[42]Personal communication to *Red and Black* editors, December 5, 1953.

[43]Leo B. Eager, *Virginia Press*, letter to Walter Lundy, December 4, 1953.

[44]Ralph N. Gregory, *Gamecock*, letter to Walter Lundy, December 8, 1953.

[45]Greg Melikov, *Miami Hurricane*, letter to Walter Lundy, May 14, 1954.

[46]Personal communication to Bill Shipp and Walter Lundy, December 9, 1953.

[47]Richard Lentz, *Symbols, the News Magazines, and Martin Luther King* (Baton Rouge: Louisiana State University Press, 1990), 35-36.

[48]Personal communication to Walter Lundy and Bill Shipp, December 11, 1953.

[49]Franklin, op. cit., 437.

[50]Donald Wheeler Jones, Morehouse staff member, personal communication to Walter Lundy, December 10, 1953.

[51]NAACP'S Jamaica, New York Branch, letter to Walter Lundy, February 16, 1954.

[52]Roy V. Harris, "Strictly Personal," *Augusta Courier*, December 14, 1953, A-2.

[53]Shipp, interview, op. cit.

[54]Greenberg, op. cit., 117; Franklin, op. cit., 366; Robert H. Brisbane, *The Black Vanguard: Origins of the Negro Social Revolution, 1900-1960* (Valley Forge: Judson Press, 1970), 239-245.

[55]Greenberg, op. cit., 4.

[56]Leon Higginbotham, Jr., *Shades of Freedom: Racial Politics and Presumptions of the American Legal Process* (New York: Oxford University Press, 1996), 188.

[57]Morton J. Horwitz, *The Warren Court and the Pursuit of Justice* (New York: Hill and Wang, 1998), 23-29; Constance Baker Motley, interview with author, New York,

NY, March 30, 1995. For the May 17, 1954, U.S. Supreme Court *Brown* decision, see *Brown v. Board of Education*, 347 U.S. 483, 74 S. Ct. 686 (1954).

[58]Francis L. Broderick and August Meier, *Negro Protest Thought in the Twentieth Century* (Indianapolis: Bobbs-Merrill Company, 1965), 255-256.

[59]"Excerpts on Segregation Decision," *Georgia Journal* 2 (May 29, 1954): 5.

[60]Horwitz, op. cit., 25.

[61]"Excerpts on Segregation Decision," op. cit., 6.

[62]Brisbane, op. cit., 245.

[63]William Madison Boyd, *WERD Radio Taped Presentation of a Report on the Supreme Court Decision on School Segregation Cases*, June 3, 1955, Atlanta, GA. William Madison Boyd was married to the former Betty Lewis and they had two sons, William M. Boyd, Jr., and Robert E. Boyd. The former Mrs. Boyd is now married to Dr. Frank Mapp. Mrs. Mapp and Dr. William M. Boyd, Jr., supplied the author with the personal papers of Dr. Boyd, including scores of newspaper clippings, journal articles, pictures, and audio tapes of Dr. Boyd's WERD radio addresses documenting his civil rights efforts to abolish segregation in Georgia in the early 1950s.

[64]Ward's army service included one year in the United States, stationed at Fort Jackson, South Carolina, and Fort Monmouth, New Jersey. During the summer of 1954, the army assigned Ward to the Artillery Corps Forward Observation Battalion near the 38th Parallel in Korea to assist in the training of the South Korean Army. By the time Ward arrived in Korea, hostilities had somewhat subsided and Ward was not involved in any form of combat, but rather in essential supply-support duties. While no significant events happened related to his lawsuit during his military service, William Madison Boyd and Austin Walden corresponded periodically with him concerning the possible reactivating of his lawsuit after his discharge. Horace Ward, interview with author, Atlanta, GA, March 3, 2001.

[65]Constance Baker Motley, interview, op. cit.

[66]Horace Ward, interview with author, Atlanta, GA, November 30, 1998.

Ward's Legal Battle for Admission: The University's Resistance

On August 25, 1955, fifteen months after the landmark *Brown* decision, Ward filed for the continuation of his case. The process of litigation that followed symbolized the massive resistance to the struggle of black men and women for equal justice. The intricacies of the state's legal maneuvering to sustain segregation, Ward's attorneys' legal strategy to try to end the centuries-old practice, and the responses and counterresponses issued during the trial, illuminate the critical steps in a process that would set the stage for the desegregation of colleges and universities in Georgia.

Following several pretrial motions and a number of legal maneuvers that stalled the lawsuit, Judge Frank A. Hooper heard the case December 17-20, 1956, and January 3, 1957. It was the first such case in Georgia history challenging segregation in colleges and universities. While Thurgood Marshall, Robert Carter, and A. T. Walden as local counsel filed Ward's lawsuit, Donald L. Hollowell of Atlanta, an emerging legal expert in civil rights, had joined the case and became chief local counsel. Walden had been Georgia's chief civil rights lawyer for more than forty years and also had become a powerful political force for blacks in Georgia. Reserved and polished in his approach, Walden continued to use his influence with the white establishment to broker services for the black community. Local NAACP leaders thought Walden had become too involved with the white political leadership to aggressively attack segregation; NAACP state conference president William Madison Boyd had expressed to Thurgood Marshall as early as 1949 concern about Walden's progress with civil rights cases. In an August 19, 1949, letter, Boyd urged Marshall not to allow Walden to let an important civil rights case "drag unnecessarily."[1] Boyd insisted that Hollowell work with Walden on the Ward case. Walden's pioneering civil rights victories certainly should not be overlooked, for he showed his valor in the Deep South at a time when it was dangerous to advocate civil rights. However, as the time approached for a changing of the guard, NAACP leaders began to embrace the young, handsome, and aggressive Hollowell as the new chief civil rights lawyer in Georgia.

Hollowell was born and raised in Wichita, Kansas, and was therefore not exposed to the Jim Crow restrictions of the South during his childhood. However, Hollowell had encountered blatant racism and segregation in the armed services during World War II, when the military was still segregated. Hollowell recounted that army officials relegated him to eating in the kitchen, sleeping in quarters adjacent to prisoners, and patronizing Jim Crow canteens. His exposure to segregation in the army and his involvement with the Southern Negro Youth Conference after he returned from World War II inspired him to pursue the study of law to help fight for social justice. Hollowell came to practice law in Atlanta in 1952 after receiving his law degree from Loyola University. Immediately after his arrival, Hollowell began to play a major role in the civil rights struggle. Hollowell and Walden sought to resume the *Ward* lawsuit at the point of its artificial postponement in 1953.[2]

Thurgood Marshall requested that Constance Baker Motley of the New York bar represent the LDF at the trial. Motley recalled that whenever Marshall and his chief assistant, Robert Carter, were busy with other civil rights cases, Marshall would send Motley or LDF counsel Jack Greenberg to represent the LDF. Motley noted that the national NAACP lawyers had become experts in segregation cases and they would assist local lawyers with writing briefs, making the necessary constitutional arguments and handling other legal matters. She assisted Hollowell and Walden with the *Ward* case and made the legal argument at the end of the trial.[3]

Born in New Haven, Connecticut, Motley, like Hollowell, had not experienced segregation as a child. Motley grew up in a working-class family and distinguished herself as a brilliant student in secondary school. Genevieve Thompson, a professional social worker, and other community activists, including Mary McLeod Bethune and Dorothy Height, influenced Motley to learn compassion for the poor, to become politically oriented, and to identify with the plight of black America. She finished high school in 1940, worked in a youth opportunity job, and served as president of the New Haven Negro Youth Council, which she helped to organize. Motley enrolled in Fisk University in 1941. She remembered that her first exposure to segregation was in the Jim Crow train cars in which she traveled to Nashville while attending Fisk. Transferring to New York University in 1942, she graduated with honors in 1943. Before Motley graduated from Columbia University Law School in 1946, Marshall hired her as a clerk with the LDF. After completing law school, Motley continued her work with the NAACP and collaborated with Marshall, Walter White, and other NAACP leaders as they fashioned the legal program to make a frontal attack on segregation.

The first case Motley worked on was *Sweatt v. Painter*, in which the LDF succeeded in gaining the admission of Heman Sweatt to the University of Texas. Motley later became the principal trial lawyer for the NAACP and appeared before state and federal courts throughout the United States in numerous civil rights matters. Motley commented succinctly on the reasons that she devoted her career to equal justice and fighting against segregation: "The fact that I'm black may have had something to do with it. I don't know anyone better to fight for me than me."[4]

Assistant Attorney General E. Freeman Leverett prepared the case for the state. B. D. "Buck" Murphy, Governor Talmadge's personal attorney and an effective advocate for segregation, handled the arguments for the defendants. Murphy, who headed most of the civil rights cases for the state during this period, had a keen understanding of segregation and an equally keen desire to see it perpetuated.[5] Other attorneys for the defendants included Eugene Cook, G. Arthur Howell, and Charles H. Bruce of Atlanta. Cook was the state attorney general and a staunch segregationist; many of his colleagues and allies throughout the Southeast joined in to support the common cause of sustaining segregation.

Before filing his lawsuit, in an April 12, 1952, letter to the UGA Board of Regents, Ward stated, "I was denied admission solely on the basis of race and color because I am a Negro."[6] Thurgood Marshall also contended in the *Ward* complaint that the university rejected Ward solely because of his color, while at the same time the university had admitted white applicants whose qualifications were equal to or less than Ward's.[7] Accordingly, Judge Hooper clearly articulated the principal issue in the case—whether the university had denied Ward admission to the law school based on his race.[8] During the proceedings, Walden, Hollowell, and Motley meticulously documented how the defendants had conspired in formulating policies to keep Ward out of the law school. The defendants responded with evasive, at times absurd, arguments that they did not practice segregation in public higher education and that they had shown absolute good faith in considering Ward's application.

Ward's attorneys presented evidence to show that Georgia's political leaders, the regents, and university officials colluded to keep Ward and other blacks from being admitted to the University of Georgia and other all-white colleges. They introduced into evidence the Appropriations Bill of 1951 to show that *shortly after* Ward's application the state had enacted legislation to deter university officials from considering even token integration.[9] Despite this bill and other state legislation that called for closing schools and threatened harsh consequences for any officials who dared to mix white and colored students in Georgia schools, the defendants contended that they denied Ward's application solely on the basis of his inferior qualifications and his refusal to comply with administrative requirements. Incredibly, Board of Regents officials testified that state laws maintaining segregation were *not* a factor in their decision to reject his application.

In the next sequence of arguments, Walden asserted that the regents had established the out-of-state aid policy to shuttle blacks to other states to keep them out of Georgia's white institutions.[10] On the other side, Murphy sought to show that the operation of the out-of-state aid program was voluntary and that it did not imply that black students would be refused admission to white institutions in Georgia. The regents' executive secretary, L. R. Siebert, insisted that the regents maintained the program "because the colored people want it, they are delighted with it."[11] Siebert also testified that the regents did not give out-of-state aid to white students because they had never requested such aid. Admissions director Walter Danner testified that applications "of that nature" (from Negroes) that he received were sent to Siebert for out-of-state aid and he did not consider such applications for potential admission to the university.[12]

Chancellor Caldwell also defended the out-of-state aid program and described how the regents made the aid available exclusively to blacks. He audaciously asserted that white students had charged that they had been discriminated against by the regents, who paid out more than $275,000 a year for Negro out-of-state aid. Moreover, shortly after Ward refused to accept out-of-state aid, in response to a letter from a Savannah, Georgia, resident who advocated Ward's admission, Caldwell questioned Ward's motives for his refusal to accept the out-of-state aid. Caldwell wrote, "Mr. Ward has not been deprived of the opportunity to secure a legal education. He has been offered scholarship aid that would enable him to attend some of the foremost law schools of the country . . . His refusal of this offer leads one to ask whether his primary concern is the securing of a legal education."[13]

Caldwell revealed in further testimony the true reason for the out-of-state aid program when he stated: "We do wish in our institutions, and so far as possible, to preserve segregation of the races."[14] Nonetheless, Caldwell continued to insist that the program did not discriminate against blacks. Caldwell then made the duplicitous statement that although the regents encouraged blacks to go out of state, they did not *send* them out of state.

Regent Charles Bloch's testimony also affirmed the true reason for the out-of-state aid:

Hollowell: Are you aware of the policy that at any time a Negro files an application to a school in the University of Georgia System, or the System of the University, that it is normally and as a matter of policy referred to Siebert?

Bloch: I don't like to use the expression, counselor, "a matter of policy," because I don't know just what that means. I do know that if a *colored man*, for the sake of illustration, wanted a technical education, that he would be *relegated* to the out-of-state aid plan.[15] [emphasis added]

The next sequence of arguments dealt with yet another ploy that Danner paraded before the court to justify his rejection of Ward. His testimony was the first time anyone in the chain of command had ever given a reason why the university had denied Ward's application for admission. Danner testified that he decided that Ward did not qualify for admission because the colleges he had attended were not members of the regional accrediting association, the Southern Association of Colleges and Secondary Schools (SACS). He said that entrance to the law school required two years of college at an accredited school.

Ward had attended Morehouse College and Atlanta University, where he had been an honor student and had attained bachelor's and master's degrees. Though SACS fully accredited both schools utilizing the same standards applied to white schools, SACS did *not* at that time allow black schools actual *membership* in SACS. Despite testimony by the executive secretary of SACS, who told the Court that Morehouse College and Atlanta University were fully accredited and in good standing, Danner maintained that because the Negro colleges were not members—which because of racial segregation they could not have been—Ward did not have sufficient credits to enter the law school.[16]

To bolster their claim that Ward was unqualified, the defendants also attacked Ward's moral character. During the application process, President Aderhold had appointed law school dean J. Alton Hosch, noted historian E. M. Coulter, and law professor Robert McWhorter to a special committee to interview Ward and review his appeal. Following the interview, which took place at the university, Hosch alleged that Ward's statements were contradictory and that he did not show the type of mind an applicant should have to successfully pursue the study of law. According to Hosch, the committee's rejection was based on three things: Ward's evasiveness, contradictory statements, and inconsistencies. Hollowell argued that the committee's findings were obviously an attempt to rationalize their rejection of Ward's application, but Hosch contended that he had reservations about Ward's ability to pursue satisfactorily either the study or the practice of law. He said that he found Ward to be elusive and that he was not the type of man whom the committee should recommend to the president for admission to the law school.

Hollowell and Walden asserted that the regents adopted the policy requiring an interview as a part of the appeals process *after* Ward insisted that the university review his application for admission rather than for out-of-state aid. Caldwell admitted that the regents revised the appeals process shortly after Ward's refusal to accept out-of-state aid, but denied that the revision was an effort to block Ward's admission.

Walden then sought to show that the special committee that interviewed Ward ignored his academic qualifications. Instead, the interview focused on matters largely unrelated to his academic qualifications. According to Ward's testimony, the interview began with questions about his draft status at the time, which was 4-F due to a medical disability caused by a hernia. The committee asked about his medical condition and he informed them that he had not had an operation for the hernia because he could not afford it. He stated that his doctors had advised him that the hernia condition was not acute and that there was no need for an immediate operation. However, Ward also told the committee that he would be able to pay his own way through law school. Committee members questioned his veracity in stating that he could pay his way through school but could not afford an operation. Committee members testified that this perceived lack of veracity was one reason that they recommended denial of Ward's appeal.

Although the special committee did not examine Ward's academic transcripts, the court record reveals that the committee did assess his ability to think on his feet, when Hosch asked him suddenly during the interview to write a statement explaining why he wanted to attend the University of Georgia. Reading from the UGA Bulletin, Hosch reminded Ward that one of the requirements for success in law is the ability to write and speak English fluently. Ward recalled that he wrote a short statement in response to the request and that the committee members made no comments on his statement after Hosch read it to them.[17]

Ward wrote that he had been a lifelong resident of Georgia and that he wanted to practice law in Georgia. Moreover, he expressed a preference for going to the school in the state, where he would come in contact with future colleagues. Ward's response was similar to the reasons Heman Sweatt offered in the Texas *Sweatt v. Painter* case, wherein the Supreme Court ordered the University of Texas to admit Sweatt.[18] Ward explained during an interview that he had studied political science at Morehouse College and Atlanta University and that he had taken a course in constitutional law. He said that at the time of the meeting with the faculty committee, he was familiar with the *Sweatt* case and similar legal cases that preceded his application to the University of Georgia.[19]

When one examines Ward's statement to the committee, it appears that he was setting the stage for legal action if the university denied him admission. While Ward himself was an astute young man, he also had the benefit of advice from the notable civil rights leaders who had already dealt significant blows to Jim Crow, such as Marshall, Boyd, and Walden.

Hollowell and Walden continued to probe university officials' testimony, exposing a pattern of duplicity, evasiveness, and contradiction. Chancellor Caldwell's assertion that he would have admitted *a qualified Negro* was one of the most controversial and hotly debated positions taken by the defendants. Caldwell described his position thusly:

> Caldwell: I have thought about that a lot, Colonel Walden, and the Regents are here, and they can fire me as soon as the meeting is over, but I'll tell you what I think about it, the way I feel about it, what I would have done then, what I will do now. If a case comes before me on appeal, and it appears on all the facts under the regulations of the Board of Regents, and the laws of the state of Georgia, that a Negro is eligible for admission to the institution, I will rule that he is eligible for admission to an institution . . . I'll take the decision to the Board of Regents and say, Here it is, this man is eligible under the regulations of the board, under the laws of the state, is eligible for admission. Now gentlemen of the board, you know what the consequence will be if you admit him. Now it is up to you to take the ball and carry it from here on.[20]

Considering Ward's superior record at Morehouse College and Atlanta University, a student whom the faculty of those institutions held in high esteem as one of their best and brightest, it is difficult to fathom Caldwell's definition of a *qualified Negro*. In a interview, Ward responded to Caldwell's comment:

> I heard that comment at the trial. I didn't really believe it because I thought I was qualified and was being denied admission. Caldwell was a very brilliant man. He was a lawyer himself, trained at Harvard and was a former Dean of the University of Georgia Law School. I think the statement was made to support the defendants' case. It made the headlines in the papers at that time because you had prominent Georgia officials saying in the days of segregation that we will admit qualified blacks. Well, I thought they were denying one qualified black. I thought I was qualified.[21]

During an interview with the author, Hollowell contended that Caldwell may have been caught up in the system and suggested that if Caldwell had done other than what he did, there may have been repercussions against him. However, Hollowell maintains that a greater responsibility rested with Caldwell than with other officials because he was the chancellor:

> There were some that I put greater responsibility upon than others. And yet I also recognized that if they had done other than what they did it could have been detrimental. At the same time, I say that they had a responsibility to be truthful and I don't think that some of them were really truthful.[22]

Caldwell's words, *a qualified Negro*, convey a sentiment that recurs repeatedly in the annals of civil rights and affirmative action debates. The absurdity of the chancellor's suggestion that Ward was not qualified is borne out in the discussions and testimony, which reveal that Danner and the special interview committee did little to assess Ward's academic merits and more to probe nonacademic considerations concerning Ward. In a telling exchange, when Hollowell asked whether the committee had examined Ward's scholastic record, Regent Coulter responded:

> Well, we considered it to the extent that we gave credit to the Director of Admissions that he considered it, and that since he had considered it, he was an official of the University and a truthful and honorable person, that his credits were not in order and probably not high enough.[23]

Hollowell and Walden also argued that university officials treated Ward differently from other students in the admissions process. They underscored that Ward held undergraduate and graduate degrees, while the entrance regulations for the law school required only two years of college work. They also made evident through Ward's testimony the time lapse between the date of his original application (September 1950) and the date of the rejection by Danner (June 7, 1951).

As another example of differential treatment, Hollowell pointed out that the entrance regulations that the law faculty recommended and the regents adopted on June 11, 1952, were put in place *after* Ward's appeal, to block his entrance. It was as if the defendants recognized that Ward not only met, but exceeded the standards for admission, so they had to adopt additional measures to block his admission. The new requirements for students entering law school included the following:

I. A series of three tests to be administered by the University Guidance Center:

(1) Ohio State Psychological test

(2) Iowa Legal Aptitude test

(3) Strong Vocational Interest Inventory

II. Additional information as to character:

(1) Additional information to be submitted as part of application for admission to the University of Georgia School of Law

(2) Recommendations from alumni of the University of Georgia School of Law

(3) Recommendations from the judge of the Superior Court of the circuit in which applicant resides[24]

Because Ward viewed these requirements as discriminatory, he refused to submit to them. In an April 12, 1952, letter to the regents, Ward stated that the requirements were not in effect at the time of his application and insisted that the regents evaluate his application based on the admissions rules in place when he filed his application.[25] The defense presented Ward's refusal to take the examinations as a major point of contention. Dean Hosch testified that the law school had considered adopting examinations well before Ward's application, and that Elliott Cheatham, a UGA alumnus teaching law at Columbia University, had recommended that the UGA law school adopt admissions tests and stricter requirements. The defendants insisted that the adoption of the requirements, occurring *shortly after* Ward's application, was purely coincidental and was unrelated to any alleged complicity by the university and regents to keep him out of the law school. Hollowell and Walden, in rejoinder, maintained that the entrance examinations and requirements for "certifi-cates of character" had been set up as stumbling blocks specifically to prevent Ward from entering the law school and that Ward was therefore justified in refusing to take the examinations.

In another attempt to validate the good faith of the entrance examinations, Murphy intensively questioned Regent Charles Bloch, the former chair of the Judiciary Council and a formidable segrega-tionist lawyer.[26] Although Bloch adamantly opposed integration, he insisted during the trial that his actions related to the establishment of entrance examinations, both as a member of the Judiciary Coun-cil and as a regent, were taken solely to improve the caliber of law-yers in Georgia.[27] Bloch contended that an American Bar Association independent study of the law school recommended that the school should exercise greater control over the applicants and implement higher standards. Bloch stated that after he read the report he ap-pointed a committee from the Judiciary Council to consider the part of the report that dealt with bar admissions.

However, under Hollowell's intense scrutiny, Bloch's testimony revealed that the regents were involved in law school admissions at the request of the Judiciary Council. In January 1952, Bloch became a member of the Board of Regents; the following month, on Febru-ary 13, 1952, the regents adopted a resolution requesting the law fac-ulty to make recommendations concerning entrance examinations. On the same day, regents' executive secretary L. R. Siebert wrote Ward that his application would be considered pending the law faculty's recommendations.[28] This regents' action stalled Ward's appeal process; moreover, the subsequent *new* entrance examinations recommended by the law faculty and adopted by the regents made it virtually im-possible for Ward to meet the requirements. Murphy asked Bloch about his motives for recommending passage of the resolution:

> Murphy: I ask if you adopted this resolution, voted for its adop-tion and proposed it, for the purpose of keeping Ward out of the School of Law, or did you do it for the purpose of getting a better class of students at the University Law School and improving the University Law School?

Bloch: I did it for the purpose of getting better students at the University of Georgia, and hoping that would affect all other law schools in the state, and for what I thought was for the betterment of the administration of justice in Georgia.[29]

Hollowell then delved into the matter of whether Bloch and the regents passed the new resolution because Ward's appeal was pending before the committee. Bloch said that as a regent, he knew the appeal was before him, and he also knew the resolution would affect Ward's application. However, he claimed that this was *not* a factor in passing the resolution. Hollowell then asked Bloch: "And the fact that that was passed, and was to have immediate effect did not in any way to you seem inequitable to a man whose application had been pending for fifteen months?"[30] Bloch said he did not think that there was anything inequitable about the regents' action.

Despite Bloch's testimony, there were a series of circumstances and coincidences that belied his statement. These include Bloch's discussion of Ward's application with the chancellor before he joined the regents; the fact that Bloch, the chair of the Judiciary Committee who recommended the review of law admissions by the regents, had then become a member of the regents' committee specifically handling Ward's application; and the regents' decision to subject Ward's application to the new admissions procedures.

Murphy questioned another regent concerning his reasons for supporting the new entrance examinations. Murphy asked Regent Frank Foley, former president of the Georgia Bar Association, whether he acted in good faith when he supported the resolution requiring Ward to conform to the new examinations or whether he did it simply to keep Ward out of the university. Foley stated that he acted in complete good faith, insisting that his primary objectives were to improve the caliber of the students at the University of Georgia and that of the lawyers in Georgia.[31] Foley said, "I think it would be proper for Ward to do like everybody else was going to, and take those tests that we prescribed which were fair and proper."[32] Walden then asked Foley bluntly whether the regents had denied Ward's application because he was a Negro. Foley replied:

No. I thought if this man had the qualifications that he claimed and set out, that he could pass the examination, or test, . . . and I thought he ought to go and take them, and I did not in any action I took on the Board of Regents, attempt by subterfuge, evasion, or conspiracy, to deprive him of getting in the Law School because he was a Negro.[33]

As part of a strategy to show that Ward was simply a figurehead for integration efforts and not a serious applicant, Murphy attempted to establish a sinister association between Ward and NAACP officials. Murphy asked Ward whether he had discussed the case with Benjamin Mays, president of Morehouse College and a noted civil rights leader.[34] Ward responded that he may have talked with Dr. Mays in passing, but said the only person from whom he had sought advice was the late William Boyd, who had been his professor and adviser. The defendants surmised that if Murphy could show that Ward had consulted with Mays or other civil rights leaders, it would lend credence to their theory that Ward was an NAACP stooge.

Further pursuing this strategy, Murphy questioned Ward in detail about his attorneys, asking "Who is financing this lawsuit? Are you doing it or is the NAACP doing it?"[35] Walden objected to Murphy's line of questioning, claiming it was irrelevant and immaterial who was financing the case. Murphy responded that the whole atmosphere of the case showed that Ward was not a bona fide applicant, but simply a tool manipulated by others for the purpose of presenting a test case. Hooper allowed the testimony on the basis that Murphy had the right to attempt to prove his theory.

Murphy persisted with questions concerning who contributed funds to help finance Ward's lawsuit. Ward responded by saying that Boyd solicited funds from various people in the community to finance the litigation, and did not know whether they were members of the NAACP. Ward explained that Boyd had been the sole custodian of the funds and that he was unaware whether others had helped Boyd to solicit the funds.

The following excerpts from a Boyd letter to Atlanta University official Dr. L. D. Reddick reveal that Boyd personally led the campaign to raise funds for the case.

> Dear Dr. Reddick:
>
> The Ward Fund of the National Association for the Advancement of Colored People was established in September 1950 for the purpose of raising funds to cover legal expenses, court fees, printing of briefs, travel to and from New York for Thurgood Marshall and for covering Ward's expenses at the University of Georgia once the law school case is won. I have had to raise the money almost alone by personal solicitations. The case has now reached a point where however much I would prefer personal contacts, I must resort to this letter on the assumption that you do not have to be sold on the idea of either the importance of the case or on supporting it.
>
> For your information, I have personally raised over $4,200 while the branches have raised $1,600. We need a minimum of $10,000. For once I am endeavoring to have the money in the bank. We want no delays due to the lack of money. Individual contributions have ranged from $5 to $250 while organizational donations have ranged from $25 to $500.
>
> In light of the above, I beg of you to join my list of contributors to the Horace Ward Fund. This contribution is apart from any other donation made to the NAACP, and will be used exclusively for the University of Georgia Law School Case.
>
> By God's grace and with your help we shall vigorously fight this case through to ultimate victory.[36]

Although the letter clearly conveyed the NAACP's support of and assistance to Ward, neither it nor other documents suggesting Ward's association with the NAACP indicate that he was not a serious applicant with the credentials to study law. Nonetheless, the defense used Ward's association with the NAACP to bolster their claim that he was merely an NAACP puppet.

Murphy specifically asked Ward whether the NAACP had paid him while he was working at a black-owned real estate company.

Ward answered that the Wilson Realty Company had paid him. Murphy again attempted to elicit information to support the state's theory that Ward was a hireling. Ward described the defendants' tactics in an interview with the author:

> The effort was to show that I didn't want to study law, but I was a tool of the NAACP being paid by the NAACP to file this case just to get rid of segregation. I hadn't been paid by anybody, and that effort was carried on down through the trial and the statement was made that they didn't consider that I was a bona fide student, but I was kind of a foot soldier for the integration efforts, but I had always planned to study law, so I was disappointed and quite hurt about it.[37]

Another line of questioning by Murphy concerning Ward's residence led to an astounding revelation. Ward stated that he had been residing in an Atlanta University dormitory since the weekend before the trial.[38] However, in response to further questions concerning his residence, Ward dropped a bombshell: he disclosed that he was residing in Chicago, Illinois, while attending the Northwestern University Law School, where he had enrolled in September 1956. Silence gripped the courtroom; Ward had not previously made known to the court that he had enrolled at Northwestern. This testimony was a defining moment in the case, as it would become a pivotal issue in the outcome of the case. Margaret Shannon, a prominent writer for the *Atlanta Journal*, later wrote:

> There were two *bombshells* in the trial: the revelation that Ward already was studying law at Northwestern and testimony by the chancellor of the University that he would approve the admission of any *qualified* black student if the appeal of the denial of the student's application reached him.[39]

After that astonishing revelation, Murphy asked Ward whether he had applied for any out-of-state aid to pay his expenses at Northwestern. Ward answered that he had not. The implication here was that if Ward had applied for out-of-state aid to pay his expenses, it would have compromised his case, in that part of his legal complaint contended that the out-of-state aid program was not an acceptable alternative to attending the only state-supported law school in one's home state.

Murphy also questioned Ward about why he refused to reveal his employment during a pretrial deposition taken in April 1956. The pertinent questions are as follows:

> Murphy: What was your reason for not being willing to say where you were working at the time?

> Ward: I was working at Alabama State College, and I was afraid that I would lose the job if publicity got out, in association with the job, in my attempt to get into the University of Georgia Law School. I had read of situations like that that had happened before, and I needed the job.

In what even the printed word reveals was an incredulous tone, Murphy then asked:

> Murphy: Alabama State College is a colored school, isn't it?

> Ward: Oh, yes.[40]

According to Ward, Murphy missed the point of his refusal to answer the question. He did not fear that the officials of Alabama State College would fire him, because they already knew about his efforts to enter the University of Georgia. His fear was that if certain state officials of Alabama found out about his lawsuit, they might pressure the college officials to dismiss him.

Although not revealed in the trial transcript, Ward stated in an interview with the author that his concern about losing his job at Alabama State appears to have been on target, because he ultimately did lose his job. Ward said:

> In the late Spring of 1956, the assistant to the president of Alabama State visited me in Mobile, Alabama, and stated that my teaching contract would not be renewed for the upcoming year

because certain state officials had learned about my lawsuit and had approached the president of the College. I have no knowledge as to how they received the information, but it came after my deposition and was a disappointment to me. However, I did not seek reemployment at that institution and entered Northwestern University School of Law in September 1956.[41]

In her closing argument, Constance Baker Motley told the court that all of the facts and circumstances showed that Ward was not admitted to the law school because of his race. Motley, who had served as counsel for Autherine Lucy in the 1955 Alabama case of *Lucy v. Adams*, asked for a decision patterned after the well-known *Lucy* case. In that ruling, a decree for the plaintiffs found that there was no written policy excluding students from admission on account of color. However, the Court found that there was a tacit policy to that effect, and that the University of Alabama denied black applicants solely because of their race. On October 10, 1955, the U.S. Supreme Court upheld a federal district court order that restrained the University of Alabama from refusing to admit black applicants based solely on race.[42]

Ward's attorneys requested a similar injunction to prohibit the University of Georgia from blocking Ward's admission, then or in the future, on account of his race. Motley, who handled most of the final argument, posited that since Ward possessed the academic qualifications and had exhausted his administrative remedies, there was no reason to keep him out of the law school. She said that Ward should be considered based on admissions rules existing at the time of his original application in 1950.[43] Motley argued that, with the proper injunction, Judge Hooper could guarantee that Ward could be considered without discrimination. She said that it was obvious from custom and usage that the regents would reject applications from blacks whether or not they were qualified.[44]

Murphy's closing arguments asserted that Ward had not exhausted administrative appeals processes and that he had brought a lawsuit prior to the regents' rendering of a final decision on his appeal. Murphy said Ward had sued prematurely and requested that the judge dismiss the suit. However, Hooper rejected the dismissal plea and said that the regents had had ample time to pass on the appeal before Ward filed the suit.[45] Murphy also maintained that the university denied Ward's application because he did not meet the minimum academic entrance requirements and because Ward did not possess the personal qualities necessary to enter the university.

Finally, Cook filed a more damaging dismissal plea based on Ward's enrollment at Northwestern University School of Law. The brief contended that since Ward had already enrolled in Northwestern, his original application was invalid since university regulations required a transfer application for him to be considered as a transfer student. Cook asserted that Ward's lawsuit, based on the rejection of his original application to enter the law school, was moot. Although Motley had asked the judge to prohibit the regents from discriminating against Ward if he sought to transfer from Northwestern later, Cook suggested that the Court could not determine hypothetical situations.

Ward lost his case on February 12, 1957. Judge Hooper dismissed the lawsuit with costs against Ward. Hooper's opinion cited the following as reasons for the dismissal: Ward's failure to file a new application after his original application was denied, which would have given the regents sufficient information on which to base a decision as to his qualifications; Ward's failure and refusal to furnish additional information as to character; the premise that Ward "expressly abandoned his formal application" to enter the law school as a first-year student when he enrolled at Northwestern and asserted the right to enter as a transfer student in the future. Hooper concluded that regardless of the foregoing grounds for dismissal, Ward's entrance at Northwestern was clearly reason enough for the court to dismiss the case.[46]

Although Hooper acknowledged that the regents adopted the requirements for additional information as to character after Ward had submitted his application, he pointed out that all other applicants admitted since then had complied with those regulations. In essence, Hooper concluded that he was unable to rule on Ward's allegation of racial discrimination due to Ward's refusal to adhere to administrative requirements imposed since his original application. Moreover, and conclusively, Hooper stated that Ward's case became moot when he entered Northwestern University, thereby disclaiming any right to enter the University of Georgia as a first-year law student.[47]

In response to Motley's request for an injunction against discrimination should Ward apply as a transfer student, Hooper ruled that in that event, if officials denied his application, he could again file a claim to the court. Hooper also expressed serious concern in his ruling that Ward's acceptance by and enrollment in Northwestern University's law school had not been revealed to the court earlier in the trial.

In addressing the validity of the stricter, more elaborate entrance regulations adopted after Ward's application, Hooper contended that even if part of the regulations were established to keep Ward out of the law school, that would not relieve Ward of the responsibility of complying with the "valid" portion of the regulations:

> Whether or not other provisions of such resolution might, or might not, be invalid would not relieve plaintiff from the necessity of complying with said valid portion thereof, nor can such regulations be reviewed by this Court until he should have complied with the valid portions and shall have made his attack upon the remaining portions before the Board of Regents, and shall have been overruled therein.[48]

Hollowell filed later to request that Hooper retain jurisdiction of the case until Ward submitted a transfer application. In the motion, Ward's lawyers said he was in the process of filing an application for transfer to the University of Georgia from Northwestern University. However, Hooper refused to retain jurisdiction over the matter, stating, "It is legally impossible for this court to retain jurisdiction . . . in view of the fact that the court has ruled that it does not have jurisdiction."[49]

Retrospectively examining this historic legal case, one must consider that Ward's application was submitted during a time in Georgia when segregation was not only a way of life, a custom, and a time-honored tradition, but also a formal social system sustained by Georgia laws. One of the most egregious statutes was an act that provided for the separation of the "white and colored races," making it a *felony* for any state official or other person to violate this provision. The act further stated that upon conviction, the offending party "shall be confined in the penitentiary for a period of not less nor more than two years; and it shall be the duty of the Attorney General to conduct the prosecution."[50] Governor Talmadge, who was elected on a pledge to preserve segregation and was one of Georgia's leading white supremacists during this period, expressed the mood of the state. In an impassioned speech to the General Assembly in 1953, Talmadge stated that, "as long as I am your governor, there will be no mixed schools and colleges in Georgia."[51] Judge Hooper, unfortunately, appeared unwilling to defy such mores, despite the soundness of Ward's legal arguments.

Ward had underestimated the power behind the forces of white supremacy in his determined quest for admission to the University of Georgia. Ward was especially encouraged in his efforts by the court decision in the Texas *Sweatt v. Painter* case. Perhaps, he surmised, the University of Georgia would admit him without a court fight:

> I somehow had the notion when I filed my application in September 1950 that there was a good chance that I might possibly be admitted to the law school without the necessity of court action. In the first place, in June of that year the Supreme Court had ruled in the case of *Sweatt v. Painter*, that the University of Texas Law School must be integrated. Also, this was 1950, before the lines were clearly drawn in terms of massive resistance to desegregation of public schools. However, I had spent too much time in political theory and had not fully accounted for the political realities.[52]

But unlike some border states, Deep South states mounted massive resistance to integration in the public schools. Governor Talmadge said that when he became aware that Horace Ward was seeking entrance to the University of Georgia, he employed his personal attorney, B. D. Murphy, as special counsel to help the state's attorney general keep Ward out of the law school.[53]

Murphy engineered multiple delays and legal maneuvers, with the result that Ward's case did not go to court until December 1956, *more than six years* after his original application. In addition to the newly adopted entrance examinations, state and regents' officials erected major obstructions to Ward's admission, including the adoption of an elaborate administrative appeals process, the passing of a state law that prohibited funding to any integrated school, and an "in-person" interview process to judge his character, which ultimately deemed him undesirable for admission. Danner even went so far as to raise questions about the credibility of Morehouse College, arguably one of the preeminent colleges in the country. Morehouse, under the leadership of Benjamin Mays, produced an annual cadre of graduates who achieved high success in other noted universities and in the professional world. Morris Phelps, who served as admissions counselor under Danner and succeeded him as admissions director, declared that using the technicality that Morehouse was not a member of SACS as a reason to reject Ward was a pure sham:

> That's just subterfuge to find a reason to keep the black student out. I mean, if this were a white student from Morehouse, they probably wouldn't pay any attention to the fact that Morehouse was not a member of the Southern Association of Colleges and Schools.[54]

Although there is no conclusive supporting evidence, some have speculated that Talmadge arranged for the drafting of Ward by the armed services to thwart his efforts to attend the university. Through the years, Talmadge has evaded the question of his role in causing Ward to be drafted. In 1986 the *Atlanta Journal* reported Talmadge's response to the question of his involvement:

> He [Talmadge] has always said he considered the timing to be coincidence, but at a symposium last year, Talmadge was asked if

he arranged for Ward to be drafted, and with a deadpan expression and twinkle in his eye, Talmadge replied, "I wasn't on the draft board."[55]

Ward says he never had any evidence that his being drafted at that particular time was anything other than coincidental,[56] but others had serious doubts about Ward's "convenient" draft notice. Bill Shipp, for example, shared this sentiment: "I believe the governor had some hand in it. Mr. Ward was drafted into the military just as he appeared about to achieve the court order forcing his admission."[57] Ward's attorneys also had their doubts about the matter; Hollowell said:

> You can be sure that we wondered whether it was a purely coincidental thing, and our better judgment told us that it was not. After all, draft boards had lots of power . . . I think we don't have to be terribly sophisticated to come to the conclusion that it just may not have been purely coincidental.[58]

Whether or not there was deliberate action by state officials behind the coincidence of Ward's being drafted thirty days before his case was to go to trial, it is irrefutable that the state employed unethical tactics, at the very least, to keep Ward and any prospective black applicants out of white institutions. It is not possible to know what was in the hearts of all who participated in thwarting Ward's efforts to enter the law school; but it is clear that parts of their testimony were contradictory, and sometimes appear to have been calculated perjury. Journalist Margaret Shannon summed up the state's defense in a caustic *Atlanta Journal* article:

> The state government's response to Ward's application was a masterpiece of demagoguery, deviousness and delay which made numerous supposedly honorable white officials into moral and legal contortionists. Many of them flirted with perjury and insulted their own intelligence by some of the things they did and said.[59]

Morehouse President Benjamin Mays, who observed the trial, recalled that he was shocked, stunned, and terribly disappointed when he heard senior officials swear in court that race had absolutely nothing to do with Ward's denial of admission. Mays concluded, "I suppose these top officials had to lie, since admission that Ward was kept out because of his race would have forced the university to admit him."[60]

President Aderhold's contradictory statements typify the highly questionable motives of university officials. For instance, he stated at one point during the trial that he could not say that the university treated Ward differently from others (i.e., whites) seeking admission to the law school because he was not involved in the admissions process. It is not credible that the president of the university was ignorant of Ward's application, especially in light of the regents' concern over it. Furthermore, correspondence discovered in the Aderhold papers between Aderhold and Elliott Cheatham revealed that Cheatham counseled Aderhold concerning the "Negro applicant" (Ward) as early as June 1951. In a June 25, 1951, letter, to Aderhold, Cheatham said, "The only question is whether Georgia is offering legal education to Negroes. Since it is not, the Negro applicant has an open and shut case—unless there is some fault in his individual application."[61]

Similarly, Chancellor Caldwell made very inconsistent statements about the out-of-state aid program. On the one hand, he indicated that the regents designed the program to encourage blacks to go to institutions out of state. However, he denied that this program meant that "we are refusing to admit them, under proper circumstances." Regent Bloch's testimony also contradicted Caldwell's insistence that the out-of-state aid program was voluntary for Negroes. Bloch testified that black applicants would be *relegated* to the out-of-state aid program.[62]

Moreover, correspondence from Robert Arnold, chair of the Board of Regents, to law school dean J. Alton Hosch during Ward's application process *contradicts his sworn testimony* that regents officials did not conspire to keep Ward out of the law school. Arnold noted in a February 25, 1952, letter to Hosch that he had been working with Hosch to handle the Ward matter. In that letter Arnold also

100

made highly condescending remarks about one liberal university student who had spoken out for the admission of blacks in a February 22, 1952, *Red and Black* article polling students' reactions to Ward's application. The letter also reveals racism of the lowest order on the part of its author:

> I wonder what she could know about the personal traits of negroes and if *B. O.* could come under the head of traits with this young lady. Maybe her education is lacking somewhere, although she is a candidate for a major in education. With her thinking, she had best be careful to locate above the Mason & Dixon line.[63]

Sentiments such as these speak for themselves and suggest the kind of attitudes underlying the shoddy tactics of the defense.

Among the defendants' most despicable tactics was the obstinate insistence that requirements for new entrance examinations and certificates of good moral character had been adopted purely to raise the educational and moral standards of the university, not to block Ward's admission. However, a letter catalogued in the J. Alton Hosch Papers reveals state and university officials' true motives. In February 7, 1952, correspondence from Chancellor Caldwell to Charles Bloch, Caldwell enclosed a copy of a resolution *"for the guidance of those who are considering the Horace Ward matter"* [emphasis added].[64] The resolution included a proposal for the dean of the law school to submit to the chancellor a plan for aptitude tests and other standards that the regents later adopted to block Ward's admission. In retrospect, even Governor Talmadge now acknowledges that the regents very likely adopted the examinations to keep Ward and other blacks out.[65]

In discussing the state's efforts to uphold segregation and to deter the *Ward* lawsuit, Attorney General Cook said, "It's ripe for a showdown, if he (Ward) wins, all he will do is close down the law school."[66] However, Attorney Earnest D. Brookins, then a law student who opposed Ward becoming his classmate, contends that Cook's statements were not sincere. Brookins, now a prominent attorney in Atlanta (and ironically a friend of Ward's) said:

101

I think the politicians were saying what they thought the people wanted to hear in order to be re-elected. For the Attorney General of Georgia to say that if blacks entered, that the school would be closed simply was not true, and I don't think any of the politicians or Mr. Cook intended that. They intended to frighten as many people as possible and get as many votes as possible.[67]

Reinforcing the state's defense before the *Ward* trial started, Cook disclosed that some of the state's most prominent attorneys were strategizing on ways to sustain segregation, including former Governor Herman Talmadge, Charles Bloch, and B. D. Murphy. Cook also revealed that he would confer with allies fighting desegregation in other Southern states and he designated two assistant attorneys to litigate antisegregation cases on a full-time basis.[68] The posture of Georgia's political leaders, armed with funds from the state treasury and in consultation with leading foes of desegregation in other Southern states, was to keep Ward out of the university.

A salient issue raised with Ward during the trial was his refusal to submit to entrance examinations beyond his original application or to provide additional information as to character. Murphy said Ward should have taken the intelligence test and submitted to other prerequisites that were set up after his application.[69] Judge Hooper supported Murphy's contention, ignoring the abundantly clear evidence that the examinations were a sham designed to keep Ward out. There were ample analogous instances in the South in which state officials used tests as devices to deny civil rights. For example, a constitutional amendment in Alabama required that voters must be able to read and write, understand and explain any article of the U.S. Constitution, and be of good character.[70] The use of such tests to prohibit blacks from voting was a widespread practice in many Southern states. Ward contended that the newly adopted admissions standards were a similar ploy to keep him out of the all-white law school.

While some readers may ask why Ward did not submit to the examinations, the answer is that given the tenor of the time, his refusal was the only reasonable choice. Even if Ward had passed the series of written examinations, some other roadblock test would have been thrown in his path. Journalist Bill Shipp has commented on how segregationists used tests to disqualify black applicants:

> If you looked at some of those tests blacks were required to pass, the Chief Justice of the United States Supreme Court today could not pass those tests. The tests were not set up to see if he was qualified for admission. The tests were set up to keep him out. Even if he had scored one hundred on the test, it didn't make any difference. They would have said he signed his name incorrectly.[71]

Former University of Georgia admissions director Morris Phelps also indicated, in an interview with the author, that the regents had adopted the new admissions examinations to exclude blacks deliberately.

> I think the test requirements were put in to keep black students from being admitted. I don't think there's any question about that, and I don't think anybody now would deny that that was why they were put in . . . I'm sure the interview itself [Board of Regents regulations requiring a three-person interview for appellants] was put in for that reason.[72]

One of the state's key defense strategists in several civil rights cases also admitted the real purpose behind the examinations. E. Freeman Leverett, former associate attorney in the Attorney General's office, concluded in a 1995 interview that the circumstances surrounding desegregation at this time undoubtedly led to the adoption of these policies.[73] Nevertheless, Judge Hooper asserted in his opinion that Ward should have submitted to the fair portions of the tests and appealed those portions deemed unfair.

Officials also said during the trial that Ward had been inconsistent, evasive, and contradictory in his statements to the special committee that interviewed him. Furthermore, they raised concerns about his character. With respect to Ward's purported evasiveness, it is understandable that he would have been cautious in responding to some questions posed by the committee. He recognized that the

committee would use any inconsistency or even marginally questionable circumstance to deny his admission. Further, it was Ward's
contention that the interview was set up for the specific purpose of
disqualifying him. His attorneys of course shared this view; Motley
stated that relying on character issues as a basis for rejecting black
applicants was a favorite strategy of Southern opposition lawyers:

> What they wanted to do, of course, was to disqualify the appli-
> cant on some ground other than race. So, whenever we filed one
> of these suits, what they would do is investigate the plaintiff from
> the day they were born to see if there was anything at all by the
> way of character defect which they could use to say well this is
> why we didn't admit them and the race had nothing to do with
> it. I don't think that we had a case in which that wasn't true.[74]

One questionable aspect of Hollowell and Motley's strategy
concerns their decision not to reveal to the court that Ward had
enrolled as a law student at Northwestern University. Ward said that
it was not part of any preplanned strategy. He stated that after the
army discharged him, he decided to try for one more year to enter
the UGA School of Law. His attorneys thought that the case would
be tried within a year and were hopeful even up to the time when
he entered Northwestern in September 1956. However, due to the
state's stalling tactics, the case was delayed until December 1956.
Because of the time that had elapsed since he first tried to enter the
law school in 1950, and as a result of his uncertainty as to whether
he was ever going to be admitted, Ward enrolled at Northwestern
under the GI Bill when his attorneys were unable to secure a trial
date before September 1956. Meanwhile, they supported his decision to enroll at Northwestern with the hope of transferring to the
UGA School of Law if he won his case.[75]

Hollowell and Motley acknowledged that the "proper discretion" had not been used in failing to reveal Ward's enrollment in
Northwestern, but they reminded the Court that Ward's application
had been pending since 1950 and they maintained that the Court
should declare that Ward had been refused admission on the basis of

race.[76] The revelation of Ward's admission to Northwestern had a twofold effect, the second of which implicitly challenged the judge's ability to be fair. It showed that Ward was qualified to attend a first-class law school, but it also compromised his application to the UGA law school as a first-year student. In the judge's mind, the latter was a reason for dismissal of his case; given the political pressures of the time, a politically prudent, if not legally upstanding decision.

The dismissal of the lawsuit brought jubilance for Georgia officials who had bitterly fought to uphold segregationist customs and traditions. However, it was, or at least should have been, apparent to even the most ardent segregationists that the question was not *if* segregation in Georgia would end, but *when*. By the end of the Ward trial, the U.S. Supreme Court had already ruled in favor of black applicants in Texas, Virginia, North Carolina, Kentucky, Tennessee, Louisiana, Maryland, and Delaware. Additionally, although Hooper refused Ward's admission, he did concede that it was established that the authorities of state-supported institutions could not refuse admission to any person solely because of race and color. Nevertheless, despite this foreshadowing of future events, segregationist forces in Georgia claimed victory and vowed to continue their effort to bar blacks from attending all-white institutions.

For Ward, however, it was time to move on to different pursuits. Although he and his advisors initially considered attempting to enroll him as a transfer student, after a period of seven years of seeking to enter the UGA School of Law, Ward and his attorneys abandoned their struggle. Hollowell said the primary reasons they did not appeal were that Ward was in his late twenties by this time, that he was already in law school, and that much of the money Boyd had raised to support the case had been spent:

> We thought it better if he go on. Since they had made a change in the administrative procedure for appeals, we were convinced that they would keep dancing us around some more. We didn't know what else they had up their sleeve or what other legal tricks they would employ. We thought it best to let Ward go on. He had certainly paid his dues, and more.[77]

Hollowell, as local counsel in collaboration with Thurgood Marshall and his LDF associates, would go on to represent black students in the Georgia cases of *Hunt v. Arnold* and *Holmes v. Danner*, wherein blacks sought to enter white universities. The issues raised in the *Ward* case would be revisited in the ensuing cases and it would become apparent that the *Ward* case provided the foundation and impetus for ending segregation in public higher education in Georgia. Many of the defendants' legal ploys would be recycled, but the civil rights lawyers would apply the lessons learned from the *Ward* case to overcome them. Ward himself would cease being a plaintiff and a foot soldier for justice, and would assume, in the years to come, a leadership role in the war against segregation.

CHAPTER 4 NOTES

[1]William M. Boyd, letter to Thurgood Marshall, August 19, 1949, in Papers of the NAACP, The Campaign for Educational Equality: Legal Department and Central Office Records, Supplement to Part 1, 1940-1955. Legal File: Schools-Irwin County, Georgia, NAACP Archives, Library of Congress, Washington. D.C.

[2]"Powell, Robeson to Speak, Sing!", *Southern Negro Youth Congress News Bulletin*, October 1946, 1-4, William Madison Boyd Collection, Special Collections, Robert W. Woodruff Library, Atlanta University Center; Louise Hollowell and Martin C. Lehfeldt, M. C., *The Sacred Call: A Tribute to Donald Hollowell——Civil Rights Champion* (Winter Park, FL: Four-G Publishers, 1997); Donald L. Hollowell, interview with author, Atlanta, GA, July 27, 1993. Donald L. Hollowell's work to secure the release of Dr. Martin Luther King, Jr., from the Reidsville State Prison, his work with Dr. King in the Albany, Georgia, civil rights movement, and his brilliant lawyering in the *Holmes v. Danner* case are a few of the legal efforts that have helped to make him a legendary figure in Georgia and throughout the country.

[3]Donald L. Hollowell, interview, ibid.; Constance Baker Motley, interview with author, New York, NY, March 30, 1995.

[4]Motley, interview, ibid. Motley was one of the lawyers who helped write the briefs in the *Brown v. Board of Education* case. In addition to appearing before state and federal courts throughout the United States, she argued ten cases before the U.S. Supreme Court, winning nine, which helped to secure equal rights for black Americans. Besides her pivotal role in the *Holmes v. Danner* case, Motley participated significantly in the litigation that resulted in the admission of James Meredith to the University of Mississippi, Vivian Malone and James Hood to the University of Ala-

bama, and Harvey Gantt to Clemson College in South Carolina. For a study of Motley's life and work, see Constance Baker Motley, *Equal Justice under Law: An Autobiography of Constance Baker Motley* (New York: Farrar, Straus & Giroux, 1998). Also see University of Georgia Third Annual Holmes-Hunter Lecture, "Abbreviated Biography on Constance Baker Motley" [brochure], Athens, GA: Holmes-Hunter Lecture Committee, 1987; Maya Angelou, et al., *Essence: 25 Years of Celebrating Black Women* (New York: Harry N. Abrams, 1995).

[5]Gwen Y. Wood, *A Unique and Fortuitous Combination: An Administrative History of the University of Georgia School of Law* (Athens: University of Georgia Press, 1998), 103; Thomas Dyer, *The University of Georgia: A Bicentennial History, 1785-1985* (Athens: University of Georgia Press, 1985), 312.

[6]Horace T. Ward, letter to Regents, April 12, 1952, Horace T. Ward Collection, Archives and Special Collections, Robert W. Woodruff Library, Atlanta University Center.

[7]*Ward Complaint*, Horace T. Ward Collection, Archives and Special Collections, Robert W. Woodruff Library, Atlanta University Center.

[8]Dyer, op. cit., 311.

[9]General Appropriations Act, Secs. 8, 9, Ga. Laws (1951), 425. Similar provisions appear in the General Appropriations Act, Secs. 8, 9, Ga. Laws Jan.-Feb. Session, (1953), 154 and General Appropriations Act, Secs. 8, 9, Ga. Laws (1956), 762.

[10]*Gaines v. Canada*, 305 U.S. 337 (1938). The out-of-state aid policy had been ruled unconstitutional in this case in 1938. However, Georgia continued this practice throughout the 1950s.

[11]*Ward v. Regents of University System of Georgia*, C.A. 4355, Trial Transcript, December 17, 18, 19, 20, 1956, 100.

[12]Ibid., 27.

[13]Ibid., 196; Harmon Caldwell to Elizabeth Parker, June 22, 1951, Hargrett Rare Book and Manuscript Library/University of Georgia Libraries, Folder: Personnel. For further study of Caldwell's views and actions related to the admission of Negroes to Georgia's colleges and universities, see Harmon Caldwell Papers, Hargrett Rare Book and Manuscript Library/University of Georgia Libraries.

[14]*Ward v. Regents*, transcript, op. cit., 198.

[15]Ibid., 379.

[16]Ibid., 454-460.

[17]See Report of the University of Georgia Faculty Committee on the Appeal of Horace T. Ward, September 13, 1951, 7. Hargrett Rare Book and Manuscript Library/University of Georgia Libraries, J. Alton Hosch Papers, Folder: Horace T. Ward case; *Ward v. Regents*, transcript, op. cit., 233-234.

[18]*Sweatt v. Painter* et al., 339 U.S. 629 (1950).

[19]Horace Ward, interview with author, Atlanta, GA, August 22, 1994.

[20]*Ward v. Regents*, op. cit., 206-207.

[21]Ward, interview, op. cit.

[22]Donald L. Hollowell, interview with author, Atlanta, GA, July 27,1993.

[23]*Ward v. Regents*, op. cit., 306.

[24]University System of Georgia, Board of Regents Minutes, June 11, 1952, 2.

[25]Ward, letter to Regents, op. cit..

[26]Biographical information on Charles J. Bloch can be found in the Hargrett Rare Book and Manuscript Library/University of Georgia Libraries, Charles J. Bloch Biographical File, Georgiana Collection, Athens, GA. Bloch graduated from the University of Georgia in 1913 with an A.B. degree and also attended Mercer University. He served as president of the Georgia Bar Association in 1944-45, and was chairman of the rules committee for the Supreme Court of Georgia for several years. He also served as vice president of the segregationist States' Rights Council of Georgia and was an active Democrat or, in the terminology of the times, "Dixiecrat," who nominated Senator Richard B. Russell for president in 1948. Bloch appeared before the House and Senate Judiciary Committees in 1957 in opposition to the Civil Rights Bill.

[27]According to Bloch's sworn testimony, state law required the Judiciary Council to investigate anything pertaining to the administration of the courts, or to the administration of justice, and make recommendations to the proper authorities of the state for the correction of any maladministration. Statutes also required the Judiciary Council to make recommendations for improvement in the administration of justice and specifically to make recommendations with respect to admission to the Georgia Bar. See *Ward v. Regents*, 343.

[28]L. R. Siebert, letter to Horace T. Ward, February 13, 1952, Horace T. Ward Collection, Archives and Special Collections, Robert W. Woodruff Library, Atlanta University Center; University of Georgia Regents Minutes, February 13, 1952, 279-281.

[29]*Ward v. Regents*, op. cit., 373-374.

[30]Ibid., 398.

[31]Ibid., 420.

[32]Ibid., 421.

[33]Ibid., 436.

[34]See Benjamin E. Mays, *Benjamin E. Mays: Born to Rebel—An Autobiography* (New York: Charles Scribner's Sons, 1971). Benjamin E. Mays was uncompromising in his assertion of dignity for blacks during a period of state-sponsored racist practices. Mays served on the board of directors for the NAACP and was a founding member of the committee to establish the NAACP Legal Defense and Educational Fund. He served as president of the United Negro College Fund and was a guiding force in several civil rights organizations. He is well known, of course, for his long and distinguished tenure as the president of Morehouse College from 1940 to 1967.

[35]*Ward v. Regents*, op. cit., 287-289.

[36]W. M. Boyd, letter to L. D. Riddick, January 29, 1953, William Madison Boyd Col-

lection, Special Collections, Robert W. Woodruff Library, Atlanta University Center.

[37]Horace Ward, interview with author, Atlanta, GA, August 22, 1994.

[38]Ward received unwavering support from the Atlanta University (AU) community in his quest to enter the law school. Political scientist Robert Brisbane, one of Ward's mentors and former professors at AU, recalls that Morehouse and AU faculty members and students wanted to do everything they could to overthrow segregation. He stated that when it became apparent that law was the profession through which the best attack could be made on segregation, individuals such as Leroy Johnson, Horace Ward, Maynard Jackson, and many others pursued the legal profession, also receiving strong support from the AU community. Robert Brisbane, interview with author, Atlanta, GA, January 19, 1995.

[39]Margaret Shannon, "Justice at Last for Horace Ward," *Atlanta Journal and Constitution Magazine*, March 13, 1977, 8, 9.

[40]*Ward v. Regents*, op. cit., 281.

[41]Horace Ward, interview with author, Atlanta, GA, November 23, 1998.

[42]*Lucy v. Adams*, 134 F. Supp. 235 (D.C.N.D. Ala 1955); *Lucy v. Adams*, 350 U.S. 1, 76 S. Ct. 33 (1955). Papers of the NAACP, The Campaign for Educational Equality: Legal Department and Central Office Records, Supplement to Part 1, 1951-1955. Legal Department Monthly Report on *Lucy v. Board of Trustees of University of Alabama* (October 1955).

[43]"Decision on Ward Suit Expected in Two Weeks," *Atlanta Journal*, January 4, 1957, 28.

[44]Bill Pickering, "Hooper Hints No Racial Edict in Ward Case," *Atlanta Journal*, January 21, 1957, 2.

[45]Margaret Shannon, "Ward Transfer Bid Hinted in Last Arguments," *Atlanta Journal*, January 3, 1957, 1.

[46]"Excerpts from Decision in the Ward Case," *Atlanta Journal*, February 13, 1957, 2, 10.

[47]Ibid., 10; also see *Ward v. Regents*, 191 F. Supp. 491 (N.D. Ga. 1957).

[48]*Ward v. Regents*, op. cit.

[49]"Ward Through, Hooper Says," *Atlanta Journal*, March 20, 1957, 2.

[50]Senate Bill 40, Georgia Laws 1955 Session, 1 Gen. Acts and Res. 174-176 (1955).

[51]"Talmadge Vows Segregation Will Remain in State," *Athens Banner Herald*, November 17, 1953, A-1.

[52]Horace Ward, "Individual Rights and Responsibilities," paper presented at the convention of the American Bar Association, Atlanta, GA, August 1991.

[53]Herman Talmadge, interview with author, Hampton, GA, January 23, 1995.

[54]Morris Phelps, interview with author, Athens, GA, August 7, 1996.

[55]Sam Heys, "Attempts to Attend UGA Law School Thwarted at Every Turn," *Atlanta Constitution*, May 2, 1986, C-4.

[56]Horace Ward, interview with author, Atlanta, GA, August 22, 1994.

[57]Bill Shipp, interview with author, Atlanta, GA, January 23, 1995.

[58]Donald Hollowell, interview with author, Atlanta, GA, July 27, 1993.

[59]Shannon, "Justice at Last for Horace Ward," op. cit.

[60]Mays, op. cit., 207.

[61]Elliott E. Cheatham, letter to O. C. Aderhold, June 25, 1951, Hargrett Rare Book and Manuscript Library/University of Georgia Libraries, O. C. Aderhold Papers, Folder: Integration of the University of Georgia.

[62]*Ward v. Regents*, op. cit., 379.

[63]"Students Turn Thumbs Down on Negro Seeking Entrance," *Red and Black*, February 22, 1952, 14; Regent Robert O. Arnold, letter to J. Alton Hosch, February 25, 1952, Horace T. Ward case folder, Hargrett Rare Book and Manuscript Library/University of Georgia Libraries, J. Alton Hosch Papers.

[64]Harmon Caldwell, letter to Charles J. Bloch, February 7, 1952, Hargrett Rare Book and Manuscript Library/University of Georgia Libraries, J. Alton Hosch Papers, Folder: Horace T. Ward case.

[65]Herman Talmadge, interview with author, Hampton, GA, January 23, 1995.

[66]Charles Pou, "Cook Gets Legal Aid in Fight to Keep Schools Segregated," *Atlanta Journal*, July 8, 1955, 1.

[67]Earnest Brookins, interview with author, Atlanta, GA, May 15, 1995.

[68]Pou, op. cit.

[69]Lerone Bennett, Jr., "Federal Judge Refuses to Dismiss Horace Ward Suit: Court Gives Regents 30 Days to Accept or Reject Student," *Atlanta Daily World*, December 16, 1952, 1.

[70]Code of Alabama, Section 181 (Recompiled 1958), Amend. 55 (Ratified 1946).

[71]Bill Shipp, interview with author, Atlanta, GA, January 23, 1995.

[72]Morris Phelps, interview with author, Athens, GA, August 7, 1996.

[73]E. Freeman Leverett, interview with author, Elberton, GA, December 8, 1995.

[74]Constance Baker Motley, interview with author, New York, NY, March 30, 1995.

[75]Louise Hollowell and Martin C. Lehfeldt, *The Sacred Call: A Tribute to Donald Hollowell—Civil Rights Champion* (Winter Park, FL: Four-G Publishers, 1997), 112.

[76]Dyer, op. cit., 313.

[77]Donald L. Hollowell, interview with author, Atlanta, GA, August 22, 1994.

Ward's Cause Reenacted: The Applications of Charlayne Hunter and Hamilton Holmes to The University of Georgia

In January 1957, after Horace Ward lost his bid to enter the University of Georgia, he returned to Chicago to complete his law degree at Northwestern University. He recalled that he was "very disappointed at the trial" in which officials had attacked his character and sought to mar his record.[1] Particularly chagrined by officials who contended during the trial that he was unfit to enter the University of Georgia, Ward said that was the first time during his six-year struggle to enter the school "that they began to hurt my feelings. I just wanted to get the trial over and go back to Chicago and be with my family."[2] Ward's wife Ruth and their young son Theodore had moved to Chicago with him in September 1956, where Ruth secured a job at the Laboratory School of the University of Chicago.

In contrast to the treatment he received in Georgia, Northwestern had become a place of refuge for Ward, and the Northwestern student body accorded him respect and decent treatment. Ward had rejected the Georgia Board of Regents' out-of-state aid offer, which the university had made available to him to keep him out of the law school. However, he was able to finance his education at Northwestern with savings, assistance from the GI Bill, and support from his wife Ruth.[3]

While Ward pursued his law degree at Northwestern, segrega-tionists in Georgia continued to clamor for ways to sustain the legal apartheid system. Governor Marvin Griffin, who had succeeded Talmadge, was quickly becoming the chief exponent in the cam-paign for massive resistance to desegregation in Georgia. In addition to his public addresses, his actions to prevent Georgia Tech Univer-sity from playing in the 1956 Sugar Bowl dramatized his alarmist view of desegregation in any form. Griffin opposed Georgia Tech's participation in this major bowl game because the opposing team from the University of Pittsburgh was racially integrated. Griffin, who had run a campaign on racial demagoguery, adamantly declared:

> We cannot make the slightest concession to the enemy in this dark and lamentable hour of struggle. There is no more differ-ence in compromising the integrity of race on the playing field than in doing so in the classroom. One break in the dike and the relentless seas will rush in and destroy us.[4]

Georgia's insistence on preserving racial traditions was also shown on the floor of the state house. On February 13, 1956, the General Assembly approved making the battle flag of the Confed-eracy part of the state flag. Griffin's floor leader, Denmark Groover, speaking for the flag bill, said that "the move should leave no doubt in anyone's mind that Georgia will not forget the teachings of Lee and Stonewall Jackson . . . this will show that we in Georgia intend to uphold what we stood for, will stand for, and will fight for."[5] In the same vein, Georgia's "interposition resolution," approved by a joint session of the General Assembly on March 9, 1956, also showed Georgia officials' penchant for racial exclusion. The defiant resolu-tion expressly called for Georgia to interpose "her sovereign power between the Court and her public schools" and to declare the Su-preme Court decisions to abolish segregation null, void, and of no effect.[6] Three days later, Georgia's congressional delegation unani-mously endorsed the "Southern Manifesto," which openly defied the Supreme Court and its 1954 *Brown v. Board of Education* decision supporting school integration.[7]

In this racially charged environment, Atlanta NAACP branch president John Calhoun had by January 1956 identified three potential black applicants to the all-white Georgia State College of Business (GSCB), now Georgia State University, and had appealed to Thurgood Marshall for help.[8] Several NAACP leaders and community activists who responded to this call for help had been involved in Ward's case and they invested what they had learned in helping the GSCB applicants. Whereas ten black students sought admission to GSCB between March 1956 and June 1956, ultimately only three of the applicants—Barbara Hunt, Myra Dinsmore, and Iris Mae Welch—were plaintiffs in the lawsuit filed for admission to GSCB. Civil rights leader and chief actuary of the black-owned Atlanta Life Insurance Company Jesse Hill led community efforts supporting the students. Opponents included several officials already known for their resistance to Horace Ward in his efforts to enter UGA. Predictably, the applicants encountered formidable obstacles, mostly related to the alumni certificate requirements and the out-of-state aid program.[9]

The Board of Regents' policy requiring applicants to secure personal character recommendations from alumni was still in effect. Judge Hooper had admonished Ward for refusing to comply with this requirement that the regents had adopted shortly after he had applied to the law school.[10] Accordingly, having learned from Ward's experience, and with the help of Jesse Hill and other NAACP leaders, the applicants made a diligent effort to comply with the policy requiring character certificates. However, GSCB alumni uniformly refused to give them the needed recommendations; uniformly also, their applications to GSCB were rejected by the college registrar.

With the help of E. E. Moore, a local black attorney active with the NAACP, the applicants then appealed to university president George M. Sparks and the regents, requesting a waiver of the alumni character certifications. The president and the regents rejected their appeal.[11] Whereas Judge Hooper in *Ward* dismissed the lawsuit in part because Ward had *refused* to seek the character recommendations, the responses to the Georgia State applicants showed that it was *futile* to ask white alumni for character certifications; any white alumni who might have been willing to provide them were undoubtedly few and reluctant. As in Ward's case, there would be no available recourse for the black applicants other than litigation.

Moore therefore sought legal help and financial assistance from the LDF. The LDF granted Moore's request and attorneys Thurgood Marshall, Robert L. Carter, and Constance Baker Motley joined the case. With added expertise gained from the *Ward* case, attorneys Donald Hollowell and Austin Walden also joined the team. More than two years after the filing of the lawsuit on behalf of Hunt, Dinsmore, and Welch (*Hunt v. Arnold*), and after vigorous efforts by state officials to dismiss the matter, the case was tried before Judge Boyd Sloan on December 8-12, 1958, in the U.S. District Court for the Northern District of Georgia.[12] Since Horace Ward had lost his heroic bid to attend the University of Georgia School of Law, the GSCB applicants, if admitted, would become the first black students admitted to a white institution in the state.

As in Ward's case, an important premise of the plaintiffs was that GSCB officials had violated the constitutional provisions of the Fourteenth Amendment. On generally the same grounds that Ward had claimed, Moore and the LDF team flatly asserted that college officials denied blacks admission to GSCB because of their race while at the same time, *with public funds*, affording whites the opportunity to attend the institution.[13] They also claimed that admissions policies requiring alumni character certificates were unreasonable and arbitrary because, due to existing social patterns, the plaintiffs were not acquaintances of any of the all-white alumni.[14]

Attorney General Eugene Cook and Deputy Assistant State Attorney General B. D. Murphy, who served as chief counsel for the defendants in *Ward*, again represented the defendants. Cook used many of the same arguments from the *Ward* trial, denying that the admissions procedures were discriminatory, and claiming that they were equally applicable to both white and black applicants. The attorneys for the state further asserted that the federal court should not rule on the matter before the courts of Georgia had, implying that a state court rather than a federal court should decide the matter.[15] Cook's argument, based on "states rights doctrine," had the strong support of Governor Griffin and Georgia's senior legislators.

Cook also borrowed another argument from the *Ward* case, claiming that the lawsuit brought by the black applicants was "not being maintained in good faith" because "it was brought at the insistence and urging of the NAACP," suggesting that the plaintiffs were mere tools of a conspiracy.[16] An additional defense strategy used before in the *Ward* case was to show that the plaintiffs lacked sufficient character to be admitted to the college. In attempting to make this argument, the defense attorneys focused intrusively on the applicants' private lives—in our contemporary court of opinion, an egregious offense against civil rights, but at the time, unfortunately a common indignity for blacks seeking legal redress.

Perhaps surprisingly, in a significant victory against the rigged admission system, on January 9, 1959, Judge Sloan found that "the effect of the alumni certificate requirement upon Negroes has been, is, and will be to prevent Negroes from meeting the admissions requirement," ruling that the alumni certification requirements were unconstitutional.[17] He also made judicial note of the fact that it was not customary for blacks and whites to interact socially and that the opportunities for the average black person to become acquainted with the average white person, and particularly with the alumni of a white educational institution, were limited.

This decision provided some vicarious recompense for Ward, who had insisted that the regents adopted post hoc requirements to keep him out of the University of Georgia. Constance Baker Motley noted that Sloan, who was considered a liberal judge, was clear-sighted enough to hold that the requirement violated black people's right to equal protection and struck it down. The arbitrary character requirements that had been major obstacles for Ward and the GSCB applicants were thereby removed from the paths of future black applicants who would seek admission to Georgia's white public colleges.[18]

Also, validating the plaintiffs' claim that the out-of-state scholarship program essentially shunted black students out of the system, Sloan ruled that the program did not meet the constitutional requirements of equal protection. Sloan exposed the program for the deceptive device it was and declared that it was not an appropriate or legal substitute for providing blacks with educational opportunities in the state, basing his ruling on the historic 1938 precedent of *Gaines v. Canada*.[19] That this program was still in practice in Georgia as late as 1958 indicated the stubbornness and arrogance of Georgia officials, particularly since the program had been ruled unconstitutional by the Supreme Court twenty years earlier. In the *Gaines* case, Chief Justice Hughes had expressly stated that it was the duty of the state to provide education for all its citizens *within the state*.[20]

Judge Sloan also responded to the defendants' claim that the applicants were not bona fide candidates, but were tools of the NAACP and had filed the case solely for the purpose of dismantling segregation. Sloan dismissed Murphy's argument that the plaintiffs' motive in applying to the GSCB was to provide grounds for filing the suit. This conclusion was also a kind of vicarious triumph for Ward, whom Murphy had claimed was merely a stooge for the integration efforts.

Regarding the applicants' qualifications, Sloan noted that while their scholastic qualifications could rightly be examined, each candidate did possess sufficient scholastic credits for admission to the college. Undoubtedly, the defendants knew—as they did when they attacked Ward's academic qualifications—that the case for disqualifying the applicants on academic grounds was weak. Therefore, exactly as in Ward's case, they focused intrusively on the plaintiffs' private lives—a practice seldom, if ever, employed in the screening of white applicants. Given the sexual mores of the time, the defendants' *ad hominem* strategy worked in this case: a background investigation by the defense revealed that two of the applicants, Holland and Hunt, had each conceived a child out of wedlock. Sloan concluded accordingly they may not have been of good moral character, and therefore perhaps not qualified for admission.[21] In addition

116

to embarrassing these women cruelly, the judge's ruling on this issue sadly proved to be the Achilles' heel of the plaintiffs' case.

Despite some broad gains for civil rights contained in the *Hunt* decision, the jubilation of the plaintiffs was muted, not only because of the attempted character assassination, but also because Sloan failed to order GSCB to admit any of the applicants. Moreover, and inevitably, the plaintiffs left the trial with a lingering sense of shame and indignity because of the defense's attack upon their moral characters. Since the court left it to college officials to guarantee that applicants meet all other valid requirements, there remained also a concern that the university might erect other obstacles to deny black applicants in the future.

This concern was well founded, since GSCB continued to deny the applications of blacks for several years. Predictably, GSCB and state officials came up with other arbitrary and capricious devices to deny or hopelessly delay the admission of black students. For example, because the Hunt plaintiffs were all adults, as indeed generally were black applicants seeking to enter white universities, Georgia officials hastily came up with an act requiring applicants to be *under twenty-one-years-old* to pursue undergraduate study.[22] Consequently, the applications of another three black women shortly after the *Hunt* case were rejected not only on the disputable basis of their academic qualifications, but, with the recent legislation as an unfortunately indisputable pretext, on the basis of *their ages*.[23] Despite the continuing official resistance to desegregation, however, the plaintiffs and their attorneys in the *Hunt* case had taken an important step toward desegregation in higher education, overcoming several obstacles that had been placed in Ward's path. Although the GSCB applicants were left in a limbo of their own, their efforts secured important legal ground that built on the foundation laid in the *Ward* case.

With this important legal groundwork and relevant expertise, the struggle to overcome racial segregation in higher education continued, but there would be yet another fierce legal battle before blacks would be admitted to a white public college in Georgia. The next

117

case would build substantially on the foundations that had been laid in the *Ward* and *Hunt* cases. The black students who later challenged segregation stood on the broad shoulders of Ward and the GSCB applicants to scale the walls of segregation in Georgia.

By January 28, 1959, two weeks after the *Hunt* decision, Ward had completed the requirements for his law degree at Northwestern University, where he received a fine legal education even though his first choice had been the law school in his home state. Following the completion of his degree, Ward worked as a claims agent for the U.S. Social Security Administration in Chicago. Meanwhile in Georgia, Donald L. Hollowell, who had represented Ward and the *Hunt* plaintiffs, had begun to attract numerous civil rights cases.[24] Such cases paid little money; because of the civil rights caseload and the need to practice other forms of law to pay the bills, Hollowell invited Ward to return to Georgia as an associate in Hollowell's firm.[25] Ward and his family moved to Atlanta during the summer of 1960, where he commenced his career as an attorney while Ruth Ward continued her education at Atlanta University, earning a B.S. degree in Library Services and working for several years thereafter as a librarian in the Atlanta public school system.

Ward passed the State Bar of Georgia in July 1960 and became Hollowell's first law partner in September of that year. In an amazingly ironic but appropriate turn of fate, Hollowell invited Ward to work with him on what was to prove an arduous, landmark case against the University of Georgia: namely, Hamilton Holmes and Charlayne Hunter's attempt to gain admission. The case was almost a carbon copy of Ward's own legal complaint eight years earlier. The celebrated *Holmes v. Danner* case emanated from the efforts of prominent Atlanta blacks, such as Hollowell and Jesse Hill, who had supported the *Ward* and *Hunt* cases.[26] The leaders decided to intensify their efforts, not only to win a lawsuit to forbid racial discrimination in principle (as in the *Hunt* case), but to win a court order actually forcing the admission of blacks to a major public university. Although the activists had also initiated efforts to desegregate Atlanta's public schools, they felt that to focus their efforts on the college level was the most effective strategy because college students would be more mature and more able to handle the resistance and controversy.

Knowing the challenges they would face, they capitalized on the hard-won experience gained in the previous lawsuits. They began by canvassing black high schools in Atlanta to identify students with superior ability and character who could withstand the intense scrutiny they would encounter if they applied to predominantly white colleges. After university officials had challenged the moral suitability of the plaintiffs in the *Hunt* case, community leaders were determined to find exceptionally wholesome candidates who would be invulnerable to character attacks. Black community leaders selected Hamilton Holmes and Charlayne Hunter as the top male and female candidates to apply to a white public institution of higher education. Both were students at the Henry McNeal Turner High School in Atlanta.

Holmes was from a prominent family in Atlanta, and had learned early the importance of asserting one's own civil and human rights. His father, Alfred "Tup" Holmes, was a businessman and a leader among local activists for racial equality. Holmes's mother, Isabella Holmes, taught school. Holmes's father, grandfather, and uncles had sued the city in 1955 to desegregate the public golf courses in Atlanta. Thanks to the able skills of black attorney R. Edwin Thomas and others, they won a 1956 Supreme Court decision on their case.[27] The golf courses actually became the first desegregated public facilities in Atlanta.

Holmes, who possessed impeccable credentials, was valedictorian of his high school graduating class, president of his senior class, an exceptional varsity football player, and recipient of the Harvard Book Award, the Danforth Book Award, and awards for excellence in mathematics and best all-around student. Holmes entered Morehouse College after high school and, like Ward, immediately became a protégé of scholar and civil rights stalwart Benjamin E. Mays.

Charlayne Hunter was born in Due West, South Carolina, but grew up in Covington, Georgia, a small town near Atlanta (now a metro area suburb). Her father, Charles S. H. Hunter, Jr., was a chaplain in the army and the family often lived on or near army bases. However, Chaplain Hunter was often away in the service, including a tour of duty in World War II, leaving Charlayne to be raised by her mother and her mother's family. Her mother worked as a secretary for the black-owned Atlanta Life Insurance Company when the family moved to Covington. Hunter attended the Negro school in Covington and at an early age observed the disparities between the facilities and resources for black schools and white schools. Hunter recalled that despite the inequities, teachers taught students to believe in themselves and sought to cultivate their self-esteem and ambition.[28]

In 1951 Hunter's mother moved the family to Atlanta where Hunter attended E. R. Carter Elementary School and Turner High School. These black schools routinely taught black history and transmitted the importance of contributing to the uplift of black people. However, not long after Hunter began classes at Turner, her mother moved the family to Alaska, where the army had stationed her husband. Hunter entered school in Alaska and discovered a striking difference from the all-black Turner High School. Hunter wrote, "I was not just the only black student in the class, I was the only black student in the school."[29] Life in Alaska exposed Hunter to interracial experiences that would later prove valuable in her challenge to Jim Crow in Georgia. After nine months in Alaska, her parents separated and Hunter returned to Atlanta with her mother and siblings. Reentering Turner High, she finished third in her class, was president of the Turner High chapter of the National Honor Society, a member of the journalism club, and editor of the Turner High newspaper. Upon graduation from high school, Hunter entered Wayne State University in Michigan.[30]

In selecting Holmes and Hunter, the activists had wisely chosen two exceptional candidates with superior academic and social skills, complemented by family and life experiences that helped prepare them for their quest. Initially, the civil rights leaders approached Hunter and Holmes about launching another attack on the Georgia State College of Business. The black leadership thought that the Atlanta environment would be safer than Athens, Georgia, for Holmes and Hunter, and that they could offer closer support if the students entered a white college in Atlanta. However, the predominantly business curriculum at GSCB was not in keeping with the aspirations of either Holmes or Hunter. Hunter was interested in journalism, and Holmes wanted to be a doctor, following the path of his grandfather. Holmes said that he had more than a few nudges from his grandfather to go into the medical field:

> I think my grandfather pushed me more than his other grandkids because my grandfather always wanted one of his sons—he had three sons—and he always wanted one of them to go into medicine. And none did. I was the oldest grandchild and a grandson. So I was probably born with a stethoscope in my hand. My granddaddy was determined that I was going to be a physician.[31]

Both students therefore told the leaders that they were not interested in attending GSCB. The civil rights leaders then approached them about applying to the Georgia Institute of Technology (Georgia Tech) in Atlanta. Holmes rejected this option as well, because neither was that curriculum suited to a premedical degree. Since the Henry Grady School of Journalism at the University of Georgia was widely considered one of the best in the country, it was a natural choice for Hunter; for Holmes, the university's liberal arts college with its depth of science courses was quite suited to his career aspirations. Hunter recalled:

> When we got together with Jesse Hill, and Hollowell, and Carl (Holman) and Whitney Young, they thought we ought to go to Georgia State. It also had journalism courses, and I really didn't know the difference . . . . We picked up applications at Georgia State, but neither one of us really liked the place; the catalog showed they really didn't offer much. We went on the steps and stood around, and Hamp said, "I want to go to Athens. That's the

place to go." And he pointed right in the direction of Athens. I said, "I'm with you."[32]

Somewhat dismayed by the decision of the two young students, the leaders were apprehensive about their ability to monitor developments in the small college town of Athens, Georgia. Holmes recalls that he and Hunter insisted that they wanted to go to the University of Georgia or nowhere, so the leaders, although reluctant, began to marshal support and assistance for them.[33] While the leaders feared that segregationist sentiment would prove formidable resistance to integration of the University of Georgia, they also realized the impact they would create if they were successful there. Jesse Hill recalled:

> We said to ourselves, "You know, Georgia State was not a residential college. It was an urban university." What we were seeking to do was to break down as many barriers as possible. We would spend the same amount of effort, finances on Georgia State, but *if we could crack the University of Georgia, then we could crack everything. Everything would come down. They would fall like dominoes.* We literally put the Georgia State case aside, and concentrated on the University of Georgia. We carefully selected students with superior academic standards and great leadership potential. And that directed us to Charlayne Hunter and Hamilton Holmes. In other situations where we've tried to desegregate certain venues, we had not been quite as careful and selective. But, in this case, it was airtight.[34] [emphasis added]

Their leading segregationist opponents included, ironically but perhaps predictably, many of the same senior-level state and university officials who had opposed Ward's admission nine years earlier. Walter Danner, the UGA admissions director, was a central figure among the opposition. Holmes and Hunter filed their applications on July 22, 1959. According to Danner, they were not admitted because of overcrowded dormitories. Holmes and Hunter requested that their applications be kept on file for the 1960 winter and spring quarters, but Danner again rejected their applications, purportedly due to space. Hunter therefore went on to complete her freshman year at Wayne State. However, limited space restrictions as a basis for keeping blacks out of the university became a problem for university officials the next year. By then, Holmes also had completed his freshman year, at Morehouse, and UGA did not require male students to live on campus after their first year.

During the summer of 1960, Holmes and Hunter filed applications to UGA for admission in the 1960 fall quarter. After Danner rejected their applications yet again, they appealed to University System Chancellor Harmon Caldwell, and when he refused to admit them, they appealed to the Board of Regents. Although Holmes and Hunter possessed exceptional credentials and had genuine professional motives to attend the university, they did not believe that the Board of Regents would admit them without a protracted battle. Georgia officials had blocked Ward for seven years, had kept blacks out of GSCB despite a federal court order banning discrimination, and had successfully sustained segregation in public schools and colleges. Nevertheless, Holmes and Hunter were determined to see their efforts through to the end.

Because of that determination, Holmes and Hunter, whose applications had been rejected repeatedly for more than a year, filed for a preliminary injunction in the U.S. District Court for the Middle District of Georgia to prohibit the university from denying them admission solely due to their race. The legal action was filed against Walter N. Danner, registrar and director of admissions. Again, the central issue in the case was simply whether the state university administered admissions in a racially discriminatory manner.[35]

Chief counsel Donald Hollowell once again sought the help of the LDF, and Thurgood Marshall again assigned Constance Baker Motley to assist Hollowell.[36] Motley had represented the LDF in the *Ward* and *Hunt* trials and had further honed her skills as a civil rights lawyer, winning several civil rights cases throughout the Southeast. Vernon Jordan, a Georgia native who had just graduated from Howard University Law School and later became a celebrated civil rights leader, also assisted Hollowell. During an interview with the author, Jordan related:

> I graduated from law school in June of 1960 on a Friday and the following Monday I went to work for Don Hollowell for $35 a week. I carried Hollowell's briefcase, I drove his car, I did his research, I studied under him, I was his law clerk, I was his intern, I was his mentee, and we had lots of little cases—too numerous to mention—having to do with violations of civil rights and asserting equal opportunity rights for plaintiffs. The most significant case by far was the University of Georgia case, which I was involved in almost as soon as I returned to Georgia [from law school].[37]

Hollowell, Motley, Ward, and Jordan would go to battle against defiant opponents. The fateful irony of Horace Ward's legal help also strengthened their purpose: they were especially determined that this case would not suffer the same fate as his unsuccessful lawsuit in 1957. Hollowell noted that Ward brought with him a special passion to see the *Holmes* case achieve what his own legal case had not been able to accomplish.[38] During an interview, Hollowell said it made him feel very good to have Ward work with him on the case against UGA because justice had not been served by the outcome of the *Ward* case.[39] Hollowell said, moreover, that "one of the most interesting things to grow out of the *Ward* case is the fact that he (Ward) had completed Northwestern University School of Law and he was able to come and be a part of the *Holmes v. Danner* case."[40]

In another scenario reminiscent of the *Ward* case, the defendant was represented by Attorney General Eugene Cook and Deputy Assistant Attorney General B. D. Murphy, both of whom had distinguished themselves as hardened opponents to desegregation. Murphy conducted most of the arguments for the defendant. The Honorable William A. Bootle presided over the hearing for the preliminary injunction.[41] Bootle refused to issue an injunction because the Board of Regents had not taken final action on the admissions applications filed by Holmes and Hunter. On the other hand, showing concern about the delays in the admission process for the two plaintiffs, Bootle ordered the regents to rule within thirty days on whether the applicants could proceed with personal interviews by university admissions officers—the admissions requirement instituted *after* Horace Ward tried to enter the university, although interviews were not always required of white applicants.[42] In response to Bootle's order, Danner and university officials scheduled interviews on November 5 for Hunter and November 18 for Holmes.

Holmes's interview amounted to little more than a crude attempt at character assassination. Danner and the admissions counselors who conducted the interview for Holmes contended that he was evasive and lied during his interview and therefore was refused recommendation for admission. According to Holmes, the university officials clearly tried to characterize him in terms of common stereotypes and biases toward blacks, in particular the belief that blacks were unintelligent, compulsive liars, and promiscuous.[43] Holmes recalled that the interviewers did not focus on his academic qualifications, but sought instead to elicit anything negative in his personal background. Based on the interview, Danner rejected Holmes in a letter stating that "on the basis of your personal interview, we are of the opinion that you do not qualify as a suitable applicant to the University of Georgia."[44]

The interview with Hunter, who had successfully completed her first year at Wayne State University, was much more positive. Nevertheless, in a convoluted, evasive letter to her, Danner declared that she could not be considered for the winter and spring quarters of 1961 because the university was accepting students only from "certain categories" such as junior college transfers and probationary students. Implying further that no dormitory space was available, Danner said that even students in those categories might not be accepted "due to limited facilities."[45]

While Holmes and Hunter's attorneys continued to press Bootle for a judicial ruling, insisting that the university was denying admission to qualified applicants on the basis of color, Attorney General Cook argued that the regents had not taken final action on the matter and denied that the university had excluded the plaintiffs because of their race. In a November 18, 1960, hearing Bootle scheduled a courtroom trial on the issues. Held in Athens, Georgia, December 13-17, 1960, the trial was an arduous process characterized by equal fervor on the part of the defendants and the plaintiffs respectively to sustain or overthrow the legal apartheid.[46]

Since the courts had already ruled segregation unconstitutional, the only position left for the defendants was to deny that they practiced any form of segregation and to shield themselves with whatever arguments they could muster. Holmes and Hunter's attorneys here had the advantage of insight into strategies used by the defendants in the *Ward* and *Hunt* cases, and the added benefit of having Ward himself as a member of the legal team. They successfully introduced testimony from the *Ward* case to show that officials used *the same reasons for rejecting Holmes that they had used more than ten years earlier to reject Ward.* After reviewing the *Ward* trial transcript during an interview with the author, Holmes observed:

> The reasons they gave for Horace Ward being rejected—"he gave inconsistent answers, he was evasive, he was not truthful"— were exactly the same things they said ten years later about me. It is very obvious that was their technique for trying to keep blacks out of the university. I don't know if whites at that time really felt all Negroes were stupid, lazy, and slovenly, and lied all the time or if they just tried to perpetuate that on society. But it's amazing the reasons were almost exactly the same, almost ten years apart.[47]

To illustrate these similarities, Hollowell asked Aderhold, the president of the university, to read from the transcript of the *Ward* trial:

> Aderhold (after reading from *Ward* transcript): Well, as I remember, Horace Ward was evasive.
>
> Hollowell: Evasive?
>
> Aderhold: Yes, inconsistent.
>
> Hollowell: Inconsistent?

Aderhold: And didn't show that he had the qualifications that we thought necessary for an applicant for admission to the law school.[48]

One momentous highlight of poetic justice during the trial occurred when Hollowell had Aderhold reveal to the court that Ward, the applicant who supposedly lacked the qualifications for admission to the UGA law school, was now a practicing attorney who had completed his degree at Northwestern University School of Law.[49] Hollowell then pursued questions designed to show that the man Aderhold had deemed unsuitable for Georgia's law school had not only completed an extremely prestigious law school, but was in the courtroom as counsel for the plaintiffs. It was most ironic (and ill-considered) that the special committee that recommended Holmes's rejection based their recommendations essentially on the same claims used to keep Ward out ten years earlier, providing a significant crack in the case. From this opening began a process whereby the plaintiffs' lawyers would show that most of the defendants' arguments, dating from the *Ward* case, were a pure sham to cover their real motive of maintaining segregation.

Paralleling their strategy in the *Ward* case, the defendants flatly denied that officials had done anything to obstruct the admission of blacks, and claimed they would indeed admit "qualified Negroes." Illustrating their meticulous research in anticipation of this kind of absurd denial, the plaintiffs' attorneys introduced a handwritten note they had discovered among official university records, written by the chancellor of the university system, Harmon Caldwell. The note showed the questionable motives behind certain new regulations regarding limited housing facilities, regulations that prevented Hunter's admission. Caldwell wrote the note to President Aderhold on behalf of a regent to help a friend's daughter (a white applicant) in the admissions process. The handwritten note revealed that officials had barred a "Negro girl" due to the purported fact that all the dormitories for women were filled.[50]

Hollowell and Motley, following their strategy in the *Ward* trial, also attempted to show that the out-of-state aid program was still a vital part of the segregationist system. L. R. Siebert, who had served as executive secretary of the regents since before the *Ward* trial, said that the out-of-state aid program "offers to colored people" funds to take educational work outside the state.[51] Despite public knowledge of the purpose of the program and the fact that Caldwell testified in the *Ward* trial that the program was set up *for blacks*, Siebert insisted that he had not offered the out-of-state aid to white students simply because white students had never applied for the assistance.

During the *Ward* trial, Hollowell and Motley often had compared the treatment of Ward to that of white applicants. In this case, with Ward's help they thoroughly examined student admissions records to show the stark difference between the treatment of Holmes and Hunter and the treatment of white students. With the expert assistance of Gerald H. Taylor, an assistant registrar at Atlanta University, Motley, Jordan, and Ward examined admissions records of students who had applied after July 22, 1959—the date that the admissions office recorded Holmes and Hunter's applications. Jordan recalled:

> Constance Motley, now a federal district court judge in New York, Gerald Taylor, Horace Ward, and myself would go to Athens every day. We would go to look through all of these records, and I was lucky enough to be the one to find the record of the woman who lived in Marietta, Georgia, Cobb County, who was a transfer student who had been admitted to the university subsequent to Charlayne's application, and Charlayne was being denied on the basis that a junior could not transfer—"some Dannerism" I would call it. This evidence convinced us that we had a case.[52]

The evidence Jordan identified was especially pertinent because the transfer applicant was interested in journalism, the discipline Hunter also desired to study. Admissions officials testified that the student admitted was Bebe Brumby, daughter of Otis A. Brumby, a prominent former member of the General Assembly, one of the university's longtime supporters, and also a relative of U.S. Senator

1. Horace Ward at age 14 (1942).

2. Ward at age 18, La Grange, Georgia (1946).

3. Ward's mother, Minnie Harrison, and stepfather, Richard Harrison.

4. Ward at his graduation from Morehouse College, age 21 (1949).

5. *Horace T. Ward in the U.S. Army, (1953).*

6. *Ruth LeFlore (Ward) at the time of her marriage to Horace Ward in 1956.*

7. *Ward as Instructor of Social Studies, Alabama State College, Mobile (1955).*

8. *William Madison Boyd addressing a radio audience over the nation's first black-owned radio sation, WERD, Atlanta, Georgia (early 1950s).*

9. *Conference between civil rights leaders William Madison Boyd and Roy Wilkins (March 1, 1955).*

10. Ward with A. T. Walden (l) and Donald Hollowell (r) on the steps of Georgia Capitol (1964).

11. *Ward, Constance Baker Motley, and Donald Hollowell (1961).*

12. *Donald L. Hollowell with Charlayne Hunter, Hamilton Holmes and Hunter's mother, Althea Hunter (1961).*

13. Reunion of partners in Hollowell's law firm, William H. Alexander, Horace T. Ward,
Donald L. Hollowell, and Howard Moore, Jr. (early 1990s).

14. *Ward with Dr. Benjamin Mays on the occasion of Ward's
appointment to the Superior Court bench (1977).*

15. *Ward (as Superior Court judge) with President Jimmy Carter.
(Portrait presentation of President Jimmy Carter to the Georgia Senate, 1979.)*

Richard Russell. Bebe Brumby had been admitted for winter quarter 1961, one of the quarters in which Hunter sought to transfer. Motley brought into evidence Brumby's academic transcript to make clear that it was *not* Brumby's exceptional academic record that justified her admission. The following is an exchange between Motley and Paul Kea, a UGA admissions counselor:

> Motley: Would you look at that transcript and tell me what kind of student she was, since you evaluate transcripts of transfer students? Was she an "A" student, a brilliant student?
>
> Kea: Well, I would say that of course she is not an "A" student because there is not an "A" on the transcript.
>
> Motley: Do you see any "Bs" on there?
>
> Kea: Yes. There are two "Bs," the rest are "Cs."[53]

Next, the plaintiffs' attorneys introduced mounting evidence of discriminatory treatment practiced by university officials, especially regarding the interview requirement—a rigorous process for Holmes, but for many white applicants, a mere rubber stamp. In the case of one student, Philip Felix Baglivo, Danner testified that Baglivo's *brother-in-law* interviewed him. Court testimony also revealed that Danner even accepted some white applicants before an interview; admissions officials merely conducted the interview on the day of registration. In other cases, testimony revealed that officials conducted the interview by telephone.

To further illustrate the disparity in the treatment of Holmes and Hunter as opposed to white applicants, Motley repeatedly asked Danner to read letters that underscored the mountain of evidence her legal team had garnered. Not only did Danner's testimony reveal the discrepancy in practice, but Motley's dissection made obvious its calculated intentionality. In one instance, she asked Danner to read the following letter showing that Danner and others advised white applicants of ways to bypass admissions barriers, whereas they extended no such guidance or opportunity to Holmes or Hunter:

Danner (reading): "Dear Miss Adams: Based on your record at Tift College, it is very doubtful that you can be admitted for the fall 1960 quarter. However, if you would like to submit a transcript covering spring quarter Tift grades in June, and if all credits are "C" or better, we'll be happy to consider you. The problem is that by that time we will in all probability have no space left for girls. I would like to suggest that you attend summer school here, if you make "C" or better in all courses. You may continue on into the fall. Please advise me."[54]

Motley then had Danner read from an admissions office letter to a *black* applicant that reflected a sharply different response:

Danner (reading): "Dear Miss McCree: Your application for admission to the University of Georgia for the fall quarter has been received. Our dormitory facilities for women students have been filled for several weeks and we have, therefore, been denying admission to all women students. Your $25 application deposit is returned herewith. Yours truly, M. O. Phelps."[55]

Another of Hollowell and Motley's tactics was to juxtapose the interview questions asked of Holmes with those asked of white students. Hollowell then interrogated admissions counselor Morris O. Phelps concerning the Holmes interview. Phelps, who claimed that he asked Holmes the same questions as other interviewees, finally revealed that he "asked the boy . . . if he had ever been arrested, and he said no, he had never been arrested."[56] Phelps further testified that he knew that Holmes's statement was untruthful because Danner had told him that Holmes had been arrested for speeding. Although Holmes testified that he did not consider the speeding ticket an arrest, officials insisted that he had lied about the matter. The mere fact that officials undertook this kind of investigation into Holmes's traffic record showed their determination to seek any excuse to mar his record and deny his application. However, Hollowell's intensive redirect questioning led to another crack in the defendants' case. Phelps contradicted his earlier testimony and revealed that the questions asked of Holmes were *not* the customary questions asked of white applicants.[57]

Paul Kea further illuminated the peculiarity of the questions asked of Holmes when he stated he "was the one who asked him if he had ever attended any of the what are so-called tea houses or beatnik houses."[58] Motley also examined Kea concerning the interview with Bebe Brumby to show that her interview was quite different from that of Holmes. In contrast to the Holmes interview, Kea testified that he did not ask Brumby about her family, whether she had an arrest record, or whether she had attended interracial parties.[59]

In addition to the testimony of the university officials, Holmes himself gave riveting testimony concerning his interview. Hollowell and Motley deliberately selected Ward himself to examine Holmes. This masterful strategy lent additional credence to their contention that Holmes's interview, like Ward's, was simply a ploy to keep blacks out of the university, since Ward obviously had demonstrated his capability to become a law student, and now, a lawyer. In retrospect, Holmes shared his view of this episode with the author.

> I think that was super strategy by them (Motley and Hollowell). Here you have the two black males that have applied, and one is now doing the direct examination on the other. I think Hollowell and Motley were sharp. . . . You couldn't have gotten two greater lawyers.[60]

The following substantial excerpt from Ward's examination of Holmes illuminates the dramatic and ironically appropriate nature of this element of the trial as well as evidence of Ward's emerging legal talent.

> Ward: Mr. Holmes, have you been interviewed by admissions officials down at the University of Georgia?
>
> Holmes: Yes, I have.
>
> Ward: During the course of that interview were you asked whether you had any traffic violations against your record?

Holmes: No.

Ward: Did they ask you whether you had ever been arrested?

Holmes: Yes, they did.

Ward: What was your answer to that question?

Holmes: I told them that I had not.

Ward: Have you ever, in fact, been arrested?

Holmes: No, I have never been arrested.

Ward: During the course of that interview did they ask you whether or not you had attended interracial parties?

Holmes: Yes.

Ward: What was your response to that question?

Holmes: I told them that I had never attended any interracial social functions, but that I had attended several interracial cultural affairs such as debates and discussions with students from Agnes Scott, Georgia Tech, et cetera.

Ward: What else did they ask you during that interview?

Holmes: I was asked to give my opinion concerning the integration crisis in New Orleans and in Atlanta and also to give some insight on the workings of the student movement in Atlanta.

Ward: How did you reply to those questions?

Holmes: I answered concerning the school integration crisis in New Orleans and in Atlanta by saying that since they were just beginning that I was not too familiar with those, and that I had— I had not actually participated in the student movement so I wasn't too familiar with it either.

Ward: Were you asked any additional questions concerning the integration situation?

Holmes: Yes. I was also asked if I participated in any of the activities of the student movement association in Atlanta, and I was asked to tell what some of these activities were.

Ward: Did they ask you anything concerning attending tea houses and red light districts in Athens?

Holmes: Yes. Kea, I believe, asked me did I know of the tea houses in Atlanta and if I had ever attended these tea houses. And he also asked me if I knew of the, I think it's the red light district in Athens, or had I heard of it.

Ward: How did you respond to those questions?

Holmes: I answered both of these questions by saying no, and in both instances that I had—that I had not heard of either of these things.

Ward: Did they ask you whether or not you had attended houses of prostitution?

Holmes: Yes, I was asked this question by, I think it was Kea also.[61]

During an interview with the author, Vernon Jordan, too, re-called the spurious tactics used by university officials to keep both Ward and Holmes out of the university:

> These were insidious character attacks on two young black appli-cants who only wanted one thing and that was equal educational opportunity. But Danner and his kind were determined to main-tain the status quo and there was no limit to what they would do—lie, cheat—to keep the university pure.[62]

Despite testimony by Kea, Phelps, and Holmes revealing that the Holmes interview was an extreme departure from customary practice, Danner fervently maintained that there was no difference in the treatment Holmes received. Moreover, although letters from his office proved disparate treatment of white and black applicants, Danner testified that he had handled the plaintiffs' applications just as he had handled others.[63]

Murphy sought to counter the assertion that admissions offi-cials treated blacks unfairly during the interview process by show-ing that the officials reached a favorable decision in the case of Charlayne Hunter's interview. In response to Murphy's line of questioning, Phelps said that Hunter's attitude and demeanor were cooperative, her answers straightforward, and her answers not eva-sive.[64] However, Hunter's testimony revealed that admissions officials had questioned her enrollment at Wayne State and failure to apply earlier for a transfer to the University of Georgia. Hunter testified that officials had asked whether she would prefer to stay at Wayne State if the regents granted her an out-of-state aid scholarship. Hollowell also pointed out that a member of the Board of Regents had traveled to Detroit to investigate Hunter's background. Hollowell questioned whether all applicants were investigated so thoroughly and whether their private lives were scrutinized so intensely.[65] The question obviously recalled the defense's shameful *ad hominem* tactics in the *Hunt* case.

The defendants summarized their position by repeating that they rated Hunter's interview favorably, but that Holmes was not a fit and suitable person for admission to UGA. However, as a practical matter, Hunter's favorable rating on the interview was worthless, because she was rejected due to purported limited dormitory space. On the other hand, while the limited housing facilities no longer restrained Holmes, he was now rejected based on his unsatisfactory interview. The dissimilar but equally "no win" responses to the Holmes and Hunter applications plainly illustrated the duplicity of university officials—they could avoid having Holmes reapply even after successfully completing a first year at Morehouse, and they could always tell Hunter that there was no dormitory space.

Murphy also relied on a tactic that led to his success in the *Ward* case. Ward lost the case, in part, because Judge Hooper ruled that he had not exhausted the appeals process before coming to court. In *Holmes*, Murphy argued that Holmes and Hunter had filed their lawsuit before Danner completed his evaluation of them, since Holmes and Hunter's interviews occurred after they filed the legal case. The Regents Committee on Education, in a report adopted October 21, 1960, detailed the regents' claims that Holmes and Hunter failed to complete the appeals process before filing the lawsuit. The regents contended that because the applicants had not followed the appeals procedures, the university could not consider their applications.[66]

Murphy had grilled Horace Ward in the original *Ward* case, asserting that he was merely a "foot soldier for the integration efforts."[67] Posing a series of questions to Holmes and Hunter that replicated his queries in *Ward*, Murphy persistently questioned Holmes on who had advised him, trying to show that Holmes was not a serious applicant. The courtroom tension heightened in proportion to the tedium and shallowness of the line of questioning. A seemingly exasperated Hollowell objected:

> Hollowell: May it please the Court, I submit that this is cross-examination and that the counselor has broad discretion and he can sift as fine as a flour sifter, but I submit that there should be some relevancy to the matter at hand, and I just can't see any relevancy to this type of questioning, as to what specific individuals have discussed with him the matter of going to the University of Georgia, and I object to it on the basis that it is irrelevant.[68]

Although Bootle allowed Murphy to continue his line of questioning, Bootle appeared to share Hollowell's sentiment concerning its irrelevancy. And in the following exchange, Murphy even impugned the relevance of his own questions to the central issue of the trial:

> Hollowell: I submit, Your Honor, that he has said—and he has said four times now, because the last time I objected it was the third time—that he did not retain the counsel, that his father retained the counsel, and that he didn't know when, exactly, his father retained the counsel. Certainly there is no relevancy.
>
> The Court: Well, I don't want to curtail counsel in anything that you tell me in your place that you bona fide think is relevant to this inquiry. Do you bona fide think it is relevant?
>
> *Murphy: I think it is relevant. I don't think it is relevant to whether or not he ought to be admitted to the University of Georgia, but—*
>
> *The Court: Well, that's the only thing we are trying, isn't it?*
>
> *(Laughter)* [emphasis added]

The Marshal: Order in court. If you are going to remain in the courtroom, you will have to be quiet. Otherwise, we'll have to clear the room.[69]

In retrospect, Holmes had this to say about Murphy:

I remember Buck Murphy very well, He was a big guy. He was a very good lawyer. A good lawyer on the wrong side. Buck was the state's top troubleshooter, and any time they had any case that involved segregation or desegregation, Buck was the man. So I guess he was considered to be an expert in this area. I remember that he cross-examined me. I think he tried to break me, especially me because I was the main one they were going after, rather than going after Charlayne so much. They were going after me like this black male thing. That was very obvious. And he was not able to break me. He was not a nice man to me. He was really after me.[70]

In a move calculated to show how ludicrous it was that a tax-supported university refused to accept any of its native black citizens, Hollowell called a secretary from the university housing office to the witness stand.

Hollowell: Miss Costa, might you indicate some of the different races or nationalities that are presently housed at the University in the dormitories?

Costa: . . .We have Japanese students, we have Chinese, we have students from India, we have students from Holland, students from France . . .

Hollowell: Do you have any students of Negroid extraction there to your knowledge?

Costa: Not to my knowledge, no.[71]

In yet another well-calculated move, Hollowell relied again on insights gained from the *Ward* case. Hollowell introduced into the record evidence from the *Ward* trial transcript concerning Ward's rejection and appeals processes that directly paralleled the processes for Holmes and Hunter. With the *Ward* record in hand, and under intense scrutiny from Hollowell and Motley, the defendants' legal arguments continued to crumble. Murphy vehemently opposed Hollowell's use of the *Ward* transcript in his examination of Aderhold. At one point, as Hollowell examined President Aderhold concerning Ward's rejection, Murphy objected: "I didn't come over here prepared to retry the *Ward* case."[72]

In response to Hollowell's questions, Aderhold responded that as president of the university since 1950, he did not know of any policy that excluded students on account of their race and as far as he knew, *they had handled applications from Negroes on "exactly" the same basis as applications from whites.*[73] Hollowell sought to show that Aderhold's statement was patently false and that the university had tried to handle Ward's application for admission as an out-of-state aid application.

> Hollowell: I wonder if we might do this, in order to save time, because I think the Doctor [Aderhold] knows, Murphy knows, and there are a half dozen other persons who know. Would you stipulate that this was a course of action that was taken when Horace Ward applied for admission to the University of Georgia Law School?[74]

Despite a strong objection from Murphy, who argued that the *Ward* case had occurred more than ten years ago and was therefore irrelevant, Bootle overruled the objection and Aderhold subsequently admitted that the manner in which they had handled Ward's application was different from the routine processing of admissions applications. Under Hollowell's questioning, Aderhold conceded that sending an application to the regents for out-of-state aid, instead of considering the application for admission, was not the usual way that applications were processed.

Aderhold's testimony also revealed that he had made several policy decisions that effectively provided a basis for the university to reject Holmes and Hunter's applications. Although his new policies were instituted shortly after plaintiffs had sought admission, Aderhold nevertheless continued to claim that he and other officials had fulfilled the duties of their offices in good faith without regard to the applicants' race. The defendants would maintain this position to the end, despite the internal contradictions and even absurdity of many of their assertions and denials. They had been successful in the earlier, related cases, but in this trial their arguments weakened under attacks from the ablest civil rights attorneys and the scrutiny of a judge who, finally, was fair-minded and evenhanded in the administration of justice, in contrast to his predecessors. Just how Judge Bootle's fair-minded jurisprudence would affect the outcome of the case would be seen when he delivered his ruling. In the meantime, with both the defendants and plaintiffs having exhausted their arguments, the court recessed for Judge Bootle to deliberate his decision.

CHAPTER 5 NOTES

[1]Horace Ward, interview with author, Atlanta, GA, June 29, 1994.

[2]Ibid.

[3]Horace Ward, interview with author, Atlanta, GA, May 28, 1999.

[4]See Charles Martin, "Racial Change and 'Big Time' College Football in Georgia: The Age of Segregation, 1892-1957," *Georgia Historical Quarterly* 80 (1996): 554-556; Griffin's quote appears on 554.

[5]The state flag change was enacted by Senate Bill 98, Georgia Laws, 1956 Session; for Denmark Groover's statement, see Mike Edwards, "State Flag Change 'Disappoints' UDC," *Atlanta Journal*, February 10, 1956, 4.

[6]Marvin Griffin, "Interposition Is an Appeal to Reason," *Interposition Address of Governor Marvin Griffin* (Atlanta: Georgia Commission on Education, 1956), 2, 3.

[7]*The Southern Manifesto*, 102nd Congressional Record 4515-16, 1956; Numan V. Bartley, *The Rise of Massive Resistance: Race and Politics in the South during the 1950s* (Baton Rouge: Louisiana State University Press, 1969), 116-117.

[8]John Calhoun, letter to Thurgood Marshall, Papers of the NAACP, Part 3: The Campaign for Educational Equality: Legal Department and Central Office Records, 1913-1950. Series D: 1956-1965, January 15, 1956. NAACP Archives, Library of Congress, Washington, D.C.

[9]Jesse Hill, interview with author, Atlanta, GA, December 17, 1996; Anne S. Emanuel,

"Turning the Tide in the Civil Rights Revolution: Elbert Tuttle and the Desegregation of the University of Georgia," *Michigan Journal of Race and Law* 5 (fall 1999): 5; "Negroes Seek to Enter Ga. College, Unused Printed Technicalities Stymie Six School Applicants," *Atlanta Daily World*, March 24, 1956, 1; "Negroes Fail in Attempt at Enrolling in Atlanta College: Fight Promised," *Macon Telegraph*, March 24, 1956. Five of the applicants did not pursue the case after the GSCB registrar returned their "incomplete" applications; one applicant moved out of state before the trial, and one plaintiff—Russell Roberts—withdrew from the case before the trial. See *Hunt v. Arnold*, Civil Action No. 5781, trial transcript (December 1958).

[10]University System of Georgia, Board of Regents Minutes, June 11, 1952, 2, Archives, Office of the Board of Regents, Atlanta, GA.

[11]Attorney E. E. Moore, letter to Dr. George M. Sparks, June 15, 1956; Sparks, letter to Moore, June 22, 1956; and Sparks, letter to Attorney General Eugene Cook, June 18, 1956; Georgia State University Special Collections, George M. Sparks Collection, Box 28, folder 357; *Hunt v. Arnold*, 172 F. Supp. 847 N.D. Ga. (1959).

[12]*Hunt v. Arnold*, Civil Action No. 5781, trial transcript, (December 1958), 8.

[13]Thomas Dyer, *The University of Georgia: A Bicentennial History, 1785-1985* (Athens: University of Georgia Press, 1985), 316, which discusses this practice.

[14]"Business College Entrance Suit Opens Monday Morning," *Atlanta Daily World*, December 7, 1958, 1; John Britton, "Negroes Have Qualifications to Enter College, One Regent Admits," *Atlanta Daily World,* December 9, 1958, 1; "Negroes Ask School Entry," *Georgia State Signal*, October 5, 1956, 1.

[15]*Hunt v. Arnold,* Civil Action No. 5781, motion of defendants to dismiss, Federal Records Center, East Point, GA, February 1957, 6.

[16]"School Suit Held Lacking in Faith," *Atlanta Journal*, October 13, 1958, 12.

[17]*Hunt v. Arnold*, 172 F. Supp. 847, N.D. Ga. (1959).

[18]Constance Baker Motley, "Remarks on Holmes-Hunter Lecture," *Harvard Blackletter Journal* 5 (1988): 3; Motley, interview with author, New York, NY, March 30, 1995.

[19]See *Gaines v. Canada*, 305 U.S. 337, 59 S. Ct. 232, 238, (1938).

[20]Ibid; see also John Hope Franklin and Alfred Moss, Jr., *From Slavery to Freedom: A History of Negro Americans* (New York: McGraw-Hill, 1988), 365.

[21]*Hunt v. Arnold*, 172 F. Supp. 847, N.D. Ga. (1959).

[22]Senate Bill 3, Georgia Laws 1959 Session, I General Acts and Res., 1959, 20-21, proposed in February 1959 and enacted before the end of the legislative session in late March.

[23]"NAACP Supports Negroes' GSC Bid," *Atlanta Journal*, May 14, 1959, 1. The three applicants, Ernestine Brown, Mary Rogers, and Alice Wyche, were all over the age of 21.

[24]See Louise Hollowell and Martin C. Lehfeldt, *The Sacred Call: A Tribute to Donald Hollowell—Civil Rights Champion* (Winter Park, FL: Four-G Publishers, 1997).

[25]Donald Hollowell, interview with author, Atlanta, GA, August, 1996.

[26]Several key leaders supporting the desegregation efforts that led to a lawsuit against the University of Georgia were involved through their association with the NAACP and the Atlanta Committee for Cooperative Action (ACCA), a progressive civic organization that advocated racial equality and economic justice.

John Wesley Dobbs was a charismatic leader who mobilized mass support for civil and human rights causes, raising over $50,000 for the LDF for the fight against segregation in the 1950s. A powerful advocate for voting rights for blacks, he also wielded considerable influence as Grand Master of the Prince Hall Grand Masonic Lodge, (Jurisdiction of Georgia) from 1932-1961. Thurgood Marshall was a Mason, and Dobbs persuasively engineered loyal and generous support for Marshall's legal program to end segregation. For an extensive review of the contributions of John Wesley Dobbs, see Juliet Dobbs Blackburn-Beamon, "The Life and Work of John Wesley Dobbs: African American Humanist, Orator and Activist," (dissertation, Clark Atlanta University, 1996).

In the 1950s and '60s Whitney M. Young, Jr., dean of the Atlanta University School of Social Work and subsequently director of the National Urban league, was a major national spokesman for civil rights as well as a community leader. Active with the NAACP and the ACCA, besides serving as Urban League director, Young advised student protesters in Atlanta to challenge segregation and helped orchestrate support for the Holmes-Hunter cause. For an analysis of Young's contributions, see Dennis Dickerson, *Militant Mediator: Whitney M. Young, Jr.* (Lexington: University Press of Kentucky, 1998).

Community activists also included M. Carl Holman, Professor of English at Clark College and editor of the *Atlanta Inquirer*. Holman was a prominent leader in the ACCA and an adviser to student activists. Several black professionals and officials from the enclave of black colleges in Atlanta also joined in their support of the ACCA and NAACP.

[27]Constance Baker Motley, *Equal Justice under Law: An Autobiography of Constance Baker Motley* (New York: Farrar, Straus & Giroux, 1998), 69; the case was *Holmes v. City of Atlanta*, 223 F. 2d 93 (5th Cir. 1955), 350 U.S. 879 (1956).

[28]Charlayne Hunter-Gault, *In My Place* (New York: First Vintage Books Edition, 1993), 16, 17, 19, 52-54.

[29]Ibid., 93.

[30]Ibid., 105-106; Charlayne Hunter to Herbert Wright, Papers of the NAACP, Part 3: The Campaign for Educational Equality: Legal Department and Central Office Records, 1913-1950. Series D: 1956-1965, Schools-University of Georgia, January 5, 1961. NAACP Archives, Library of Congress, Washington, D.C.

[31]Hamilton E. Holmes, interview with author, Atlanta, GA, February 24, 1995.

[32]Calvin Trillin, *An Education in Georgia: Charlayne Hunter, Hamilton Holmes, and the Integration of the University of Georgia* (Athens: University of Georgia Press, 1991), 22.

[33]Holmes, interview, op. cit.

[34]Hill, interview, op. cit.

[35]Motley, "Remarks," op. cit., 5.

[36]Motley, *Equal Justice*, op. cit., 145.

[37]Vernon Jordan, interview with author, Washington, D.C., February 28, 1997.

[38]Hollowell and Lehfeldt, op. cit., 5.

[39]Donald L. Hollowell, interview with author, Atlanta, GA, July 27, 1993.

[40]Ibid.

[41]William Augustus Bootle was born in Colleton County, South Carolina, in 1902. He received the A.B., L.L.B., and L.L.D. (honorary) degrees from Mercer University in 1924, 1925, and 1982, respectively. Appointed to the federal bench in 1954 by President Dwight Eisenhower, Bootle served as judge for the middle district of Georgia for twenty-one years, becoming a senior judge for the district in 1971. Bootle often raised the ire of white segregationists and is credited with several decisions overturning segregationist practices in the South, including school desegregation rulings and rulings banning discrimination against blacks in voter registration and public transportation. For more information on Bootle, see Charles R. Adams, III, "An Oral Interview with Judge W. A. Bootle," *Journal of Southern Legal History* 7 (1999): 115-201.

[42]Dyer, op. cit., 326-327.

[43]Holmes, interview, op. cit.

[44]Walter N. Danner, letter to Hamilton Holmes, Hargrett Rare Book and Manuscript Library/University of Georgia Libraries, Walter N. Danner Subject File, November 29, 1960.

[45]Walter N. Danner, letter to Charlayne Hunter, Hargrett Rare Book and Manuscript Library/University of Georgia Libraries, Walter N. Danner Subject File, November 29, 1960.

[46] The trial opinion is reported as *Holmes v. Danner*, 191 F. Supp. 394 (M.D. Ga. 1961).

[47]Holmes, interview, op. cit.

[48]The complete trial transcript is archived as *Hamilton E. Holmes, et al. v. Walter N. Danner, et al.*, Civil Action No. 450, Federal Records Center, East Point, GA, December (1960); the quote of this testimony is from vol. II, 142. The author obtained the *Holmes* trial record (three volumes) from the National Archives. Information in endnotes 50-51, 53-59, 61, 63-64, 68-69, and 71-74 is from the trial record, subsequently short-titled as *Holmes v. Danner*.

[49]Ibid., 143.

[50]Trillin, op. cit., 41; *Holmes v. Danner*, vol. I , 27.

[51]*Holmes v. Danner*, vol. I , 37.

[52]Jordan, interview, op. cit.

[53]*Holmes v. Danner*, vol. I, 123.

[54]*Holmes v. Danner*, vol. III, 42-43.

[55]Ibid., 43-44.

[56]*Holmes v. Danner*, vol. I, 69-71.

[57]Ibid., 92-94, 108.

[58]Ibid., 151-155.

[59]Ibid., 135-136.

[60]Holmes, interview, op. cit.

[61]*Holmes v. Danner*, vol. II, 1-3.

[62]Jordan, interview, op. cit.

[63]*Holmes v. Danner*, vol. II, 255.

[64]*Holmes v. Danner*, vol. I, 83-84.

[65]"Lawyers Charge Bias," *Atlanta Inquirer*, December 17, 1960, 1, 8; *Holmes v. Danner*, vol. I, 108-109.

[66]*Holmes v. Danner*, 191 F. Supp. 394, 398 (M.D. Ga. 1961).

[67]Ward, interview, June 29, 1994, op. cit.

[68]*Holmes v. Danner*, vol. II, 51-54.

[69]Ibid., 59-60.

[70]Holmes, interview, op. cit.

[71]*Holmes v. Danner*, vol. II, 132-133.

[72]Ibid., 142.

[73]Ibid., 202-207.

[74]Ibid., 206.

CHAPTER 6

Ward's Vindication:
The Outcome of the Trial and Its Aftermath

On January 6, 1961, Judge Bootle delivered his eagerly awaited ruling. The ruling was to prove a triumph for the plaintiffs and the cause of desegregation. Judge William A. Bootle found that university and regents officials were not free to admit Negroes to UGA by virtue of the Appropriations Act that required withholding of funds in the event that a Negro entered an all-white college.[1] He also found that the appellate procedures, set up *after* Ward's application, did not require action by officials within any prescribed time limit. He noted that under the existing appellate regulations, if Hunter and Holmes were to pursue appeals, they would probably use up the normal four-year college attendance period before a final decision on their admission. Bootle also substantiated the claim made by Ward ten years before that regulations had been created to thwart his entrance. Bootle stated in his decision, "It might be noted, collaterally, that the regulation creating the administrative remedy was adopted November 8, 1950, six weeks after the application of Horace Ward, a Negro, for admission to the University of Georgia Law School."[2]

Having Vernon Jordan drive the team of lawyers from Atlanta to the admissions office in Athens to compare the records of Holmes and Hunter with those of other applicants also paid dividends. A document Jordan found, showing a discrepancy in treatment between Hunter's application and that of a white student interested in journalism, provided unassailable evidence supporting the plaintiffs' claim of discrimination. Concluding, then, that had Holmes and Hunter been *white* both would have been admitted, Bootle found that although no written policy excluded Negroes from admission, university officials had practiced a tacit policy to that effect, and that Danner had enforced it. Citing several of President Aderhold's actions that blocked Holmes and Hunter's admission, Bootle found that Aderhold had instructed Danner not to admit any additional students a few weeks *after* Holmes and Hunter filed their admissions applications.[3]

Bootle also found that Danner rejected Holmes's application for fall quarter 1960 because Holmes had not satisfied the personal interview requirement. However, evidence disclosed that Danner had accepted several white applicants, pending the personal interview upon their arrival, and even had accepted some students whose files contained no record whatever of an interview. Bootle accordingly affirmed the plaintiffs' claim of a sharp contrast between extremely loose interview requirements for white applicants and the stringent requirements applied to Holmes and Hunter. Agreeing with Holmes's contention that officials had conducted the interview with the intention of rejecting him, Bootle noted that the questions they asked Holmes probably had never been asked of any other applicant.[4] In yet another indirect vindication for Horace Ward, Bootle noted that Aderhold's testimony confirmed that Ward had been denied admission because the interview committee had asserted that he was evasive, inconsistent, and contradictory—virtually the same things said about Holmes.

In an interview with the author, the defendants' attorney E. Freeman Leverett, who assisted Murphy and Cook at the trial, described the reasoning behind the attack on Holmes's character with trumped-up, alleged character defects. Leverett said that anything the defense could produce to defend their case would have been used, because previous court decisions barring discrimination did not leave them much legal ground.[5] This essential weakness was perceived by Judge Bootle and led to the long awaited outcome.

The court ruled that Danner and other officials *now must do what-ever was necessary* to permit Holmes and Hunter to enroll in the university. Bootle found that since the plaintiffs would have already been admitted to the university had it not been for their race, the plaintiffs were entitled to immediate enrollment at UGA for winter quarter 1961.

The *Ward* case was pivotal in shaping the strategies of Hollowell and Motley and in influencing Bootle's final ruling. Hollowell observed in an interview with the author that the *Ward* case "laid the groundwork and helped us to show the kind of duplicity that the system engaged in to thwart these young people."[6] Hollowell concluded that the *Ward* case had been very instructive and that the important lessons learned there helped to win the victory for Holmes and Hunter. To the absolute frustration of Murphy, at every opportunity Hollowell and Motley made references to and comparisons with Ward's rejection by UGA officials. Although Ward had lost his legal case, the *Holmes* finding belatedly validated his legal complaint. In recalling this historic victory years afterward, Ward said, "I feel vindication because these two people who were superstars in terms of academic achievement had now fought the battle and had won."[7]

During the years when Georgia officials bragged about maintaining segregation, Danner testified that his office had not discriminated against blacks. Bootle found Danner's testimony and that of other officials to be false. Curiously enough, although Danner steadfastly had defended segregation, Morris Phelps, Danner's former assistant, has indicated that Danner was neither a segregationist nor a racist:

> Walter Danner was basically an engineer, and so his social atmosphere was pretty technical. He and university president O. C. Aderhold were very good friends, personal friends and professional friends. So anything that Dr. Aderhold suggested, I'm sure Danner went along with it. He was from Northern Virginia and I think he really didn't have any feelings one way or the other. And if the officials above him said, "Enroll black students," he would

have enrolled black students. If they said, "Don't enroll black students," he probably wouldn't enroll black students. That's the technical way he seemed to approach sociological issues.[8]

According to Phelps, Danner was merely following orders, while his superiors masked their tacit discrimination in professed innocence, over and over again.

However, it does appear that Danner participated in even more absurd and reprehensible acts to block Holmes and Hunter than those exposed during the trial. Archival documents from Danner's office reveal confidential informant reports on Holmes and Hunter during 1959-1960. The unsubstantiated reports show that informants closely monitored the activities of Holmes and Hunter, their parents, and their associates after Holmes and Hunter sought entrance to the university. For example, excerpts from informant reports on Holmes stated:

> Confidential Informant of known reliability advised that Hamilton Holmes and Charlayne Alberta Hunter dated during their senior year at Turner High School. The night of graduation, Hamilton Holmes, Charlayne Hunter, and another boy and girl, after the graduation dance stayed out together until about 4:00 A. M. in the morning.
>
> Reportedly Hamilton Holmes has bragged that he intends to be in the University of Georgia next September. Information has also been developed indicating that the college group is frequenting a House of Ill Repute believed to be on Sunset somewhere near Magnolia. This spot reportedly has "Pot parties, tea parties, beatnik parties." . . . Reportedly this house has white girls as well as colored for the proper price. There were approximately twenty-five white boys and girls ranging from the ages of 18 to 25 also at this dance. Hamilton and his friends were drinking beer, scotch, and Thunderbird wine. Informant is of the opinion that possibly some form of narcotic was being smoked.[9]

Danner's files also included confidential reports from informants who spied on Hunter during her attendance at Wayne State University. The following excerpt is an example in which one may note the generally positive conclusions; the point, however, is the reprehensible practice of such an investigation:

> Charlayne was very popular among the Wayne students; however she never dated or gave any indication of wanting to date white students, dating Negro students only. There is no record of Charlayne Alberta Hunter contained in the files of governmental agencies which maintained a record of all persons living in the Detroit area who are, or have been, a member of the Communist party or affiliated with any of its front organizations. A check of the Wayne County and City of Detroit birth records failed to reflect that any child has been born to Charlayne Alberta Hunter.[10]

A review of many of the reports shows that the informants focused specifically on any interracial interactions of Holmes and Hunter or their associates. Since state laws at that time forbade interracial sexual relationships, even a hint that desegregation would engender such relationships would derail any white public sentiment for integration. Long after the end of slavery, segregationists played on white fears of racial mixing despite the fact that miscegenation had occurred primarily as a result of the "subjection of Negro women to the whims and desires of white men."[11] Fears of "the Red menace" were also prevalent and civil rights activists were frequently accused of Communist support or influence. The confidential informants therefore sought also to elicit any information on Holmes or Hunter's possible involvement in Communist or so-called "Communist-influenced" organizations. In both areas of investigation, the confidential reports failed to produce credible damaging evidence against either Holmes or Hunter.

However, Danner and UGA admissions officials posed interview questions to Holmes and Hunter, especially Holmes, clearly based on the informants' insinuations in the confidential reports. Although Danner and the admissions officials treated the reports' information as unequivocal truth, the confidential informants routinely prefaced possibly character-damaging statements with words such as "reportedly" and "possibly." Nevertheless, as reported during the trial, officials attempted to use this kind of intrusive, atypical character investigation—worthy of a clearance investigation by the FBI for "Top Secret" clearance—as part of their rationale for denying admission to the two outstanding applicants.

In retrospect, Holmes described how the absurdity of Danner's claims became even more evident:

> Danner got up on the stand in that trial and said if they had to take somebody, okay, they might take Char [referring to Charlayne Hunter] some day, but I wasn't qualified. That made me mad. But look, that guy said I wasn't qualified and here I end up with one of the highest averages in the school . . . I was raring to come down here and show them. That's why I got such a kick out of Danner coming up after my election to Phi Kappa Phi and congratulating me. He's in Phi Kappa Phi too. It used to be he wouldn't talk to me on the campus. Now he almost crosses the street to see me.[12]

Constance Baker Motley also commented on the absurdities of the defendants' tactics to preserve segregation:

> The [legal] system is based on people getting on the stand and telling the truth. But people who talk about their respect for tradition and integrity and the Constitution get involved in one lie after another. They're willing to break down the system to keep a Negro out. In Mississippi, university officials got up on the stand and said they had never even discussed the Meredith case. They do the same kind of thing in voting cases. People are denied the right to vote, not because they are Negroes but because they didn't dot an "i" or they interpreted the Constitution incorrectly.[13]

The rehearsed arguments and unresolved issues in the *Ward* and *Hunt* cases that previous judges either dismissed or left to the discretion of university officials were invalidated by Bootle's ruling in a way that the officials could not elude or evade. Most importantly, Bootle issued a court order for Holmes and Hunter's immediate admission to the university. Bootle also affirmed Ward's central complaints: that the admissions requirements were rigged for the purpose

of disqualifying him and that officials upheld a tacit policy of discrimination. Vernon Jordan has commented on Bootle's progressive
decision, pointing out that judicial integrity was an important factor
in the successful outcome of the suit:

> Judge Bootle was a very impressive man, modest, quite stern. He
> was a man of dignity, and was one of those Eisenhower-appointed
> judges. One of those twenty-eight lonely men in the South who
> stepped up to his judicial and constitutional responsibility and
> ruled correctly in the University of Georgia case.[14]

During an interview with the author, Holmes concurred that
Bootle's integrity should not be overlooked in examining the *Holmes
v. Danner* case:

> Bootle, who I got to know, and he got to know me after the trial,
> was a segregationist also. He said he was, but after hearing all the
> facts, he said he had to do what he thought was right, even though
> he didn't want to do it. You had to have judges like Bootle . . .
> who believed things should be right.[15]

In discussing the reasons for the triumph in the *Holmes v. Danner*
case, Jordan also brought up other key factors; his retrospective view
captures well the causes and implications of the victory:

> Well, number one . . . Hollowell and Motley were good law-
> yers. Number two, and equally as important, they were com-
> mitted to this process. They were acting out of a sense of duty
> and obligation, not just to their clients but to black people and
> to the country and to the Constitution. Because there was
> Hollowell's talent and Connie Motley's talent, combined with
> their commitment, it's over, it's history. The combination of
> the two, extraordinary legal talent plus commitment and devo-
> tion, added up to victory and it was a significant victory to
> open up the state university who had denied Horace Ward years
> earlier based on race. And then to have Horace, who was de-
> nied admission based on race, who goes to Northwestern,
> comes back and is admitted to the Georgia Bar by the same

judge who had denied him admission to the university. So there's a lot of poetic justice there that Horace could be denied himself and come back and be counsel to Charlayne Hunter and Hamilton Holmes . . . as my mother would say, *the Lord works in mysterious ways.*[16]

Many UGA students responded to the victory of Hollowell, Motley, and Ward in Judge Bootle's courtroom with resistance and hostility. The first student demonstration on campus came on the Friday evening following Bootle's decision. A crowd of one hundred and fifty to two hundred students gathered by the historic archway to the campus and hung an effigy of Holmes.[17] The following night, some two dozen students gathered to burn a cross made of two-by-fours, "but owing to a lack of kerosene and a lack of experience in the art, they were unable to get it ablaze."[18] Meanwhile, state and university officials continued their resistance with legal maneuvers intended to circumvent Bootle's order. Predictably, admissions director Walter Danner and other officials remained determined to prevent Hunter and Holmes from enrolling. Thus was triggered a series of moves and countermoves by the plaintiffs and defendants.

On January 9, 1961, Murphy was able to get a stay of the court order for the enrollment of Holmes and Hunter. On the same day, Ward and Vernon Jordan, along with Althea Hunter and Alfred Holmes (Hunter's mother and Holmes's father), traveled to the UGA campus with Holmes and Hunter to register them. Ward recalled that they drove to Athens and marched directly, without precautions, through the hostile crowd and the media reporters gathered at the university's archway. Amidst insults and chants such as "Nigger go home" and "There goes the nigger," Ward escorted Holmes and Jordan escorted Hunter through the historic gateway to the central campus; Ward recalled that an onlooker told him, "Attorney, don't ever come back to this campus."[19] The huge Confederate flag at the Kappa Alpha fraternity house, flown at half-mast to protest the enrollment of Holmes and Hunter, symbolized the determination of some students to maintain the status quo against what segregationists termed "judicial tyranny."[20] Although no physical incident occurred, as he reflected on the day, Ward said they probably should have been more careful to protect themselves against possible danger.[21] And as Ward and Jordan ushered Holmes and Hunter through the registration process, they discovered to their dismay that Bootle had granted the stay of his court order. When onlookers outside the registration office learned of the stay, a cheer rose from the crowd; one student yelled at Jordan, "The nigger lawyer ain't smiling no more."[22]

However, after Hollowell and Motley rushed an appeal to Judge Elbert Tuttle, Chief Judge of the Fifth Circuit in Atlanta, Tuttle rescinded Bootle's stay the *same day*. Tuttle opined that "the Supreme Court has held many, many times in higher education that you can't exclude people on account of race . . . So, I will enter an Order directing that they be admitted immediately."[23] Tuttle's decision even generated the memorable headline "Tuttle Boots Bootle."[24] The next day, the state appealed Tuttle's order to the Supreme Court. However, recognizing the correctness of Tuttle's ruling, all nine justices affirmed it with unprecedented swiftness. Hollowell telephoned the Athens residence of civic leader Ray Ware, where Holmes and Hunter had been waiting since the university halted their registration, and informed them of Tuttle's decision. Again, escorted by Ward and Jordan and their parents, they returned to the university, resuming their registrations and filing their academic schedules. After completing the registration process, Holmes, Hunter, and their escorts went back to Atlanta with plans to return for classes on the following morning.[25]

Meanwhile, at midnight, January 9, 1961, Governor Ernest Vandiver, seeking to uphold his campaign promise of "no, not one," had issued a public statement cutting off all funds appropriated to the University of Georgia, as required by the Appropriations Act of 1956.[26] Vandiver said that this move was one weapon the state had in reserve to prevent integration and ordered the university closed for at least one week, beginning at noon, January 10, 1961. To counter Vandiver's order, Hollowell, Motley, and Ward filed for a temporary restraining order of the governor's threat to close the university. They contended that by virtue of Bootle's rulings, UGA officials would violate the rights of Holmes and Hunter by closing the university, the plaintiffs would continue to suffer irreparable injury to their constitutional rights for each day of schooling lost, and the closure would also bring harm to the other students enrolled at the university.

As the political and legal maneuvering continued, Holmes and Hunter returned to campus on the afternoon of January 10, 1961. They tried unsuccessfully to elude the protesters who chanted "2, 4, 6, 8, we don't want to integrate; 8,6,4,2, we don't want no jig-a-boo," as university officials escorted them on the campus. Notwithstanding the racially charged environment, on the following morning, eleven years after Ward originally submitted his application to the university, Holmes and Hunter entered classes at the university, breaking the 175-year color line.

Although no serious incident occurred during the day, on the night of January 11, 1961, a riot erupted: "Rioters set fires in the woods near Hunter's dormitory, threw bricks and other missiles at the dorm windows, tossed rocks and firecrackers at reporters, and scuffled with police."[27] Despite local officials' requests for help, Vandiver failed to order out the state patrol to assist local police in quelling the disturbance. After waiting in vain for the state patrol, with the help of the unflappable dean of men William Tate and a few concerned faculty, local law enforcement officers and firefighters used tear gas and fire hoses to disperse the mob, quieting the disturbance by midnight. Their actions were most fortunate; historian Robert Cohen, in a revealing article on the riot, provides extensive documentation, including notes from FBI files, that shows the potential for more brutality and the rioters' complicity with the Ku Klux Klan and segregationist political figures.[28]

It is noteworthy that the leaders of the mob were law students. Dean Tate recalled, "The leaders of that group had been law students, who seemed to be interested in practical politics rather than political theory, and who apparently thought that resisting desegregation was the way to the legislature."[29] Another event that fueled the violence was the UGA men's basketball game loss to arch rival

Georgia Tech, which occurred shortly before the riot. One student, expressing his frustration before the riot, said, "We got beat by Georgia Tech and we got beat by the niggers."[30]

Taking advantage of the university policy that required only freshmen to live on campus, Holmes found a safe refuge off-campus at the home of black restaurateur Ruth Moon Killian and her sons Archibald and Alfred. The Killians had agreed to house Holmes after several black families, understandably fearful of reprisals, declined to provide him a room in their home. On the night of the riot at Hunter's dormitory, local terrorists threatened to burn a cross at the Killian home. But by then, the Killian home had become an armed base camp. Archibald, a U.S. Air Force Korean War veteran who returned from military service in Germany in 1960, recalled,

> We had between twenty and thirty black Athenians, with about thirty shotguns, with about thirty cases of shotgun shells, and we were ready to do whatever, *Malcolm X*, by whatever means necessary. I told them, if you burn a cross at my house, you will not have to ask who came. All you gotta do is turn them over in the morning, pull that sheet off, and you will know because we are going to stand up![31]

The Killians cut the hedges in front of their home for a clear view of potential troublemakers, installed "rabbit wire" over the windows to prevent Molotov cocktails or other objects that could be thrown from the streets, and rotated shifts of armed guards to protect Hamilton Holmes. The Klan, whose modus operandi depended on intimidation, did not burn a cross or incite other violent acts at the well-armed Killian household. While Hollowell, Motley, and Ward had won a pivotal court battle to dismantle the state-sanctioned apartheid system, civil rights activists such as the Killians were also important in the struggle to desegregate UGA.[32] Ruth, Archibald, and Alfred Killian (also a U.S. Air Force veteran), symbolized an emerging militant form of protest as blacks became increasingly intolerant of racial oppression, particularly black veterans who had fought for freedom abroad. The militancy of Martin Luther King,

153

Jr., and the new Student Nonviolent Coordinating Committee also
helped embolden blacks to resist racism and join in the civil rights
struggle.[33]

Back on campus, shortly after the suppression of the demonstration at Hunter's dormitory, Dean of Students J. A. Williams suspended Holmes and Hunter from the university. In a January 12,
1961, letter to Holmes, Williams stated that "last night the events
which took place on the University campus were due to the enrollment of you and Charlayne Hunter at the University of Georgia.
These events placed in jeopardy the lives of you and Charlayne as
well as university students, university officials and city police."[34] It is
more than ironic that they suspended Holmes and Hunter while
most of the rioters stayed in school.

State troopers returned Holmes and Hunter to their homes in
Atlanta. One leading public official praised the riotous behavior. Peter Zach Geer, the governor's executive assistant, issued a statement
saying, "The students at the university have demonstrated that Georgia youth are possessed with the character and courage not to submit to dictatorship and tyranny."[35] On the other hand, in a January
12, 1961, press release, NAACP leader Roy Wilkins denounced the
mob action and suggested that the Civil War was still being fought.
Condemning the students who stoned Hunter's dormitory, he said,
"Young white Georgians feel the odds are about right when a thousand of them can stone a single Negro girl."[36]

Although Bootle had equivocated in his decision to admit
Holmes and Hunter by delaying their enrollment pending the state's
appeal, he did not equivocate on two subsequent rulings. At a hearing on January 12, 1961, Bootle ordered Vandiver *not* to cut off funds
to the university based on the admission of Negroes. He found that
the Appropriations Act, originally instituted ten years earlier to
thwart Ward, was unconstitutional; the Supreme Court had recently
held that similar provisions failed to meet the tests of constitutionality. Shortly thereafter, Bootle also examined the legality of the sus-
pensions of Holmes and Hunter. Regarding Vandiver's failure to
dispatch state police on the night of the riot, Vandiver advised the

Court that "if and when he is notified by the appropriate local authorities that their efforts to maintain order under protest demonstrations have failed, he will immediately dispatch adequate state
police forces."[37] In his declaration Bootle concluded that the constitutional rights of plaintiffs were not to be sacrificed or yielded to
violence and disorder. Therefore, Bootle ordered that the university
should lift and vacate the suspension of Holmes and Hunter by 8:00
A.M., January 16, 1961.[38] Holmes and Hunter returned to campus
that morning without serious incident.

In recalling these events, Vandiver said that ultraconservatives
wanted him to fight and stand in the door to stop Holmes and
Hunter from entering. Governor Ross Barnett of Mississippi later
used this ploy in blocking James Meredith from entering the University of Mississippi as did Governor George Wallace in blocking
the entry of two Negro students to the University of Alabama.[39]
Vandiver asserted that there was a feeling of impending doom:

> Had a case been filed against Georgia Tech, I think there probably
> would have been a difference because Tech had so many out-of-
> state students and didn't have the ties to every family in Georgia
> that the University of Georgia has. I mean the University of Geor-
> gia is just part of the fabric of Georgia. Every [white] family in
> Georgia has somebody that went to the University of Georgia.[40]

Speaking passionately to the author during an interview,
Vandiver continued:

> I knew that we had to make a change and had to make a radical
> change in our political system. So I called over fifty people who
> are my political friends, who helped me get elected governor. I
> called them out to the executive mansion. This was when Judge
> Tuttle had intercepted Judge Bootle and had rendered the deci-
> sion about the University of Georgia. I went around the room,
> doctor, and of those fifty people who was there, forty-eight said,
> "Let's close the schools." There were two people in that group
> that said, "We cannot close the schools." One of them was Carl
> Sanders, who later succeeded me as governor. The other was Frank

Twitty, a man from deep south Georgia who was my floor leader in the House.[41]

On January 19, 1961, Vandiver, reluctantly influenced by Sanders and Twitty, proposed that the legislature repeal several segregation laws. However, Vandiver's legislative proposal, the Child Protection Freedom of Association Defense Package, also had the aspect of a pro-segregationist bill to appease the die-hard segregationists and to protect his political future. Vandiver says the proposal and his speech to the general assembly supporting the bill were designed to convey that "I'm still a segregationist, yet we have reached the point in time that we got to change."[42] The legislature overwhelmingly passed his proposal. Interestingly, the Hollowell, Motley, and Ward legal team had not only won a pivotal court order, but their victory helped influence the governor who had crafted the "Vandiver segregation bills" to initiate legislation to abandon some forms of segregation, ultimately ending Georgia's massive resistance to desegregation.

No doubt, efforts by Vandiver to stand in the door or close the schools would have failed. Nevertheless, his decision to opt for a conservative political solution probably lessened the potential for more intense violence and strife. Vandiver said:

> The popular thing to do would have been to go to jail and make a big media event out of this thing. . . . So, I finally made the decision that we would have to comply with the order of the federal government. We had no choice as long as we were part of this country and were under the jurisdiction of the courts of this country. As a lawyer, I was an officer of the court. As a governor, I was sworn to uphold the constitution and laws of this country.[43]

On the other hand, Vernon Jordan commented that Vandiver was a progressive governor in some areas, but his vitriolic words and actions related to segregation overshadow this progress. Jordan said:

> I think Governor Vandiver in my mind will live on as the governor who had his feet and his head in cement and his famous statement "no, not one" is what he will be remembered for, not

that he supported Kennedy, not that he was progressive or an agent of change. He was the guy that said "no, not one will enter" and it turned out that he was lying.[44]

Hollowell, Motley, and Ward had led the efforts to overcome the major legal and political barriers to the desegregation of the public university, but in many ways the struggle for the first two black students to pursue their aspirations at the university was just beginning. Nevertheless, both of them were distinctly successful in their academic pursuits and the university awarded them degrees on June 1, 1963, in their respective disciplines. Phi Beta Kappa and Phi Kappa Phi recognized Holmes's superior achievement and inducted him into their honor societies. Overall, the record of Holmes's and Hunter's experiences with students, faculty, and the university community was filled with jubilance, frustration, and a great deal of tolerance on the part of Holmes and Hunter.[45]

The march to desegregate the University of Georgia begun by the dauntless William Madison Boyd and Horace T. Ward had reached a pinnacle. State and university officials had used every possible legal and political tactic to sustain segregation. Nevertheless, they lost, and this loss represented a turning point for civil rights in Georgia history. The doors of opportunity for blacks in all-white colleges and universities in Georgia had been opened, and blacks (in small numbers) began to enter other white institutions within a few months. Jesse Hill's prediction was right: "If they could crack the University of Georgia, they [other institutions] would fall like dominoes."[46]

In the fall of 1961, Georgia Tech opened its doors to black students for the first time, admitting three—Ford Greene, Ralph Long, Jr., and Lawrence Williams.[47] Although the Georgia State College of Business had been under a federal court order banning discrimination for three years, the college did not admit its first black student, Annette Lucille Hall, until one year after the admission of Holmes and Hunter.[48] Other leading all-white public and private colleges in Georgia admitted black students for the first time during the 1960s, including Mercer University (Sam Oni, 1963) and the Medical College of Georgia (Frank Rumph and John Harper, 1967).

After an FBI-style background check and interrogation by university officials, the University of Georgia admitted Mary Frances Early to its graduate school for the summer quarter of 1961. Early, who transferred from the University of Michigan, completed her graduate degree in music education on August 16, 1962, and thus became the first black student to actually graduate from the University of Georgia.[49]

Within the labyrinth of Georgia segregation laws lurked a statute that made private educational institutions ineligible for tax exemptions if black students were admitted. In 1962, carried by the momentum created by the *Holmes v. Danner* victory, Emory University sued the tax commissioner of DeKalb County, Georgia. Emory wanted to maintain its tax-exempt status if it admitted a black student. In October 1962 the Supreme Court of Georgia found that Emory was entitled to a tax exemption and that the county could not deprive the university of such an exemption because of the admission of a black student. Emory University admitted its first black student, Neverda E. Jackson, shortly before the final resolution of the court case.[50]

The desegregation of Georgia's flagship university also had an immediate impact on public secondary education. On August 30, 1961, nine black children entered four previously all-white schools in Atlanta. They entered the schools without violence. Noted historian Alton Hornsby, Jr., concluded that the *Holmes v. Danner* victory at the University of Georgia not only had opened the state's institutions of higher learning to blacks, but also forced the state to abandon massive resistance to school desegregation at all levels.[51] Before the court-ordered admission of Holmes and Hunter, Georgia's political leaders were adamant in their stance that they would stop desegregation at any cost, including the disruption of public education. However, Hollowell, Motley, and Ward's defeat of Georgia's leading political figures in the University of Georgia crisis served the critical, perhaps invaluable, purpose of forestalling any interruption of public education in Georgia.[52]

CHAPTER 6 NOTES

[1]See General Appropriations Act, Secs, 8, 9, Ga. Laws 1951, 425. Similar provisions appear in the General Appropriations Act, Secs. 8, 9, Ga. Laws Jan.-Feb. Sess. 1953, 154 and General Appropriations Act, Secs. 8, 9, Ga. Laws 1956, 762.

[2]*Holmes v. Danner*, 191 F. Supp. 394 (M.D. Ga. 1961).

[3]Ibid.

[4]*Holmes v. Danner*, 191 F. Supp. 394, 407 (M.D. Ga. 1961).

[5]E. Freeman Leverett, interview with author, Elberton, GA, December 8, 1995.

[6]Donald Hollowell, interview with author, Atlanta, GA, August 27, 1993.

[7]Horace Ward, interview with author, Atlanta, GA, May 28, 1999.

[8]Morris Phelps, interview with author, Athens, GA, August 7, 1996.

[9]Confidential informant report on Hamilton Holmes, Hargrett Rare Book and Manuscript Library/University of Georgia Libraries, Walter N. Danner Subject File, 1959-60.

[10]Confidential informant report on Charlayne Hunter, Hargrett Rare Book and Manuscript Library/University of Georgia Libraries, Walter N. Danner Subject File, 1959-60. The concern for possible Communist affiliation is typical of the times.

[11]John Hope Franklin and Alfred Moss, Jr., *From Slavery to Freedom: A History of Negro Americans* (New York: McGraw-Hill, 1998), 128-129.

[12]Quoted in Calvin Trillin, *An Education in Georgia: Charlayne Hunter, Hamilton Holmes, and the Integration of the University of Georgia* (Athens: University of Georgia Press, 1991), 84.

[13]Ibid., 42.

[14]Vernon Jordan, interview with author, Washington, D.C., February 28, 1997.

[15]Hamilton E. Holmes, interview with author, Atlanta, GA, February 24, 1995.

[16]Jordan, interview with author, op. cit.

[17]Robert Cohen, "Two, Four, Six, Eight, We Don't Want to Integrate: White Student Attitudes toward the University of Georgia's Desegregation," *Georgia Historical Quarterly* 80 (1996): 617.

[18]Trillin, op. cit., 51.

[19]Horace Ward, interview with author, Athens, GA, April 15, 1996.

[20]Calvin Trillin, op. cit., 71.

[21]Horace Ward, interview with author, Atlanta, GA, May 28, 1999.

[22]Jack Greenberg, *Crusaders in the Courts: How a Dedicated Band of Lawyers Fought for the Civil Rights Revolution* (New York: Basic Books, 1994), 282.

[23]Judge Elbert Tuttle, interview with Clifford Kuhn, April 10, 1992. Judge Elbert Tuttle

grew up in Hawaii and traces his philosophy on civil rights to his multicultural upbringing. He earned the A.B. and LL.B. degrees from Cornell University in 1918 and 1923, respectively. Tuttle, a lifelong Republican, orchestrated key support that helped Dwight Eisenhower win the 1952 Republican nomination. Eisenhower named Tuttle to the Fifth U.S. Circuit Court of Appeals in 1954. Tuttle took senior status in 1967, and moved to the Eleventh Judicial circuit in 1981. Tuttle issued rulings during the tumultuous period of the 1950s and 1960s when there was massive resistance to the civil rights movement; undeterred, he made numerous historic and pivotal rulings that favored social justice for blacks, translating the Supreme Court *Brown v. Board of Education* ruling into a broad mandate for racial justice. During the 1960s, he enraged segregationists by ordering the desegregation of colleges in Alabama, Georgia, and Mississippi. See Anne S. Emanuel, "Turning the Tide in the Civil Rights Revolution: Elbert Tuttle and the Desegregation of the University of Georgia," *Michigan Journal of Race and Law* 5 (fall 1999); Jack Bass, *Unlikely Heroes: The Dramatic Story of the Southern Judges of the Fifth Circuit Who Translated the Supreme Court's Brown Decision into a Revolution for Equality* (New York: Simon and Schuster, 1981). Also see Bill Rankin and Peter Mantius, "True Judicial Hero of Civil Rights Battles Mourned," *Atlanta Constitution*, June 25, 1986, A-6, 8-9; T. Thompson, "Judge Tuttle an Unyielding Activist at 85," *Atlanta Journal,* October 5, 1982, A-1, 20; Bill Rankin, "At 95, Judge Still Lays Down the Law," *Atlanta Constitution*, May 5, 1993, A-1, 10.

[24]Quoted in Charlayne Hunter-Gault, *In My Place* (New York: First Vintage Books Edition, 1993), 175.

[25]Constance Baker Motley, "Remarks on Holmes-Hunter Lecture," *Harvard Blackletter Journal* 5 (spring 1988): 5; Ray Ware, interview with author, Athens, GA, May 19, 2001. Ware, a Morehouse graduate, U.S. Army Air Force veteran, and prominent businessman, organized local support and hospitality for Holmes, Hunter, and their legal team.

[26]Trillin, op. cit., 40, 45, 46.

[27]Cohen, op. cit., 619.

[28]Robert Cohen, "G-men in Georgia: The FBI and the Segregationist Riot at the University of Georgia, 1961," *Georgia Historical Quarterly* 83 (1999): 3, 508-538. According to Cohen, the FBI's probe turned up several pieces of evidence indicating that state politicians encouraged lawless behavior by segregationist students. Whereas the FBI documents do not show that the Ku Klux Klan masterminded the riot, they do reveal that the Klan joined in the already organized student riot. The FBI files also undermine the myth of the riot as a wholly spontaneous event and suggest that segregationist organizers had made advance preparation for the riot. Fortunately, no serious injury occurred during the rioting despite the potential for such. Police arrested eight Klansmen on the campus on charges of disorderly conduct and carrying a deadly weapon to a public gathering. Athens police found in the men's car one

.45, two .22, and three .38-caliber guns, all loaded, and two belts of ammunition. Because the FBI probe ended prematurely and many of its files are censored, despite the criminal acts and the preliminary evidence of rioters' collusion with state officials, there is no conclusive account of the events or all of those responsible. Also see Bill Shipp, *Murder at Broad River Bridge* (Atlanta, GA: Peachtree Publishers, 1981), 23.

[29]Trillin, op. cit., 81–82.

[30]Hunter-Gault, op. cit., 189.

[31]Archibald Killian, interview with author, Athens, GA, July 9, 1997.

[32]Alfred Killian, interview with author, Athens, GA, July 9, 1997; Archibald Killian, interview, op. cit.

[33]Robert H. Brisbane, *The Black Vanguard: Origins of the Negro Social Revolution, 1900-1960* (Valley Forge, PA: Judson Press, 1970), 220, 250; for more information on grassroots activism during the civil rights movement, see Clayborne Carson, *In Struggle: SNCC and the Black Awakening of the 1960s* (Cambridge: Harvard University Press, 1981), Chana Kai Lee, *For Freedom's Sake: The Life of Fannie Lou Hamer* (Chicago: University of Illinois Press, 1999), and Stokely Carmichael and Charles V. Hamilton, *Black Power: The Politics of Liberation in America* (New York: Random House, 1967).

[34]J. A. Williams, letter to Hamilton Holmes, January 12, 1961. Hargrett Rare Book and Manuscript Library/University of Georgia Libraries, O. C. Aderhold Papers, Folder: Integration-University at UGA.

[35]Trillin, op. cit., 58.

[36]NAACP press release, January 12, 1961, "NAACP Deplores Campus Mob Action in Georgia," Papers of the NAACP, Part 3: The Campaign for Educational Equality: Legal Department and Central Office Records, 1913-1950. Series D: 1956-1965, Schools, University of Georgia. NAACP Archives, Library of Congress, Washington, D.C. In addition to Roy Wilkins's condemnation of the riotous mob, while the UGA faculty had not been proactive in the desegregation struggle, some three hundred UGA faculty members (approximately 50 percent of the faculty) signed a petition that deplored the riotous behavior. Led by Professor Horace Montgomery, the faculty members insisted that "the two suspended Negro students be returned to the University and that the state provide the school with adequate protection." Hargrett Rare Book and Manuscript Library/University of Georgia Libraries, Walter Danner File.

[37]Eugene Cook, telegram to W. A. Bootle, January 13, 1961, Hargrett Rare Book and Manuscript Library/University of Georgia Libraries, O. C. Aderhold Papers, Folder Heading: Integration at UGA; *Holmes v. Danner*, 191 F. Supp. 394 (M.D. Ga. 1961).

[38]In his decision ordering university officials to allow Holmes and Hunter to return to the university, Bootle cited *Lucy v. Adams* and *Cooper v. Aaron*, which dealt with the constitutional rights of plaintiffs. See *Cooper v. Aaron*, 358 U.S. 1, 16, 78 S. Ct. 1401, 1409, (1958).

HORACE T. WARD

[39]Greenberg, op. cit., 323, 340.
[40]Ernest Vandiver, interviews with Dr. Charles Pyles, March 20 and July 28, 1986, Georgia State University, Special Collections.
[41]Ernest Vandiver, interview with author, Sky Valley, GA, August 14, 1996.
[42]Ibid.; also Trillin, op. cit., 46; James F. Cook, *The Governors of Georgia, 1754-1995* (Macon, GA: Mercer University Press, 1995), 269.
[43]Vandiver, interview with Dr. Pyles, op. cit. Also see Ernest Vandiver, letter to O. C. Aderhold, February 16, 1961, Hargrett Rare Book and Manuscript Library/University of Georgia Libraries, O. C. Aderhold Papers, Folder: Integration at UGA.
[44]Jordan, interview, op. cit.
[45]For a more in-depth documentation of the events surrounding the desegregation of the University of Georgia, see Hunter-Gault, op. cit.; Trillin, op. cit.; Thomas Dyer, *University of Georgia: A Bicentennial History, 1785-1985* (Athens: University of Georgia Press, 1985), 303-334; Robert Cohen, "Two, Four, Six, Eight," op. cit.; Robert Cohen, "G-men in Georgia," op. cit.; *Foot Soldier for Equal Justice: Horace T. Ward and the Desegregation of the University of Georgia*, Maurice C. Daniels, ex. prod., Janice Reaves, prod., University of Georgia Center for Continuing Education, 2000, videocassette; Louise Hollowell and Martin C. Lehfeldt, *The Sacred Call: A Tribute to Donald Hollowell—Civil Rights Champion* (Winter Park, FL: Four-G Publishers, Inc., 1997).
[46]Jesse Hill, interview with author, Atlanta, GA, December 17, 1996.
[47]Benjamin Griessman, Sarah Jackson, and Annibel Jenkins, *Images and Memories of GA Tech: 1885-1985* (Atlanta: Georgia Institute of Technology Foundation, 1985), 208.
[48]"Ga. State Admits First Negro," *Atlanta Inquirer*, June 23, 1962, 1.
[49]Alan Scot Willis, "A Baptist's Dilemma: Christianity, Discrimination and the Desegregation of Mercer University," *Georgia Historical Quarterly* 80 (1996), 611; Phinizy Spalding and Charles Epps, Jr., "First African-American Graduates of U.S. Medical School," *African-American Medical Pioneers*, ed. Charles Epps, Jr., Gilman Johnson and Audrey Vaughan (Rockville, MD: Betz Publishing, 1994), 149; Phinizy Spalding, *The History of the Medical College of Georgia* (Athens: University of Georgia Press, 1987), 209.

Mary Frances Early, valedictorian of her 1953 Turner High School class and 1957 Clark College class, taught school in the Atlanta Public Schools. Beginning in 1957 she pursued a master's degree in music education at the University of Michigan during the summers, supported by a Georgia Board of Regents "out-of-state aid scholarship." On January 12, 1961, Early observed a picture of Charlayne in the newspaper "clutching a Madonna and looking so despondent," after Charlayne and Hamilton had been suspended from the university. Early knew Hamilton and Charlayne from Turner High School and decided that she would "join the struggle to help these two young people and do what I could to help end the segregation that was so prevalent in the South," subsequently pursuing her transfer to the University of Georgia. Mary Frances Early, interview with author, Atlanta, GA, February 19, 1997. Also see *Foot Soldier for Equal Justice: Horace T. Ward and the Desegregation of the University of Georgia*, Maurice C. Daniels, ex. prod., Janice Reaves, prod., University of Georgia Center for Continuing Education, 2000; Confidential Informant Report on Mary Frances Early, Hargrett Rare Book and Manuscript Library/University of Georgia Libraries, Walter N. Danner Subject File-Integration.

[50]Thomas H. English, *Emory University 1915-1965: A Semi-centennial History* (Atlanta, GA: Higgins-McArthur Company: 1966), 101; *Emory University v. Nash,* No. 21731, Supreme Court of Georgia, September, 1962 (218 Ga. 317, 127 S. E. 2d 798).

[51]Alton Hornsby, Jr., "Black Public Education in Atlanta, Georgia, 1954-1973: From Segregation to Segregation," *Journal of Negro History* 76 (fall 1991): 21-29.

[52]Ibid., 27.

CHAPTER 7

Ward's Emerging Career:
Civil Rights Attorney and State Senator

Having won his spurs in the celebrated *Holmes v. Danner* case, Ward now entered the forum of civil rights litigation as a practicing attorney. Ward's early exposure to civil rights pioneers such as Austin Walden, William Madison Boyd, and Benjamin Mays, and his personal quest for equal justice were shaping motives of his emerging career: the discrimination he had faced and conquered reinforced his desire to advocate justice for all. After Ward's seven-year battle to win his constitutional right to attend law school in his home state and his completion of a law degree at the prestigious Northwestern School of Law, as an attorney Ward became intensely involved in fighting for civil rights.

As we have seen, he actually began his career as a civil rights lawyer working under Donald L. Hollowell's tutelage with the barristers who eventually achieved the desegregation of the University of Georgia. Ward had joined the Hollowell law office in 1960 as an associate and became a partner in 1962. In 1963, Hollowell invited two other promising young lawyers to become partners in his now quite substantial law firm. In addition to Hollowell and Ward, the principals in the firm were William H. Alexander, who later became a superior court judge, and Howard Moore, Jr., who later represented black activist Angela Davis in her celebrated California trial. Among the other lawyers associated with the Hollowell firm were such dynamic figures as Vernon Jordan, who moved to the forefront of the civil rights movement as the National Urban League's executive director in 1972.

During his tenure with the Hollowell firm, Ward joined Hollowell in litigating several far-reaching civil rights cases in various state and federal courts, including the Supreme Court of Georgia and the U.S. Court of Appeals for the Fifth Circuit. His areas of litigation covered a broad spectrum, from equal educational opportunity to fairness in the criminal justice system, and the cases with which he was involved can be likened to battering rams against the walls of segregation and racial discrimination. His valuable role in the UGA *Holmes v. Danner* case was an historically significant, highly public entrée into the arena of civil rights litigation and a prophecy of a long line of cases that demonstrated his commitment to equal justice.

Technically, though, *Holmes* was not quite the first civil rights case in which he played a role. In *King v. State of Georgia* (1960), shortly before the actual trial of *Holmes v. Danner*, Ward joined chief counsel Hollowell to challenge the sentencing of Dr. Martin Luther King, Jr., to twelve months of hard labor for a traffic offense and the subsequent revocation of King's probation. This case arose from King's 1960 conviction for operating a motor vehicle without a valid Georgia driver's license in DeKalb County. On September 23, 1960, King pled guilty before the Civil and Criminal Court of DeKalb County and the court sentenced him to twelve months on the public works camp. Initially, the sentence was probated upon the payment of a $25 fine. However, on October 19, 1960, police arrested King for leading a group of student demonstrators, charging him with violating his probation. In protest of the Jim Crow practices among Atlanta's white restaurateurs, Atlanta's student movement leaders, King, A. D. King (King's brother), and more than eighty demonstrators were seeking luncheon service at several prominent stores in downtown Atlanta, including Rich's, Newberry's, and Woolworth's. Using the pretext of the state's antitrespass law, Atlanta and Fulton County police arrested more than fifty demonstrators at Rich's, including King. Judge James Webb set bond at $500 pending trial. When King refused release on bail, insisting that he would come out of jail only if the police dropped charges, police hustled King off to spend the first night of his life behind bars. The student demonstrators, including Student Nonviolent Coordinating Committee (SNCC) leaders and five student body presidents from the Atlanta University complex, joined King in jail.[1]

In response to the demonstration crisis, Atlanta mayor William Hartsfield, unlike his counterparts in other Southern cities such as Birmingham, sought to work with the demonstrators and the business community toward desegregating public venues. Seeking to end the demonstrations and reach a peaceful resolution, Hartsfield ordered the immediate release of all twenty-two Negroes in the Atlanta city jail and vowed to work with county and state officials for the release of other demonstrators in the Fulton County jail, over which Hartsfield had no jurisdiction. In a move characteristic of Atlanta's white leaders during the civil rights era, Rich's sought to settle the matter to avoid a more militant crisis in the thriving Atlanta business community. Working with Hartsfield to have the trespass charges dropped, Rich's officials announced that they had "no desire to prosecute Dr. King or the Negro students arrested in the store."[2] In about a week the authorities had released all of the jailed demonstrators—with the exception of King.

DeKalb County solicitor Jack Smith insisted that King show cause in court as to why he should not be sent to public works camp to serve his originally imposed sentence. After a court hearing on October 25, 1960, Judge Oscar Mitchell of the Criminal Court of DeKalb County revoked King's probation and he was sentenced for four months "to be put to work and labor on the Public Works Camp of DeKalb County, or otherwise, as the proper authorities may direct.[3]

This sentence constituted an unusual and extreme form of punishment, considering that it stemmed from a mere misdemeanor traffic offense. Moreover, under cover of night DeKalb County officials whisked King off, not to a public works camp, but to the maximum security prison in rural Reidsville, Georgia.[4] The incident prompted Democratic presidential nominee John F. Kennedy to telephone

Georgia's Governor Vandiver to ask for King's release. The politically astute Vandiver, who had aspirations for the United States Senate, supported Kennedy in the upcoming November 1960 presidential election and wanted to help King, but feared political repercussions from his strong segregationist constituency. After Judge Mitchell sentenced King, Vandiver's press agent praised the decision; however, in an interview with the author, Vandiver revealed that he opted to work behind the scenes with Kennedy's brother, Robert Kennedy, who telephoned DeKalb County judge Oscar Mitchell on King's behalf.[5]

As Dr. King's arrest and sentence began to attract national and international attention, both protests and praise poured in for Atlanta officials. In a telegram to Mayor Hartsfield, Eleanor Roosevelt said, "I wish to protest the imprisonment of Dr. Martin Luther King and hope you will use your good office to correct this injustice."[6] John F. Kennedy also called Mrs. King to express his concern. Some journalists and historians have even attributed Kennedy's close win in the presidential election to his gesture of support for Dr. King, which prompted increased black voter support for him. In 1956, Negro voters had voted Republican by approximately a 60 to 40 percent margin; in 1960, the Democrats won 70 percent of the black vote.[7]

While Kennedy, Vandiver, and Hartsfield continued to deliberate behind the scenes on possible ways to secure King's release, Hollowell and Ward represented King at the revocation hearing and handled his appeal before the Georgia Court of Appeals, where they challenged both the original sentence and the probation revocation. They argued that the four-month term was "harsh, excessive, and cruel" punishment for a minor traffic offense and that the original twelve-month sentence was longer than the law allowed.[8] During the appeal, Hollowell and Ward secured King's release from the Reidsville State Prison on appeals bond, eight days and eight nights after police jailed him in Atlanta.

The Court of Appeals reversed King's sentence and the probation revocation, holding that the original twelve-month sentence was indeed excessive, and that the subsequent revocation was thereby invalid.[9] In fact, the court declared that the maximum penalty for the misdemeanor offense of operating a motor vehicle without a license was a fine not to exceed $50 and imprisonment not to exceed six months, as Hollowell had correctly pointed out before the court. The court further ruled that King did not violate his probation, because Judge Mitchell had not imposed any conditions upon the probation. Sustaining the arguments of Hollowell and Ward, the Court of Appeals remanded the case to the trial court for appropriate action consistent with its mandate.[10] While the effect of high-level, behind-the-scenes political influence on the outcome of King's case is not entirely clear, King said after his release from prison that he was "deeply indebted to Senator [John F.] Kennedy," who, he said, "served as a great force in making his release possible."[11] However, even recognizing the likelihood of political influence on King's probationary release from prison, it is clear from the appeals court ruling that Hollowell and Ward had appealed the case on sound legal grounds, and the court cited their legal reasoning in its final ruling.

Continuing their pressure against an oppressive criminal justice system, less than a year later Hollowell and Ward prevented the electrocution of a fifteen-year-old black youth from Monticello, Georgia, five days before the scheduled execution. On June 1, 1961, Preston Cobb was indicted for the murder of Frank Coleman Dumas, an elderly white man, on whose farm Cobb lived and worked with his mother and family.[12] Dumas had been found shot to death and the same day sheriff's deputies arrested Cobb and a friend riding in Dumas's car. Upon interrogation by sheriff's deputies, Cobb had admitted to the murder, claiming Dumas had told him that "he was going to blow his brains out."[13] On August 16, 1961, an all-white, all-male Jasper Superior Court jury deliberated only forty-five minutes before finding Cobb guilty. Cobb was sentenced to be executed at the Reidsville State Prison.[14]

Shortly thereafter, Ward answered a telephone call in the Hollowell law office from a frantic Leathy Cobb, Preston's mother, who contacted the firm regarding her son's scheduled execution. Ward and Vernon Jordan subsequently met with Cobb's mother to discuss her son's case. Due to her fear of white reprisals for challenging the system, she would only meet with Ward and Jordan late at night. The way whites in Monticello had dealt with Daniel Barber and his family, who dared to challenge white authority in 1915, was no doubt well-remembered in the small rural community.[15] When the local police chief attempted to arrest Barber on a bootlegging charge, Barber and his family forcibly resisted the officer. After police subdued and detained the Barbers, a white mob stormed the jail, dragging Barber, his son, and his two married daughters to a tree in the black section of Monticello where the entire family, one by one, was hanged, and their bodies riddled with bullets. In response to the quadruple lynching, the *Crisis* published an article quoting various newspaper responses, including even the following from the *Atlanta Journal*: "Savage lawlessness seldom grows so monstrous as it did in the mob which hanged four Negro prisoners, two of them women . . . That was murder, cold-blooded and cowardly."[16] While these kinds of public lynchings had largely ended by the 1960s, their intimidating effects remained, and blacks continued to be victims of more subtle forms of violence for challenging the white-controlled system. Moreover, often unable to vote, serve on juries, or hold public office in Jim Crow towns, they possessed no available means to bring whites to justice for brutality against blacks.[17]

Despite her justifiable fears, Cobb's mother decided to appeal to the Hollowell firm, traveling from Monticello to Atlanta and retaining the firm to represent her son. Soon thereafter, the LDF accepted the case and designated Hollowell as chief counsel. Cobb had been sentenced to die about a month after the trial, but his court-appointed white attorney had not appealed the verdict. With the scheduled execution only a few days away, Hollowell and Ward rushed to halt it. In a motion for a new trial, Hollowell and Ward challenged the exclusion of blacks from the grand and trial juries in Jasper County, Georgia. They asserted on appeal that the court-appointed white attorney was inexperienced in raising legal issues related to racial discrimination and that because his fee-paying clients were predominantly white, economic reasons would keep him from challenging the selection of an all-white jury.[18] As the prominent white lawyer (and later judge) Charles Weltner observed, when the American Civil Liberties Union approached him to take the case, "raising the issue of systematic inclusion of Negroes . . . would brand him as a civil rights lawyer and, worse still, an integrator."[19] Most white lawyers and even some of the few black lawyers in the South during this era simply were not willing to risk alienating themselves from the white power structure.

In gathering evidence to prove that blacks were systematically and arbitrarily excluded from jury rolls, Hollowell, Ward, and Vernon Jordan traveled to Monticello to review records at the Jasper County courthouse. Complacently affirming that blacks were not on the jury rolls, the clerk of the court remarked to Hollowell, Ward, and Jordan that "there ain't no niggers on the books."[20] Despite the overwhelming evidence, however, the trial court judge denied the motion for a new trial. The lawyers then appealed the case to the Supreme Court of Georgia, which affirmed the judgment of the trial court.[21] The Supreme Court's failure to recognize the exclusion of blacks was particularly egregious since the 1960 census demonstrated that Jasper County, like so many counties in Georgia that also excluded blacks from jury pools, possessed a majority black population.

The death sentence of the youthful Cobb imposed by an oppressive criminal justice system attracted international attention. President Kennedy received requests to intercede, Eleanor Roosevelt sent a telegram to Governor Vandiver for intervention, and two Dutch court officials, speaking for the people of the Netherlands, traveled to the United States to advocate for Cobb.[22] Nonetheless, the Supreme Court of Georgia also denied an extraordinary motion for a new trial filed by Hollowell and Ward.

Because the federal courts had provided decisive leadership on race issues during the 1950s and 1960s, Hollowell and Ward then turned to the federal courts for relief. The two lawyers filed a petition for habeas corpus (a writ requiring that a detained person be brought before a court to decide the legality of the imprisonment) in the federal courts on the grounds of systematic exclusion of black persons from the grand and trial juries. The United States District

Court denied the petition; however, on appeal, the United States Court of Appeals for the Fifth Circuit reversed that decision. After the long series of legal maneuvers and denials, the Court of Appeals held that local officials had systematically excluded blacks from grand and trial juries in Jasper County, Georgia. The court remanded the case with direction that the state provide a new trial.

Subsequently, with some blacks now on the jury rolls, a grand jury in Jasper County reindicted Cobb, whereupon Cobb's attorneys requested a change of venue to move the case outside Jasper County. Although the court had denied several pleas filed by Hollowell and Ward, they were able to secure a change of venue to Bibb County, where Cobb was retried. The jury rolls in Bibb County also contained black persons; however, Hollowell and Ward challenged the jury selection based on the court's use of racially segregated tax digests. Despite this objection, the Bibb County court also convicted Cobb, and sentenced him to life imprisonment. Hollowell and Ward appealed the case to the Supreme Court of Georgia for a *third* time, but the Court affirmed the conviction and sentence of the lower court. The attorneys then took their cause to the federal courts again, appealing to the United States Supreme Court; here the judgment of the Georgia Supreme Court was reversed, sending the case back to Georgia for a new trial. The U.S. Supreme Court held that while there were *some* black persons on the rolls of the grand and trial juries, the procedure used to select jurors by the use of segregated tax digest books constituted a *prima facie* case for purposeful discrimination based on race.[23]

By the time of the third appeal to the Supreme Court of Georgia and the appeal to the U.S. Supreme Court, Howard Moore, Jr., had become chief counsel for Preston Cobb, with Ward assisting; Hollowell had left the private practice of law to direct the Equal Employment Opportunity Commission for the Southern Region. Before Cobb's case was tried for the third time, he decided to plead guilty, and after receiving credit for seven years of time served, prison officials eventually released him. In representing Cobb, Hollowell, Ward, and Moore had presented evidence that finally convinced the courts that excluding blacks from jury pools using segregated tax digests constituted a double standard of justice, with the U.S. Supreme Court declaring such practices unconstitutional. The legal work of Hollowell, Ward, and Moore thus helped advance a new doctrine of fairness in Georgia's criminal justice system.

More importantly, they prevented the electrocution of a fifteen-year-old youth and helped create an important judicial precedent for the inclusion of blacks on jury rolls in a non-discriminatory manner. As far back as 1935, in a unanimous opinion written by Chief Justice Charles Evan Hughes, the U.S. Supreme Court had affirmed in the *Norris v. Alabama* case that the arbitrary and systematic exclusion of Negroes from jury rolls violated the equal protection clause of the Fourteenth Amendment. The fact that many state and local officials continued to exclude blacks from the jury rolls in the 1960s showed the disrespect for the federal courts by Southern officials. Moreover, despite previous U.S. Supreme Court orders such as *Norris v. Alabama*, these actions did not produce sweeping changes in the South. Legal advocates such as Hollowell, Ward, and Moore had to fight a case-by-case battle to win rights for blacks in the Jim Crow South, even those rights guaranteed by the Constitution and ordered by the Supreme Court.[24]

In addition to advocating for fair criminal justice for black youths such as Preston Cobb, Hollowell and Ward recognized the importance of equal educational opportunities for black youth. In this context Hollowell, Motley, and Ward handled the case of *Harris v. Gibson* in 1963, after a federal district court issued an injunction preventing six black youths from attending the all-white Glynn Academy in Brunswick, Georgia.[25] A group of white citizens brought this case in 1963 after the Glynn County School Board promulgated a voluntary plan for the desegregation of its schools in the eleventh and twelfth grades. As a result of the lawsuit, Frank Scarlett, the United States District Court judge for the Southern District of Georgia, issued a restraining order that halted this *voluntary* desegregation plan and prevented black students from entering Glynn Academy. Hollowell, Motley, and Ward intervened on behalf of the six black applicants, and Ward appeared before Judge Scarlett at several hearings seeking to dissolve the injunction.

After unsuccessful legal proceedings before Judge Scarlett, Hollowell, Motley, and Ward brought the matter before Judge Griffin B. Bell, presiding for the Fifth Circuit Court of Appeals.[26] Ironically, Bell had earlier served as chief of staff for segregationist Governor Ernest Vandiver. Nonetheless, Judge Bell, who had been appointed in 1960 by President Kennedy, granted a stay of Judge Scarlett's decision, allowing the six black students to attend Glynn Academy until the case was tried and final judgment rendered.

In 1964 the courts combined the *Harris v. Gibson* case for appeal with a related Savannah school desegregation case (*Stell v. Savannah-Chatham County Board of Education*), wherein blacks were also seeking equal educational opportunities in Savannah and Chatham County schools. Constance Baker Motley handled the combined case with prominent NAACP Legal Defense and Educational Fund lawyers Derrick A. Bell, Jack Greenberg, and others. Judge Bell declared that it was indisputable that the Glynn County schools and the Savannah-Chatham County schools "were being operated on a segregated basis," in violation of the Fourteenth Amendment. The case ultimately led to the desegregation of both school systems.[27]

Interestingly, Judge Bell, who had grown up in the racially segregated community of Americus, Georgia; had attended Jim Crow schools and colleges in south Georgia; and directed the staff of a governor steeped in prejudice, made a decisive declaration for equal rights for blacks. Bell's 1964 ruling against the segregationist establishment is one example of the dramatic social changes that were occurring in the Deep South during the period of the 1950s and 1960s. The ruling also suggests the fracturing of the solidarity of those white Southerners who had maintained a virtually united stance for racial oppression of blacks since Reconstruction. Undoubtedly, Bell was influenced by the liberal Kennedy administration and the sweeping social changes being legislated, prompted by civil rights protesters demanding an equitable society. While Bell does not possess the progressive judicial record of such forward-looking federal judges as Elbert Tuttle, his moderate rulings on issues of equal rights for blacks clearly transcended his upbringing and earlier career in environments ensconced in Southern racial traditions.

During the years 1963-1965, in a quest for equal access to professional opportunities, Hollowell and Ward championed the causes of black health-care professionals who were barred from membership in the white local and state medical associations, and of those who were denied opportunities to attend the white nursing school or practice at Grady Memorial Hospital in Atlanta. It was Horace Ward who served as the lead counsel in these cases in 1964. In *R. C. Bell, et al. v. Fulton/DeKalb Hospital Authority, et al.*, Hollowell and Ward, along with LDF lawyer Michael Meltsner of New York, represented three groups of plaintiffs: black dentists excluded from local and state dental associations; black physicians excluded from local and state medical associations; and black nursing school applicants restricted to a segregated nursing school at Grady. One of these companion lawsuits also challenged the denial of staff appointments to black dentists and physicians at Grady.

The outcome of these suits represented a substantial victory for Ward. After extensive litigation on various motions to dismiss filed by the defendants, the medical associations and Grady Hospital Authority entered consent judgments with the plaintiffs, resulting in the desegregation of the nursing school at Grady Memorial Hospital, the admission of black physicians and dentists to the staff at Grady Hospital, and the enrollment of black physicians as members in the medical associations.[28]

However, the dental associations did not join the consent judgment and insisted on a separate court hearing on their case. The case was tried in 1964 before Judge Frank Hooper, U.S. District Court, Northern District of Georgia. In *Bell v. Georgia Dental Association*, the defendants contended that the dental associations constituted "voluntary associations of professional men," whose acts were not governed by the Fourteenth Amendment.[29] They further insisted that because the associations were private professional organizations, they possessed the right to admit such dentists "as they see fit."[30] Ward, as lead counsel, argued that the dental associations acted as agencies of the state, since state law prescribed that the Georgia Dental Association would nominate practicing dentists to the Board of Dental Examiners of Georgia. Ward contended that because the Georgia Dental Association excluded Negro dentists from its membership, only white dentists could be nominated to the Board of Examiners; therefore, Negro dentists had no voice in the selection processes.

On February 3, 1964, Judge Frank Hooper found the exclusion of blacks from the state and district dental associations to be a violation of the Equal Protection Clause of the U.S. Constitution.[31] Hooper agreed with Ward's contention, concluding that because the Georgia legislature granted the dental association the right to nominate members to state agencies, that legislative act made the dental association an agent of the state. This decisive victory was especially exhilarating for Ward, who won this ruling before Federal Judge Hooper, the same judge who had ruled against him in his own lawsuit in 1957 that challenged the exclusion of blacks from the University of Georgia.

In yet another case tried before Judge Hooper during 1963-64, *Johnson v. Georgia State Board for Vocational Education*, Ward was chief counsel for two black students seeking admission to the Coosa Valley Area Technical School. Their case recalled his own lawsuit against the University of Georgia years before, with the plaintiffs filing a lawsuit to desegregate the school. Once again Attorney General Eugene Cook, who had stubbornly resisted Ward's entrance to the University of Georgia, represented the defense, in this case against the Georgia State Board for Vocational Education. On generally the same grounds used in the *Holmes v. Danner* case, specifically the violation of the Fourteenth Amendment, the action filed by Ward resulted in a judgment in favor of one of the plaintiffs and against the other.[32] Although he had not achieved a victory for both of his clients, Ward had again been notably successful as chief counsel, and before the federal judge who had originally dismissed his lawsuit

176

and against the attorney general who had fought to keep him out of the University of Georgia Law School. This victory, indeed, typifies the many ironies in Ward's struggle and vindication as he succeeded as a lawyer.

Ward also represented student protesters on the front lines of the civil rights movement during the early 1960s. For example, he was counsel for approximately fifty high school-aged black students who were arrested for sitting-in at downtown lunch counters in Rome, Georgia. All of the cases were tried in the Rome Municipal Court, with most of the defendants being convicted of city ordinance violations. Four of the cases were appealed to the Superior Court and Ward made arguments on behalf of the appellants. However, the Superior Court affirmed the judgments of the lower court and no further appeals were taken. Although the court ruled against the plaintiffs, the significance of these cases was that issues involving constitutional rights of black citizens were raised for the first time in the courts in the rural area of Rome.[33]

The above cases are significant highlights in Ward's career, but by no means singular; during the early to mid-1960s, Ward, with the Hollowell law firm, was involved in several important civil rights cases. Two 1962 cases, filed in federal district courts in Macon and Augusta, Georgia, *Alexander v. Bibb Transit Company* and *Taylor v. City of Augusta,* enabled blacks to ride desegregated buses in those cities. In the *Taylor* case (February 1962), before a three-judge U.S. District Court panel in Augusta that included Judges Tuttle and Bootle, who rendered decisions in the celebrated *Holmes* case, the panel declared certain segregation statutes of the City of Augusta, Public Service Commission, and State of Georgia unconstitutional, prohibiting Augusta officials from racially segregating passengers on its buses. The *Alexander* case emanated from a few strong-willed black ministers including Reverends Van J. Malone, Ellis S. Evans, Elisha B. Paschal, Hosea R. Rancifer, Jeff Lorenza Key, Cameron Alexander, and Booker Chambers, who challenged the Jim Crow bus statutes in Macon. Reminiscent of the courageous Rosa Parks, tired of the second-class citizenship, on February 9, 1962, Malone, Evans, Paschal, and Rancifer boarded a Bibb

Transit bus, taking seats near the *front* of the bus. Refusing the bus operator's request to move to the rear, stating they were *comfortable* in the seats they occupied, the Macon city police arrested the ministers for violating the segregation statutes and racial practice that required blacks to sit in the rear. A few days later, Hollowell and Ward filed a complaint before Judge Bootle of the U.S. District Court, Middle District, to restrain the bus company from discriminating against black passengers. In a swift, unequivocal ruling, on March 1, 1962, Bootle declared the racial segregation unconstitutional and issued a permanent injunction that restricted the Bibb Transit Company from segregating its passengers.[34]

In the historic Atlanta sit-in cases of 1960–61, Ward represented student protesters in the Municipal Court of Atlanta and the Criminal Court of Fulton County. The rulings in favor of the protesters helped to dismantle segregation in public facilities in Atlanta. In these and in numerous other civil rights cases, Ward helped move America toward greater freedom and equality. Although the University of Georgia never opened its doors to Ward, he played a major role in winning landmark cases that opened the doors for blacks in Georgia to participate in a free society.

Ward's determination to help others achieve equal access by 1964 motivated him to move into the more public political domain. He recognized that the battle for equal rights had to be fought not only in the courts, but where the laws were being enacted. Consequently, in 1964, Ward ran for a seat in the Georgia Senate in the Thirty-ninth Senatorial District in Fulton County, a majority white district. Ward garnered significant support from business, community, and civic leaders. On August 18, 1964, at a community-based Thirty-ninth Senatorial District Convention sponsored by a number of predominantly black political and social organizations, Ward won the endorsement of the district convention. Community leader Vernon Jordan, who in 1962 became field secretary for the Georgia branch of the NAACP, gave the nomination speech for Ward. Austin Walden, Ward's former attorney and mentor and Georgia's foremost veteran civil rights leader, seconded Jordan's nominating speech. In endorsing Ward, he emphasized the value of electing a "capable young man who has demonstrated his worth and integrity as a student and a lawyer."[35] Walden also cited the groundbreaking role Ward had played in his own lawsuit to enter the University of Georgia and in the *Holmes* case. Walden's endorsement represented an especially defining moment in Ward's life, since Walden had been the first black lawyer who had inspired Ward to study law and fight for social justice.

In September 1964 Ward won an upset Democratic primary victory in a contested election. Ward overcame an early lead by his white opponent, incumbent Senator Oby T. Brewer, Sr., defeating Brewer by a margin of 4,973 votes to 3,376. Commenting modestly on what was indeed a breathtaking triumph, Ward remarked, "This is a happy day for me and my family in that we actually see history being made in the city of Atlanta . . . I take this opportunity to pay special tribute to my wife who performed yeoman service all during the summer."[36] During an interview with the author, Ward said that his wife, Ruth, had encouraged him to become a candidate and had strongly supported his senatorial campaign. Ward also attributed his election to his campaign manager, Ben Brown, a young black attorney who had strong political aspirations, and to the support and financial contributions from civil rights leaders Jesse Hill and Benjamin Mays.[37]

Shortly after the primary election, Ward began a vigorous campaign to defeat his Republican opponent in the November 1964 general election. Ward faced insurance businessman Robert Shaw, who led a formidable campaign to win the senate seat. To bolster his political bid, Ward sought grassroots community support for his campaign, which was operating on a shoestring budget.[38] Community leaders who had supported Ward in the Democratic primary helped galvanize support for his general election bid. The Know Your Neighbor Community Club, which had spearheaded voter registration drives in the Atlanta community, launched a fund drive with other community clubs to help finance the Ward campaign.

Ward, who made a campaign promise to support legislative reapportionment that would make election possible for other blacks, also won endorsements from Atlanta's black-owned newspapers, *At-*

lanta Daily World and *Atlanta Inquirer*. An *Atlanta Daily World* editorial highlighted his reputation as a tireless advocate for equal justice:

> About twelve years ago a young local man came to our attention when he took courageous leadership in attempting to break down one of the barriers which denied Negroes full participation in the democratic way of life. He brought suit against the University of Georgia Law School after he was denied admittance, solely because of this racial identification . . . We endorse, support, and recommend to voters in the Thirty-ninth Senatorial District to elect Atty. Horace T. Ward to the State Senate . . . Atty. Ward promises to support a plan for reapportionment which will make election possible for members of our race.[39]

The major Atlanta newspaper, the *Atlanta Constitution*, urged voters to vote Democratic in the November election, but stopped short of endorsing Ward individually. In an *Atlanta Constitution* editorial, the editors stated that Republican candidate Shaw as well as Ward "impress us as being well qualified for the office."[40] Ward's chances for election seemed realistically no more than fair, given the time and context of his bid.

However, despite the fact that this was Ward's first campaign for elected office, running in a majority white district against a formidable Republican opponent, Ward did indeed win the state senate seat in November 1964. Moreover, Ward defeated Shaw by a nearly two to one margin, polling 10,289 votes to Shaw's 5,423.[41]

Ward's triumph was also framed by the November 1964 presidential election in which President Lyndon Johnson defeated Republican opponent Senator Barry Goldwater. Several prominent Atlantans such as Mayor Ivan Allen, Morehouse President Benjamin E. Mays, Senator Leroy Johnson, and others actively supported the reelection of the liberal President Johnson, who had already developed a progressive civil rights record and had a major civil rights agenda. In a hard-hitting front page editorial, the *Atlanta Inquirer* advocated that "the man opposing President Johnson must be beaten in Georgia as well as nationally, in order to keep the Georgia racial climate at least tolerantly moderate. Senator Barry Goldwater as a presidential possibility is a nightmare."[42] The *Atlanta Constitution* also supported President Johnson for reelection and urged a strong voter turnout.[43] And the turnout was strong: 80 percent of registered Negro voters and 68 percent of whites cast votes in the November general election. Without question, an overwhelming majority of voters in the Thirty-ninth District favored Ward, but the impressive black voter turnout aided by the strong campaigns to reelect President Johnson no doubt helped to increase his margin of victory.[44]

Ward attributed his successful bid, in part, to the celebrity—perhaps in some quarters, notoriety—gained from his civil rights advocacy.[45] Ward's active membership in the Atlanta Voter's League, the Fulton County Democratic Club, the NAACP, and other progressive groups that cultivated black political influence also helped his election bid. This victory represented a dramatically notable milestone in his life. Ward's success in becoming the second black elected to the state's highest law-making body was a crowning achievement for him at this time, a further vindication of a long, arduous struggle dating back to those days in the early 1950s when the legislature adopted measures to thwart his admission to the University of Georgia.

In 1962 Ward's friend and former Morehouse classmate, Senator Leroy Johnson, had become the first black to be elected to the Georgia Senate. But the prestige of the position did not automatically confer mainstream social acceptance.[46] Johnson has described how his election provided him little immunity from the vestiges of second-class citizenship for blacks. During a 1996 interview with the author, Johnson recalled that the state cafeteria refused to serve him, that the senate chamber still had separate water fountains for "colored" and "white," and that once he integrated the cafeteria, his colleagues refused to sit at the same table with him.[47] Such experiences strengthened his commitment to equal rights.

However, Johnson said, as time passed and white politicians sometimes needed a single vote to pass a bill, the same politicians who had never spoken to him before began to seek his support. As Johnson put it, "instead of seeing a black senator, they saw a vote, a vote that could either get their bill out of committee or kill it in committee."[48] Both Johnson and Ward were shrewd politicians, although of differing styles and temperaments—Johnson the consummate legislator and "horse trader," Ward characteristically more modest and reserved. But they were of one mind in capitalizing on the value of their votes and bargaining with their colleagues for improved resources and services for their primarily black constituents. One notable example, in 1970, is Ward's and Johnson's opposition to Senate Resolution No. 234, which placed the Senate on record as being against the Black Panther Party members using state educational facilities. Voicing his passionate opposition on the Senate floor, Ward stated, "Let the record show that this Senator did not favor the Resolution, . . . Although I am opposed to the violent overthrow of our government, I strongly favor academic freedom and freedom of speech."[49]

Johnson's two years in the Senate before Ward's election had somewhat neutralized the racial atmosphere, and in general Ward did not experience the blatant forms of racism that Johnson had encountered. Nonetheless, over many preceding years the Georgia General Assembly had created a virtual fortress of statutes obstructing social equity for blacks. And so, Ward (almost inevitably) played a leadership role in legislative initiatives designed to end this oppressive system and empower blacks in Georgia. Ward recalls that at the time he was elected to the Senate, there were no blacks in the Georgia House of Representatives, on the Atlanta City Council, or on the Fulton County Commission. Ward and Johnson therefore took it upon themselves to fashion a reapportionment plan that would create opportunities for blacks to be elected to the Georgia House of Representatives for the first time since Reconstruction.[50]

As Ward had promised during his election campaign, he participated in reapportionment sessions in which he strongly advocated a reconfiguration of voting districts for the Georgia House of Representatives that would make possible the election of blacks. These efforts were largely successful in the 1965 session of the General Assembly, when the legislature created several single-member House districts. Creating single-member districts increased the opportunities for blacks to be elected since blacks constituted a majority in some single-member districts—unlike the at-large districts in which whites usually constituted a majority. Consequently, blacks became more politically active, often supporting black candidates to represent their interests in the newly created black majority districts.

This chain of events resulted in the historic election of eight black persons, including Julian Bond, Ward's former campaign manager Ben Brown, and Grace Hamilton, to the Georgia House of Representatives in 1966. Similarly, Ward served on the charter commission of the city of Atlanta, which recommended to the legislature the adoption of a new charter that included twelve single-member districts and six at-large districts. In 1973 the Georgia General Assembly adopted legislation creating a new charter, separating the powers of the mayor and council, and providing for twelve single-member districts and six at-large districts. The charter also provided for a "bill of rights," which prohibited discrimination based on race, religion, sex, or national origin.

In the election of 1973, pursuant to the new charter, the voters of Atlanta elected Maynard Jackson mayor and increased black persons on the city council from five to nine. The new charter of the city of Atlanta also dealt with the Atlanta Board of Education, changing the election process from selecting all members at-large to selecting six by districts and three at-large. Also in the 1973 election, the voters elected five black persons to the board of education, including educator/civil rights activist Benjamin Mays. Moreover, Ward and other legislators from the Fulton County delegation secured the passage of legislation reorganizing the board of commissioners of Fulton County. The General Assembly enacted the legislation into law in 1973, which changed the membership on the board of commissioners from three to seven members and created single-member districts. This law further provided for the election of three members from at-large districts and four members from single-member districts. Subsequently, in the 1974 election, the voters elected two black members to the board of commissioners, whereas previously no black member had served.[51]

Although known for his civil rights pursuits, Ward also championed fundamental human rights issues as a legislator, beginning with his first term in 1965–66. He opposed the death penalty and on March 12, 1965, proposed Senate Resolution 107 to create a Senate Capital Punishment Study Committee.[52] Although several influential senators supported Ward's effort to abolish the death sentence in Georgia, their actions were initially unsuccessful. However, based on Ward's resolution, the senate established a committee to study the issue, ultimately resulting in a reclassification of several crimes so that those convicted could no longer be given the death penalty: the legislation reduced the number of capital crimes from more than twenty—an archaic, appalling legacy of the past—to five. Demonstrating his continued fervent opposition to the death penalty and showing concern for racial and economic justice during his eighth year in the Senate, in a 1973 session of the legislature, Ward stated:

> History has pointed out for all to see that the death sentence laws have not been fairly administered and applied. There is considerable evidence which demonstrates arbitrary action, and racial and economic bias in the enforcement of these laws. Very often a person's station in life has a bearing on whether he was tried and sentenced to prison or to death.[53]

Ward's expressed concerns for justice in the administration of the death penalty were prophetic; in 1976 the United States Supreme Court reduced the number of crimes for which a state defendant could receive the death sentence to one, murder under aggravating circumstances.

Ward's human rights concern also included an effort to establish a Human Development Commission, originally proposed to his Senate colleagues in 1969.[54] The proposal did not pass the Senate, but the legislature subsequently created such a commission after Ward left the Senate.[55] Reflecting his long-standing commitment to civil rights,

Ward also opposed in 1971 a Congressional District Plan adopted by the Senate that disenfranchised black voters in the Fifth Congressional District (the district in which Andrew Young and John Lewis later won congressional seats). Ward chided the Senate as follows:

> The plan is especially unfair for the black people of the state of Georgia who constitute over one million people. . . . The Fifth District is particularly arbitrary and discriminatory as it relates to black people in Atlanta and Fulton County. . . . The new plan is a deliberate scheme to dilute the black vote in the Fifth District.[56]

Such excerpts from Ward's years of human and civil rights advocacy in the Senate are characteristic, but certainly not exhaustive, examples of his commitment and leadership. They do help explain, however, his popularity that won him constant reelection: For ten years, Ward's constituents continued to choose him for their state senator. Moreover, Ward succeeded in garnering support across racial lines. For the first three elections Ward was elected by a majority white district; for the last two elections, a majority black district (reflecting the effect of redistricting as well as population shifts).

During the period of his Senate service, Ward left the Hollowell law firm, to become deputy city attorney in 1969 and in 1970 to open his own legal practice. While practicing law in his own firm, he continued to focus on general civil litigation, as well as real estate and commercial law. During that time he represented the estate of the late Dr. Martin Luther King, Jr., and the Martin Luther King, Jr., Center for Social Change. Ward handled the initial incorporation of the predecessor organization to the King Center and represented it for two years. Continuing to show his commitment to civil rights, Ward also represented the Atlanta Chapter of the NAACP and the Atlanta Urban League in various business matters during the period he worked as a sole practitioner.[57] Ward also served as Assistant Fulton County Attorney from 1971 to 1974. In these varied roles, he continued to reveal his acumen as a litigator, which he had continually developed since his auspicious start as a partner with Donald Hollowell.

In one notable case in 1970, *Flanigan v. Preferred Development Corporation*, Ward represented the Mayor and Board of Aldermen of the City of Atlanta. The lawsuit challenged the zoning ordinances of the City of Atlanta and the power of the mayor to veto zoning ordinances. Ward ultimately represented the Mayor and Board of Aldermen before the Supreme Court of Georgia, in which the court reversed the decision of the lower court that abrogated the mayor's veto power. The particular significance of this case is that the Supreme Court upheld the power of the mayor to veto zoning ordinances, an important judicial precedent in one of the nation's largest- and fastest-growing cities with an increasing minority population.[58]

Given such a varied and energetic commitment, by 1974 Ward had distinguished himself as an attorney, civil rights activist, and legislator. In the latter role, he became respected for his leadership within the legislature, both on the floor and in committees. He rendered able service on the Senate Business, Trade and Commerce Committee; the County and Municipal Government Committee; the Penal and Correctional Affairs Committee; and, for seven years, the Senate Judiciary Committee.

Ward's outstanding service in the Senate and his active role in the Democratic Party also led to his selection as a delegate to the famous (or infamous) 1968 Democratic National Convention in Chicago. Despite the selection of Ward and his colleague, Leroy Johnson, Georgia's 107-man delegation was predominantly white and included only six blacks in a state that comprised a black population of 25 percent. Julian Bond, an outspoken civil rights activist, Ben Brown, and a few other political leaders opposed the predominantly white delegation led by supporters of Georgia's notoriously segregationist governor, Lester Maddox. Bond and Brown, who joined a group of prominent white liberal political leaders and labor organizers, formed a rival group of delegates. After much political wrangling and heated exchange, the challenge delegation won almost half of Georgia's delegate votes, prompting Maddox and some other regular delegates to walk out of the convention, and catapulting Bond to national visibility. The rival delegates, some of whom had not even been admitted to the convention floor, subsequently joined Ward, Johnson, and several of the regular delegates who had not walked out in protest.[59]

Political considerations aside, Ward's success in breaking into nontraditional roles for blacks had placed him in a position whereby friends, civil rights advocates, and even his former campaign manager opposed his having joined the conservative, white-establishment delegation. Ward recalled that before the convention, the SCLC and NAACP sought to dissuade him, Johnson, and the other black members from participating in the regular delegation, and instead resign and demand more black representation. However, Ward, who had become only the second black elected to the general assembly less than four years earlier, took the position that "it was a gain to have as many [blacks] as we had."[60] Whereas Ward was a close friend of Bond and Brown and the rival group did not target him personally, nonetheless, Ward, known as a civil rights advocate, acknowledges that it was an awkward position for him.[61]

While one can retrospectively debate whether Ward and other blacks should have resigned from the Maddox-led delegation, any objective and fair analysis supports the principles of the challenge delegation, which objected to the disenfranchisement of black Georgians. Although Ward certainly was not identified with Maddox's segregationist stands, it was a strange twist of fate that in this situation, his refusal to resign and oppose the Maddox-led delegation placed him in a position of antithesis to his own civil rights beliefs. However, despite his choice, which went against the grain of civil rights leaders and his previous advocacy, Ward was reelected in 1970 and 1972 to the Georgia Senate in a majority black district. No doubt, his record as a civil rights pioneer and advocate continued to resonate with his constituents.

Fortuitously, Ward's first term in the Georgia Senate coincided with Senator Jimmy Carter's last term in that body. According to Ward, on the first day of the term, Carter congratulated him on his election and offered any assistance that he could provide. Ward stated in an interview with the author that Carter's intelligence and independence impressed him, and that the Atlanta newspapers had rated Carter as one of the five outstanding members of the Senate. Ward also stated that he generally shared Senator Carter's interests in education and other progressive proposals, often voting with him on proposed legislation.[62]

After Jimmy Carter became governor in 1971, Ward, as a state senator, developed a close working relationship with him and supported many of his programs and initiatives, some of which were hotly contested in the senate. One of the governor's top priorities was the reorganization of the executive branch of state government, which, when adopted, resulted in a substantial reduction of state agencies. Another priority of Carter's was the preservation of Georgia's natural resources and historical sites, opposing projects he considered damaging to the environment. Governor Carter's efforts also included the improvement and upgrading of prison facilities in Georgia, an issue of unfortunately particular significance to black Georgians, who constituted a disproportionately large percentage of the prison population (and still do). Explaining his fervent support for Governor Carter, Ward stated that he deemed Carter one of the most resourceful persons he had encountered in public office, a man genuinely committed to human rights, coinciding with his own passion for human rights.[63]

By the 1974 session of the General Assembly, the legislature created a new superior court judgeship in Fulton County. Senator Leroy Johnson sponsored the bill to create the judgeship. Carter appointed a judge on the Civil Court of Fulton County to the new Superior Court judgeship and appointed Ward to the vacant civil court position. State law prohibited Ward from being appointed to the new Superior Court position, as the legislature created that position during a legislative session in which he served. Nonetheless, there was some controversy surrounding the issue.

Georgia Legislative Black Caucus members, including senior member Leroy Johnson, contended that the caucus influenced the passage of the bill to create the new judgeship with the express purpose of gaining the Ward appointment. Ben Brown, a prominent member of the Georgia Legislative Black Caucus, stated that "Carter had a commitment to the caucus to integrate the judicial system," while another caucus member, Fulton County representative Billy McKinney, said that Carter "made a legislative tradeoff on the final day of the session to insure that Ward would get the appointment."[64] Other caucus members stated that Carter had "committed" himself to making the Ward appointment as part of a promise to appoint blacks to high court positions.[65]

Black Caucus members thus generally saw Carter's appointment of Ward as the fulfillment of a longtime promise to integrate the higher echelons of the state government. On the other hand, the *Atlanta Constitution* asserted that Carter's appointment was a move to win favor with state representative Julian Bond, the nationally prominent black leader who had an avid interest in running for Ward's senatorial seat, but not against Ward.[66] Political forecasters contended that Carter would benefit from Bond's considerable influence if Carter were to pursue his strong ambitions for national office. In response, Carter noted his longstanding admiration for Ward, praised Ward's competence, and resolutely stated that his judicial appointment was based strictly on merit. When the author raised the matter with Ward, Ward stated that while he was not aware of Carter's aspiration for national office at the time, he was certain that his appointment did not result from a political deal. However, he disclosed that before the legislature convened for the 1974 session, Carter had called him to the governor's office and informed him that if a judicial vacancy occurred in Fulton County before the end of his term as governor, he would appoint Ward to a judgeship.[67]

After a period of political commentaries and speculations on reasons for Ward's anticipated appointment, in May, 1974, in a historic and progressive move, Governor Carter appointed Ward to the vacancy on the Fulton County Civil Court (now State Court), making him the highest-ranking black judicial official in the state. This appointment represented the first time in history a governor had appointed a black person to a judgeship in Georgia. Ward's swearing-in as judge of the civil court took place before a standing-room-only crowd in the House chambers in the state capitol building. In remarks before the formal swearing-in, Governor Carter reflected on the appropriateness of Ward's triumph. Carter said:

> Senator Ward, many years ago, in a different age, under different circumstances, attempted to enroll in the University of Georgia and was denied that opportunity because he was black. I am very proud today to be participating in this ceremony and the selection of a man without regard to race. It's very gratifying to me to be able to choose him strictly on his own personal merits.[68]

Despite political speculations that Ward's race played a part in his judicial appointment, the record showed a scholar who graduated with honors from Morehouse College, who excelled at the Northwestern University School of Law, and who had demonstrated exceptional acumen as a lawyer and solid achievement as an elected official.

Ward's wife, Ruth, who had been so instrumental in supporting Ward since his days in law school, joined him for the swearing-in ceremony. During an interview with the author, Ward credited her with contributing significantly to his education and career: "She helped me get through Northwestern School of Law . . . she completely supported my efforts as a lawyer, civil rights lawyer, and as a state senator."[69] Tragically, however, she was not destined to be a mainstay of his subsequent judicial career. Less than two years after his appointment to the civil court judgeship, on February 17, 1976, a nineteen-year-old next-door neighbor, Randy Darnell Mitchell, murdered Ward's wife Ruth in a random act of violence, the day before her fiftieth birthday. With no apparent motive, Mitchell entered the couple's home near Morehouse College and Atlanta University, Ward's college alma maters. Ward returned home from work and found his wife lying face down in the study of their home with multiple stab wounds. According to Detective Sidney Dorsey, Mitchell became a prime suspect when samples of his blood type were found in the Ward home. Also, blood of Ruth Ward's type was found on a pair of shoes belonging to Mitchell. Atlanta police arrested Mitchell one month after the slaying; he was tried, convicted of Ruth Ward's murder, and sentenced to life imprisonment.[70]

Ruth Ward's tragic, senseless death was unquestionably the most devastating experience of Horace Ward's life. But despite this personal tragedy, Ward continued his service on the bench; with all of the support Ruth had provided him, Ward said he knew she would have wanted him to do so.[71] And in January 1977, Governor George Busbee, recognizing Ward's astuteness as a judge, appointed him to the Fulton County Superior Court.[72] In an event that Georgia's political leaders hailed as "a milestone occasion" in state history, Ward was sworn in on January 25, 1977, by Governor Busbee in a special ceremony before a packed senate chamber in the state capitol. Before such dignitaries as Mayor Maynard Jackson and members of the General Assembly in which he had served for ten years, the poor kid who grew up in La Grange and was denied entrance to the state law school pledged to "administer justice without respect to person and do equal rights to the poor and rich." The audience gave him a standing ovation, undoubtedly reflecting its appreciation of his historic journey: from victim of racial injustice to litigator, to senator, to jurist. Ward's only regret, as he said during the ceremony, was that his wife, Ruth, "is not here to share the moment with me."[73]

CHAPTER 7 NOTES

[1]Taylor Branch, *Parting the Waters: America in the King Years 1954-1963* (New York: Simon and Schuster, 1988), 351-352; "Negroes Agree to Halt Sit-ins for 30 Days Here," *Atlanta Journal*, October 23, 1960, 18. For more information on the 1960s Atlanta student movement and two of its emerging leaders, Lonnie King and Julian Bond, see Howell Raines, *My Soul is Rested: Movement Days in the Deep South Remembered* (New York: G. P. Putnam's Sons, 1977), 83-93.

[2]"Rich's Declines to Prosecute Pastor King on Sit-in Count," *Atlanta Journal*, October 24, 1960, 4.

[3]*King v. State*, 119 S.E. 2d 77, 79 (Ga. App. 1961).

[4]Raines, op. cit., 90.

[5]Ernest Vandiver, interview with author, August 14, 1996, Sky Valley, GA; Branch, op. cit., 359, 367.

[6]Mike Edwards, "Telegrams About Dr. King, Pro and Con, Pour In," *Atlanta Journal*, October 26, 1960, 2.

[7]Branch, op. cit., 374–375; Raines, op. cit., 90, 94–95.

[8]Margaret Shannon and Gordon Roberts, "King at Reidsville as Hearing Held," *Atlanta Journal*, October 26, 1960, 1, 2, 18; Margaret Shannon and Fred Powledge, "King Fights Term on Driving Charge," *Atlanta Journal*, October 25, 1960, 7.

[9]*King v. State*, 110 S.E. 2d 77, 81 (Ga. App. 1961).

[10]Ibid.

[11]Margaret Shannon and Douglas Kiker, "Out on Bond, King to Name Choice," *Atlanta Journal*, October 28, 1960, 4.

[12]*Cobb v. State*, 126 S.E. 2d 231, 233 (Ga. 1962).

[13]Ibid.

[14]Louise Hollowell and Martin Lehfeldt, *The Sacred Call: A Tribute to Donald Hollowell— Civil Rights Champion* (Winter Park, FL: Four-G Publishers, 1997), 145; William Osborne, "Commutation Hearing Due in Case of Jasper Slayer, 15," *Atlanta Journal*, August 17, 1961, 32; *Cobb v. State*, op. cit., 597.

[15]Leon F. Litwack, *Trouble in Mind: Black Southerners in the Age of Jim Crow* (New York: Alfred A. Knopf, 1998), 291.

[16]"Lynching," *The Crisis*, March 1915, 225–228.

[17]Litwack, op. cit., 291; Robert L. Zangrando, *The NAACP Crusade against Lynching, 1909-1950* (Philadelphia: Temple University Press, 1980), 8.

[18]Hollowell and Lehfeldt, op. cit., 145–146; *Cobb v. State*, 126 S. E. 2d 231, 239 (Ga. 1962).

[19]Charles Longstreet Weltner, *Southerner* (Philadelphia: J. B. Lippincott, 1966), 43–44.

[20]Hollowell and Lehfeldt, op. cit., 147.

[21]*Cobb v. State*, op. cit., 237 (affirming denial of new trial).

[22]Hollowell and Lehfeldt, op. cit.

[23]*Cobb v. State*, op. cit.; *Cobb v. State*, 133 S. E. 2d 596, 601 (Ga. 1963), denying extraordinary motion for new trial; *Cobb v. Balkom*, 339 F. 2d 95 (5th Cir. 1964); *Cobb v. State*, 222 Ga. 733 (1966); *Cobb v. State*, 389 S. Ct. 12 (1967), relying on *Whitus v. State of Georgia*, 385 U.S. 545 (1967); Hollowell and Lehfeldt, op. cit.

[24]*Norris v. State of Alabama*, 55 S. Ct., 294 U.S. 587 (1934); James Goodman, *Stories of Scottsboro* (New York: Pantheon Books, 1994), 243, 249.

[25]*Harris v. Gibson*, 322 F. 2d 780 (5th Cir. 1963).

[26]President Jimmy Carter appointed Griffin Bell to the position of U.S. Attorney General in 1977. For more information on Griffin Bell, see Griffin Bell, interview with Clifford Kuhn and William L. Bost, June 12, 1990, Georgia State University, Special Collections, Box B-1; Folder 4.

[27]*Stell v. Savannah-Chatham County Board of Education*, 333 F. 2d 55 (5th Cir. 1964); *Harris v. Gibson*, op. cit.

[28]*Bell et al. v. Fulton/DeKalb Hospital Authority*, Federal District Court for Northern

District of Georgia, Civil Action #7966 (1964), settled out of court.

[29] *Bell v. Georgia Dental Association*, 231 F. Supp. 299 (N.D. Ga. 1964).

[30] Ibid., 300.

[31] Ibid., 301.

[32] Civil Action No. 1523, (N.D. Ga., Rome Division, 1964); Horace T. Ward, "Ten Significant Litigated Matters," unpublished manuscript, 1998, personal papers of Judge Horace T. Ward.

[33] Rome Sit-in Cases, *Viola Lions et al.* These cases were not reported in law reports. See Ward, "Ten Significant Litigated Matters," op. cit.

[34] *Alexander v. Bibb Transit Company*, C.A. no. 1822 (M.D. Ga. 1962); *Taylor v. City of Augusta*, Civil Action No. 972 (S.D. Ga. 1962); Van J. Malone, interview with author, Macon, GA., May 1, 2001.

[35] "39th District Convention Endorses Ward for Senate," *Atlanta Inquirer*, August 22, 1964, 12; "39th District Convention Set for Tonight," *Atlanta Daily World*, August 18, 1964, 3.

[36] "Ward Wins Senate Race," *Atlanta Inquirer*, September 12, 1964, 1, 3.

[37] Horace Ward, interviews with author, Atlanta, GA, November 30, 1998, and February 13, 2001.

[38] "Fund Launched for Ward Race," *Atlanta Inquirer*, September 19, 1964, 3.

[39] "Our Choice for 38th, 39th Senators," *Atlanta Daily World*, October 25, 1964, 6.; "Straight Demo Vote: LBJ All the Way," *Atlanta Inquirer*, October 24, 1964, 1, 4.

[40] "In a Critically Important Election, the Democrats Offer the Best Choice," *Atlanta Constitution*, November 2, 1964, 4.

[41] "Atlanta Elects Two Negro Senators: Turnout of 80% Stops 'Goldwaterites'," *Atlanta Inquirer*, November 7, 1964, 1, 2.

[42] "Help Get Out the Vote, Don't Be Confused; Vote Straight Democratic Ticket," *Atlanta Inquirer*, October 23, 1964, 1.

[43] "In a Critically Important Election," op. cit.

[44] "Atlanta Elects Two Negro Senators," op. cit.

[45] Horace Ward, interview with author, Atlanta, GA, August 22, 1994.

[46] Leroy Johnson, interview with author, Atlanta, GA, December 17, 1996; Nicholas C. Chriss, "Senator Ward Says He'll 'Play Role of Freshman'," *Atlanta Daily World*, January 12, 1965, 4.

[47] Johnson, interview, op. cit.

[48] Ibid.

[49] Journal of the Senate of the State of Georgia at Regular Session, January 12-February 21, 1970, Atlanta, GA.

[50] Horace Ward, interview with author, Atlanta, GA, May 28, 1999.

[51] Georgia Laws, 1973 Session, City of Atlanta, Board of Education Reorganized, Etc., No. 52 (Senate Bill No. 49); City Charter, City of Atlanta, Adopted by General Assembly and Approved by Governor, March 16, 1973, City of Atlanta Charter Com-

mission; City of Atlanta Election, October 2, 1973, and City of Atlanta Runoff Election, October 16, 1973, Summary Reports.

[52]Journal of the Senate, op. cit., January 11-March 12, 1965. The Senate Capital Punishment Committee issued a report in 1966. Data supplied by the Georgia State Board of Corrections contained in the report show legal executions in Georgia between 1924-1964 as follows: for murder, 75 white males, 267 colored males, 1 colored female; for rape, 3 white males, 63 colored males; for robbery by force, 6 colored males. Of the total 415 executions, 333 were blacks.

[53]Ibid., January 8-March 16, 1973.

[54]Ibid., January 13-March 26, 1969.

[55]Horace Ward, "Politics and the State Senate," unpublished manuscript, 1998, 12-13; Horace T. Ward Personal Papers. Horace Ward, interview with author, Atlanta, GA, February 13, 2001.

[56]Journal of the Senate of the State of Georgia at the Extraordinary Session, September 24-October 8, 1971, Atlanta, GA.

[57]Horace Ward, letter to author, January 6, 1999.

[58]*Flanigan v. Preferred Development Corporation*, 226 Ga. 267 (1970).

[59]Roger M. Williams, *The Bonds: An American Family* (New York: Atheneum, 1971), 241-245; Ward, interview, February 13, 2001, op. cit.

[60]Ward, interview, February 13, 2001, op. cit.

[61]Ward, interview, October 29, 2000, op. cit.

[62]Ward, interview, May 28, 1999, op. cit.

[63]Ibid.

[64]Rex Granum, "Carter Names Senator Ward as Fulton Judge," *Atlanta Constitution*, May 4, 1974, A-5.

[65]Ibid.; Johnson, interview, op. cit.

[66]Granum, op. cit.; Julian Bond grew up in Pennsylvania where his father (Dr. Horace Mann Bond) was president of Lincoln University and a prominent champion of racial justice. Following his father's example of activism, Julian Bond, while in his early twenties, became cofounder of two significant civil rights groups—the Atlanta Committee on Appeal for Human Rights and the Student Nonviolent Coordinating Committee (SNCC); he also played a significant role in establishing the progressive black newspaper *Atlanta Inquirer*. Bond was elected to the Georgia General Assembly in 1966, first gaining national attention when the Georgia legislature refused to seat him because of his public endorsement of SNCC's opposition to the Vietnam War. Bond ardently defended his right to his seat and the U.S. Supreme Court unanimously ruled that the Georgia legislature had violated his right of free expression. On the floor of the 1968 Democratic Convention, Bond became the Democratic Party's first black nominee for the U.S. vice presidency, although the convention declared him ineligible due to his youth. Bond's U.S. Supreme Court victory, his political shrewdness, and his ascension to civil rights leadership made

him into a rallying figure for the rebuilding of grassroots support in the Democratic Party. See George R. Metcalf, *Up from Within: Today's New Black Leaders* (New York: McGraw-Hill Book Company, 1971), 144, 153, 164, 171; John Neary, *Julian Bond: Black Rebel* (New York: William Morrow and Company, 1971), 13, 25, 36, 46, 90; Barbara Carlisle Bigelow et al., "Julian Bond, Civil Rights Activist, Politician," *Contemporary Black Biography* (Detroit, MI: Gale Research International, 1992), 22-27; Howell Raines, op. cit.; Roger M. Williams, *The Bonds: An American Family* (New York: Atheneum, 1971).

[67] Ward, interview, May 28, 1999, op. cit.

[68] Governor James Earl Carter, remarks at the swearing-in ceremony of Horace T. Ward as Fulton County Civil Court Judge, Georgia State Capitol Building, Atlanta, GA, May 1974.

[69] Ward, interview, May 28, 1999, op. cit.

[70] James D. Heath, "Vicious Slaying of Judge Horace Ward's Wife Probed By Police," *Atlanta Daily World*, March 19, 1976, 1; Yvonne Shinhoster, "Wednesday Hearing Set for Mrs. Ward's Accused Killer," *Atlanta Daily World*, March 21 1976, 1, 4; "Stepped Up Probe Gets Break in Ward Slaying," *Atlanta Inquirer*, March 20, 1976, 1; Ed Jahn, "Officer Says Ward Suspect Confessed," *Atlanta Journal*, March 24, 1976, A-3; "Teen Convicted of Ward Killing," *Atlanta Journal*, August 19, 1976, A-2.

[71] Ward, interview, May 28, 1999, op. cit.

[72] David Morrison, "Ward Becomes 1st Black Georgia Superior Court Judge," *Atlanta Constitution*, January 25, 1977, A-2. (Romae Turner Powell, appointed to Fulton County Juvenile Court by judges on the Fulton Superior Court in 1973, became the first black person to preside over a state court in Georgia.)

[73] Ibid.

Ward's Culminating Triumph: State and Federal Jurist

In the years when Ward was pursuing his lawsuit against the University of Georgia, Attorney General Eugene Cook, supported by segregationist Georgia governors, adamantly defended segregation in Georgia and vowed to maintain the status quo against all odds. Cook dubbed Ward and his supporters, "a few irresponsible people and outsiders."[1] As fate would have it, Ward and several of those so-called "irresponsible people" achieved unparalleled success, attaining high positions in government, law, and politics. In many cases, just a few years after their efforts dismantled legal segregation, they became government-appointed arbiters of justice.

Horace Ward was an outstanding exemplar in this process of significant change. Having already achieved a noteworthy record as a litigator and state senator, with civil rights issues heading his agenda of priorities, in 1974 Ward made history as the first African American state civil court judge appointed in Georgia. A few appointments of blacks to lower court judgeships such as traffic and juvenile court appointments had occurred, but a gubernatorial appointment of an African American to a trial court judgeship was a "first" for Georgia as well as Ward. Then-governor Jimmy Carter's admiration of and friendship with Ward was, of course, a significant factor in his selection of Ward for this historic appointment, but so was Ward's record of legal and political achievement for the preceding fifteen years, which had created widespread respect for

Ward among Georgia's leadership, including former adversaries (or even enemies).

Ward's actual term of service on the Fulton County Civil Court began on July 1, 1974, following the expiration of his predecessor's term. The entire court consisted of five judges who had broad civil jurisdiction, but criminal jurisdiction restricted to misdemeanor prosecutions. During the next two and one-half years, Ward presided over a wide range of lawsuits between private litigants, covering the domain of the civil law field (excepting equity, domestic relations, land title, and personal injury cases). The cases he handled, though numbering several hundred, were not of historical significance. Moreover, civil court judgments were not then and are not now published in any official law reports, unless challenged on appeal—a matter we shall return to when considering Ward's next judicial appointment. It is thus Ward's precedent-setting appointment to this position that is, in itself, of main significance. Providing Ward a judicial apprenticeship, it also served to establish for him a record of fairness and competence that earned the respect of colleagues, professional organizations, and political leaders. As a result, within three years he was recognized as a candidate for higher judicial appointment.

That appointment came in January 1977 when Governor George Busbee appointed him judge of Fulton County Superior Court. In the case of this appointment, merit alone was the criterion, since Busbee, while not the kind of close personal acquaintance and supporter of Ward that Carter was, nonetheless recognized Ward's legal expertise, dedication, and hard-won professional respect. His selection of Ward was based upon close review of a list of nominees furnished by the Judicial Nominating Commission of the State of Georgia.[2] But just as Ward's appointment by Governor Jimmy Carter to the civil court bench was a historic event, so was Governor Busbee's appointment of Ward to the Fulton County Superior Court judgeship: Ward, on January 25, 1977, became the first African American appointed to a Superior Court judgeship in Georgia.

Ward continued to develop his judicial acumen and reputation during his precedent-setting appointment to the superior court judgeship. Similar to his historic civil court service, the cases he adjudicated, though much more important, were generally not of historical significance. In the superior court, the main trial court in Georgia, Ward held a general jurisdiction that covered the full spectrum of state cases. His civil cases included tort actions, domestic relations, equity cases, and appeals from lower courts and state agencies. In addition to this array of civil cases, Ward tried a multitude of felony criminal cases such as murder, rape, armed robbery, arson, and larceny. The hundreds of such cases he tried as a superior court judge provided a higher level of judicial apprenticeship than the civil court cases—an important learning and proving ground that positioned him for his highest judicial appointment almost three years later.

Evidence of Ward's success in both civil and superior courts can be determined from the percentage of rulings sustained upon appeal. As with the civil courts, superior court judgments (notwithstanding their manifestly greater importance) are not published in official reports; however, when either civil or superior court cases are appealed, rulings of the appellate courts are published. An examination by the author of Ward's cases thus reported reveals that appellate courts affirmed both his civil and superior court judgments in a substantial majority of the cases appealed: The Georgia Court of Appeals or the Georgia Supreme Court affirmed Ward's decisions in 74 percent of the reported cases; affirmed in part and reversed in part his decisions in 9 percent of the cases; and reversed his decisions in 17 percent of the cases.[3]

The cumulative affirmation by appellate courts of more than three-fourths of Ward's rulings represents a significantly high percentage, well exceeding the judicial norm. In fact, a November 1979 article in the *Atlanta Constitution* even went so far as to assert that "a survey of court records by the *Atlanta Constitution* found that Ward has been overturned on appeal fewer times on a percentage basis than almost all of his colleagues."[4]

Despite such evidence of judicial competence, some lawyers were critical of the length of time often taken by Ward in issuing his rulings. By 1979, according to Fulton County court records, Ward still had 794 cases pending trial or judgment, more than any other of Fulton County's eleven superior court judges. However, the undisputed gravity of Ward's judicial deliberations may be regarded more as a virtue than an implied lack of timely effort. As noted above, the *Atlanta Constitution* was impressed by Ward's high percentage of sustained rulings.[5] In a subsequent *Atlanta Constitution* article, an experienced Atlanta lawyer said, "Horace is a very sensitive man, and he hates to make anyone unhappy, and he hates to make mistakes, and that's one reason why it takes him forever to rule on a case."[6] In a recent interview with the author, prominent attorney Charles S. Johnson III (also current chair of the Atlanta Bar Association's Bar Poll Committee) questioned the criticisms of Ward for judicial tardiness: "If the purpose of justice is to be correct, isn't it better to issue a careful and correct ruling? I prefer to characterize Judge Ward as a scholar who is deliberate and careful, as opposed to slow."[7]

Notwithstanding such criticism, the primary conclusion to be drawn is that by 1979 Ward, in his first two historic judgeships, had developed a reputation as a meticulous adjudicator whose judicial temperament, fairness, and dedication were winning him praise and respect—in the legal community, and among the press and public officials. And in that year, fortuitously or perhaps providentially, came the occasion for a third historic, culminating judicial appointment for this leader, no longer a foot soldier, in the cause of legal justice—and one that would, finally, allow him to adjudicate civil rights cases, many of them highly publicized.

In 1978 the U.S. Congress approved five new federal judgeships in the United States District Court for the Northern District of Georgia. The United States District Court is the trial court in the federal judicial system created under Article III of the United States Constitution, and extends lifetime tenure to judges. The court handles federal cases such as civil rights, securities, and antitrust cases. In 1979, Jimmy Carter, by then in his third year as the president of the United States, appointed Horace T. Ward to one of these judgeships. As a result, Ward made history once more by becoming Georgia's first black U.S. District Court judge. Ward's brilliance and outstanding legal track record were, of course, prime factors in his appointment to this important benchship. But his cordial relationship of mutual respect with the politically liberal Carter certainly proved helpful. President Carter appointed not only the very first African Americans to federal judgeships in the South, but appointed more African Americans to the federal bench than all previous presidents combined.[8]

For Ward, who had already proven his mastery of legal skills in the courtroom and who had earlier won the support and confidence of the electorate in his senatorial district, the confidence shown him by the highest executive officials in both the state and federal governments marked the culmination and validation of everything for which he had worked. Ward's appointment to the United States District Court bench was a powerful rebuttal to everything that University of Georgia officials had said about him during his quest to enter the UGA Law School. In another of many instances of poetic justice that marked Ward's struggles and triumphs, Carter's appointment placed him behind the bench in the same venue—the U.S. District Court for the Northern District of Georgia—in which his lawsuit to enter the University of Georgia had been lost in 1957.

In perhaps one of the most remarkable turns of events, U.S. Senator Herman Talmadge, the former virulently segregationist governor who had unleashed the state treasury to keep Ward out of the UGA Law School, not only supported Ward's confirmation, but actually nominated him for the federal judgeship. Under a tradition of senatorial courtesy, a state's two U.S. senators must approve new district court judges before they are appointed by the president.[9] Accordingly, the Federal Merits Review Council for the Northern District of Georgia screened a large number of nominees for the new judgeships, furnishing Senators Talmadge and Sam Nunn with a list of well-qualified candidates.

In an interview with the author, Talmadge noted that he had first considered another black attorney from one of Georgia's most prestigious law firms. However, Talmadge said that after consulting with several black constituents concerning the appointment, they opposed the candidate because they wanted not only an able jurist, but also someone who "had marched" and been part of the civil rights movement. That consideration led Talmadge, the pragmatic politician, to nominate Ward. Summing up this remarkable reversal, Talmadge exclaimed, "Well, I kept him out of the University of Georgia Law School, but made him a federal judge!"[10] While such a statement may be viewed as grandstanding on Talmadge's part, those who understand the system acknowledge that even with Ward's outstanding credentials and record, the support from both of his home senators was pivotal for his United States Senate confirmation. Ward has acknowledged that Talmadge's support of his nomination may have been politically pragmatic, but also that he would not have been confirmed without that support.[11]

Talmadge maintained his support for Ward despite opposition from some lawyers who contended that Ward did not have the background to preside over federal cases. Ward recalled that the opposition asserted that he had only been a general practitioner with some civil rights experience, but may not have had sufficient experience in some of the more complicated areas of the law such as antitrust, income tax, patent, and securities law. However, Ward noted that when Talmadge learned of this, he contacted Ward and stated that he would stand by his appointment unless Ward withdrew or the president would not support him.[12]

While Talmadge's support for Ward was powerful testimony to Ward's achievements as a lawyer and a jurist, the changing political climate and the emergence of black political power also influenced that support. By 1979, when the United States Senate confirmed Ward as a district court judge, Congress had long since enacted the 1965 Voting Rights Act, and its enforcement over the years had helped blacks make important political gains. In Georgia, black voter influence was now significant and Talmadge, consequently, had drastically changed his stance on race matters—indeed, to such an extent that the predominantly black Morris Brown College awarded him an honorary degree in 1975. [13] Talmadge, however, has insisted that he had never had any animosity toward blacks and has attempted to explain his segregationist actions solely in terms of political survival and the racial customs of the time. Defending his actions that thwarted Ward's efforts to enter the University of Georgia, Talmadge said,

> The mood of the state at that time [the 1950s] was overwhelmingly in favor of segregation, particularly in the white schools. I was elected on a platform to preserve segregation. My position as governor of Georgia was that he [Ward] was black. The laws prohibited integration of the blacks and that is the policy that I followed. [14]

Talmadge, who ran successful gubernatorial and senatorial campaigns with the frequent use of racial demagoguery and even proposed new laws to disfranchise black voters, exemplified the massive resistance to racial equality during the 1950s and 1960s. [15] However, during the author's interview with Talmadge, just as he attributed his earlier segregationist policies to prevailing custom and law, Talmadge concluded that general changes in racial attitudes and customs accounted for actions such as his nomination of Ward for the federal judgeship. Constance Baker Motley, also in an interview, noted that Southern leaders were capable of changing their course to adjust to new political realities. Motley asserted that "they realized the Old South was either dead or dying and that if they were going to survive in their chosen profession, politics, they would have to change their oratory, which they did. Talmadge and George Wallace decided to do that." [16]

Having prevailed over the racist practices of the "Old South," Ward's academic achievements, his legal work in the civil rights movement, his personal crusade for social justice waged on the Georgia Senate floor, and his distinguished service as a civil and superior court judge culminated in his selection as a federal jurist—a lifetime appointment. On December 27, 1979, Ward was sworn in as a federal judge in the same courtroom in which Judge Hooper had dismissed his case twenty-two years earlier. Donald L. Hollowell robed him and described how Ward's early mentors and advisers, such as William Madison Boyd and Austin T. Walden, had helped to lay the foundation for this historic event.[17] Reflecting on Ward's previous struggle, Hollowell said, "I congratulate you today for myself. I congratulate you for . . . Austin T. Walden, who with me and others in this courtroom, handled your case when you were seeking to enter the University of Georgia. I congratulate you for Dr. William Madison Boyd, who worked his heart out going back and forth across this state trying to raise money to support that case."[18] It was indeed a day of triumph for Hollowell as well, who described the swearing-in ceremony for his former client and law partner as "history in the making."[19]

Ward's oath of office ceremony was a day of success and happiness, but also a time to reflect on the many challenges that both he and his supporters had overcome for him to reach this triumphant day. Ward's longtime friend, Reverend Martin Luther King, Sr., noted at the ceremony Ward's perseverance and his struggles to achieve. King said:

> I have prayed for and talked for this day. I know no man that has earned more of a right to become a Judge of this Court. He has moved up step by step and much of it has been difficult and rugged. We have much and many people to thank for this, not one, more than one, many, that helped to bring this to fruition. This is a happy day in Atlanta and in Georgia and we are looking forward to seeing more of this. It has been said by one—and I agree with it—great men need not that we praise them. The deed is to know them. So we know you whether we praise you or not.[20]

When Reverend King, Sr., talked about "many people" who helped bring to fruition Ward's appointment as Georgia's first black federal judge, he must have reflected on his own struggles and sacrifices as a civil rights leader and the ultimate sacrifice of his son, Dr. Martin Luther King, Jr. Notwithstanding the importance of Ward's own achievements, he indeed is the beneficiary of many persons (such as the Kings) who had been involved in direct-action strategies (marches, protests, sit-ins, freedom rides, etc.) to help create a social, political, and economic climate for black progress and the recognition of black achievements.[21] The combination of civil rights lawyers who destroyed the legal foundation for racial discrimination, and civil rights workers who used direct action tactics to demand constitutional guarantees such as voting rights, helped bring about the socio-political environment that made Ward's historic appointment possible. Although the quiet, reserved Horace Ward had not been involved in direct action strategies, he legally represented civil rights advocates involved in social protests such as sit-ins, boycotts, picket lines, and marches, using his legal skills to undergird those courageous actions with precedent-making court orders. Commenting on the necessity for both direct action and legal advocacy in the quest for social justice, Dr. Martin Luther King, Jr., observed, "Direct action is not a substitute for work in the courts and the halls of government . . . Indeed, direct action and legal action complement one another; when skillfully employed, each becomes more effective."[22]

Griffin Bell, former U.S. attorney general and U.S. appellate judge, who presided over the *Harris v. Gibson* school desegregation case in which Ward served as a counsel for the plaintiffs, also remarked during the oath of office ceremony on Ward's fitness for the federal judgeship, alluding to Ward's excellent service as a state judge and noting his dedication to truth and justice for all people. Russell De Bow, chair of the Judicial Council of the National Bar Association, also shared insights on Ward's outstanding success. De Bow applauded Ward's skill, service, and sacrifice and spoke of the importance of Ward's legacy, noting, "This is a story that we must tell our children."[23]

With an already impressive judicial record established during the preceding five years, Ward assumed his third historic bench appointment shortly after the swearing-in ceremony, supported by widespread professional and community respect. It was a well-deserved honor for the man who had initiated and fought a protracted legal battle to dismantle segregation in Georgia's colleges and universities. It was also the beginning of virtually a third career spanning over twenty years. As a federal judge Ward has presided over many significant cases covering essentially the entire legal spectrum, with civil rights cases several times at the forefront.

The 1981 *Georgia Association of Retarded Citizens v. McDaniel* is among the many noteworthy cases tried before Ward in which higher courts, as in his earlier civil and superior court rulings, generally sustained his decisions. The case involved a lawsuit against state and local school officials concerning the practice of limiting the education term for mentally retarded children to the traditional 180-day school year. Fundamentally a civil rights case for retarded children, the case was tried before Ward without a jury. Plaintiffs claimed that the defendants had violated two federal statutes: the Education for Handicapped Children's Act and Section 504 of the Rehabilitation Act. Ward ruled in favor of the plaintiffs and granted an injunction that prohibited school officials from refusing to provide more than 180 days of school for retarded children when their individual educational plans showed the need for more.

The effect of Ward's ruling was to provide handicapped children with year-round schooling when needed. After an unsuccessful appeal to the Eleventh Circuit Court of Appeals, which affirmed Ward's ruling, school officials appealed the case to the U.S. Supreme Court, which modified and remanded the decision of the Eleventh Circuit. On a second appeal, the Supreme Court declined further review, allowing Ward's ruling under the Education for Handicapped Children's Act to remain in effect.[24] Ward's ruling established an important judicial precedent for the civil rights of handicapped persons. In rendering the judgment, Ward must have reflected on his own civil rights struggle and his legal representation of other civil rights advocates. He noted in an interview with the author that he considers his ruling in this case to be one of his most significant judicial decisions.[25]

In addition to civil matters, Ward heard and ruled on major criminal cases. In 1985 he presided over a drug case (*United States v. Rivera*) that arose when a federal grand jury returned indictments against more than twenty-five defendants, alleging a conspiracy to distribute heroin and cocaine in the Atlanta area. The case came to trial before a jury, lasting six months before the jury decision. The prosecution originally consisted of nineteen of the indicted defendants, but the court dismissed eight before the case was submitted to the jury. The remaining eleven prosecuted were found guilty, and Ward sentenced all eleven to federal prison terms. In accordance with the jury's verdict, Ward also ordered the forfeiture to the government of significant amounts of property owned by some of the defendants. Defense attorneys appealed the case to the Eleventh Circuit Court of Appeals, but the court affirmed Ward's judgment and the convictions of ten of the eleven defendants.[26]

In another high profile criminal case, *United States v. Evans*, Ward presided over a jury trial involving a DeKalb County commissioner in 1989. The commissioner had allegedly accepted $8,000 from a government agent, acting under cover, who told the commissioner he was seeking zoning changes by the DeKalb County Board of Commissioners before which an application was pending and asked the commissioner for his assistance before paying the $8,000. The commissioner did not report the money on federal income tax returns for the year in question, and was indicted and tried for attempted extortion under the Hobbes Act and for income tax evasion. He was convicted on both the extortion and tax evasion charges. Appeals to the U.S. Court of Appeals and later to the United States Supreme Court were unsuccessful; both higher courts affirmed Ward's ruling. In affirming the decision, the Supreme Court also noted and approved Ward's instructions to the jury on the extortion charge, which the defendant had challenged.[27]

In perhaps his most dramatic case, Ward was presented the opportunity of moral and emotional recompense for his earlier struggle against the University of Georgia. In yet another of a long series of uncannily ironic twists, Ward encountered University of

Georgia officials and regents once again, but this time from the other side of the judicial bench. The occasion was a First Amendment case that led to the toppling of the University of Georgia's highest officials: the nationally reported, controversial Jan Kemp "freedom of speech" suit against the university in 1986, over which Ward presided.

In February 1982, Dr. Jan Kemp, UGA Coordinator of Developmental Studies, filed a civil rights suit in federal court against Dr. Leroy Ervin, assistant vice president for Academic Affairs and director of Developmental Studies, and Dr. Virginia Trotter, vice president of Academic Affairs, alleging that they had first demoted and subsequently fired her because she spoke out against preferential treatment of student–athletes and children of financial contributors. Kemp claimed that her dismissal violated her constitutional right to free speech, suing the university for reinstatement and compensatory and punitive damages.

Ward heard Kemp's case in 1986. Trotter and Ervin contended that there was no connection between Kemp's dismissal and her outspokenness related to student–athletes. They asserted that Kemp did not conduct adequate research, was insubordinate, and had difficulty getting along with peers and others. However, overriding objections from the defendant's attorneys, Ward allowed the plaintiff to present evidence substantiating her claim that certain athletes received favorable treatment and impugning the motives and state of mind of the administrators. The evidence showed that Trotter, by virtue of her authority as vice president, administratively transferred nine student–athletes from the developmental studies program into the regular university curriculum, though each had received a "D" in English during their fourth quarter in the program. Trotter's transfer of the nine students violated university policy requiring students in the program to achieve a minimum grade of "C" in English during the fourth quarter.[28]

Although the evidence presented by the defendants suggested that Kemp was often insubordinate and caustic, the jury, after a long trial, found that Trotter and Ervin had fired her maliciously. The jury awarded Kemp $280,000 in compensatory damages and $2.3 million in punitive damages.[29] Ward declared the following in his ruling:

> The evidence in the record supports a finding of various aspects of preferential treatment given to revenue-producing athletes (scholarship athletes) . . . While the court does not believe that the evidence presented showed that either of the defendants was motivated by evil motive or intent, the court concludes that the evidence is strong enough to support a finding that the conduct of both defendants involved reckless or callous indifference to the federally protected rights of the plaintiff.[30]

Because the University of Georgia had a strong football tradition and placed a high value on athletic glory, many Georgia alumni and football fans lamented the decision as an assault on a cherished tradition and a threat to the university's athletic pursuits. The jury decision against the university and the huge award for the plaintiff sent shock waves throughout the university community and state. Some fifteen hundred UGA boosters rallied in Atlanta after the verdict, praising the university and berating Jan Kemp.[31] The plethora of print and electronic media reports of academic abuses and preferential treatment for athletes provoked other alumni to chide the media for its coverage of the Kemp case and the resulting "terrible publicity" for the university.[32]

Ward, whose character had been besmirched by university officials some thirty-five years before, also became a target of disgruntled UGA supporters. Despite the evidence of wrongdoing and the state's mishandling of the case, university loyalists blamed the verdict on what they termed Ward's "liberal hand" in allowing the plaintiff's attorneys to present damaging evidence of official malfeasance. Surprisingly, columnist Bill Shipp, formerly the editor of the *Red and Black* who had passionately advocated Ward's admission to the UGA School of Law thirty-four years earlier, remarked rather sourly in an *Atlanta Constitution* article that Ward, "known in the courthouse trade as 'Let-it-all-hang-out Horace', stood by while UGA's skeletons publicly haunted the courtroom."[33]

Some university and state officials even asserted that Ward should have recused himself from the case because of his previous litigation against the university and the possibility of a conflict of interest that could provide the basis for a successful appeal. However, the defendants never filed any motion for Ward to recuse himself. Even Bill Shipp questioned why attorney general Michael Bowers did not intervene since, "There were good grounds to ask Judge Ward to recuse himself from the case. He had once been denied admission to the University of Georgia law school because he is black."[34] However, Ward's long-standing and well-earned reputation for fairness had apparently influenced the attorney general *not* to challenge Ward as the presiding judge. Responding to Shipp in a letter to the editor of the *Atlanta Constitution*, Michael Bowers stated that "while I disagree with Judge Ward's ruling, I believe that he is fair."[35] Given the national notoriety the Kemp case generated, Bowers undoubtedly also wanted to avoid further embarrassment to the university by reviving the issue of Ward's shameful treatment by the university in the 1950s.

Ward, characteristically, remained above the fray. While Ward let stand the judgment for compensatory damages, he declared the jury award for punitive damages excessive and that the court had a duty to keep an award within reasonable bounds. He noted, "The purpose of punitive damages is to punish and to deter; its purpose is not to destroy."[36] Ward obviously had the opportunity to let the jury award stand, thereby punishing the university for having kept him out of its law school. However, he demonstrated a charitable disinclination to vindictiveness by reducing the punitive award from $2.3 million to $400 thousand, while sustaining the compensatory award of $280 thousand. Ward simultaneously granted the motion of the defendants for a new trial, unless Kemp filed a remittitur of all punitive damage awards above the sum of $400 thousand. University officials and Kemp ultimately reached an out-of-court settlement for $1 million and cleared the path for Kemp to resume her academic position. In the aftermath of the Kemp case, the regents delayed action on renewing university president Fred Davison's contract and

ordered an audit of the developmental studies program; Davison pro-
tested the regents' delay of his contract as an insult and subsequently
resigned his position.[37] Virginia Trotter, Leroy Ervin, and several other
senior level administrators also either resigned or were forced from
their administrative positions by university officials.[38]

Ward has not discussed the Kemp case, suggesting that it would
be inappropriate for him to do so. However, displaying an uncom-
monly forgiving spirit that might be difficult for many to fathom,
Ward said in an interview with the author:

> It's best to deal in a live-and-let-live philosophy, and to stand on
> whatever foundation you have built rather than to go back and
> live in the past. I don't harbor any ill will against anyone because
> of their efforts to keep me out of the University of Georgia. I
> think they were wrong, especially on a constitutional basis; as a
> matter of fact, I know they were, but I don't live in the past. I
> know some of these people now, they're getting old like I am,
> some of them are my friends now, but I don't have any bitterness
> toward them; it would be counterproductive to do so.[39]

The fact that Ward harbors no ill will towards the university that
rejected him and officials who questioned his integrity speaks volumes about his character.

He also apparently has taken in stride, and perhaps even in good
humor (despite some initial disappointment), the criticisms of his
"judicial tardiness" that originated during his Superior Court judgeship and followed him into his federal appointment. According to a
1983 survey of attorneys by the Lawyers Club of Atlanta, the Atlanta
Bar Association, and the Gate City Bar Association, Ward had irritated attorneys with his slowness; the *Atlanta Constitution* reported
that Ward was overwhelmingly regarded as the slowest of the eleven
federal judges in his district.[40] And in a 1992 Atlanta Bar Association
survey attorneys again ranked Ward as the slowest of judges in his
rulings and docket management. On the other hand, Ward received
good marks from the attorneys for his patience, courtesy, and absence of bias in criminal and civil cases.[41]

In retrospect, it is the latter part of that survey's conclusion that has carried the most weight in characterizing Horace Ward's perceived reputation. In spite of attorneys' pique at having to wait for his rulings, those rulings have been consistently respected, even admired, and Ward has consequently won the friendship and admiration of lawyers who have appeared before him. For example, Terrence Lee Croft, who appeared before Ward in both state and federal courts, praised Ward not only for his legal insight but also for his gracious personal demeanor and his sense of fairness. Croft noted that some of the things he most appreciated about Ward were that he was a gentleman, he was courteous, and he listened. The former Atlanta Bar president said Ward exhibited those qualities on the bench, in his chambers, or on the street—to lawyers, jurors, courthouse personnel; indeed, to everyone. Speaking at a ceremony commemorating Ward's senior status as a federal judge, Croft said:

> The really interesting thing about Horace Ward as a judge is that he treats other people the way that all of us should, the way we should treat each other; and he does it all the time. He's patient, he's polite, even when he's being firm with you. He seems to look for something in fellow human beings to respect, and he finds it. If you were going to strike the mold for judicial temperament and demeanor, Horace Ward would define it.[42]

The reputation for fortitude and character established during Ward's heroic struggle to enter the University's School of Law, together with his humble manner and judicial record, won him the respect of the legal community. Summing up the views of Ward's colleagues, a fellow judge praised his sense of fairness and his desire for justice: "Horace Ward believes the best about everybody. You're dealing with somebody who's got the outlook and temperament of a saint."[43]

Ward's career as a public servant and judge has brought him into contact with many of his former segregationist adversaries, and it is an appropriate tribute to him that they praised his fitness as an able man and judge. In sharp contrast to the officials who assailed his character during his bid to enter the law school, as in the case of Talmadge's turnaround in nominating Ward for the federal judgeship, former foes now attest to Ward's impeccable character. One such convert is former assistant attorney general E. Freeman Leverett, who helped construct the state's "legalized" rejection of Ward's application to the University of Georgia. In a 1995 interview with the author, Leverett said that Ward "is a person of impeccable honesty and integrity ... an outstanding citizen, a lawyer, and a great judge."[44]

UGA law graduate Earnest Brookins, who had adamantly opposed Ward's entry to the law school while he himself was a student there, had a similar change of heart. Brookins, who had served as an investigator for the Georgia Bar investigating and interviewing Ward for admission to the Georgia Bar in 1960, said in an interview with the author that he realized that he had formed an opinion of Ward that "just didn't fit the man," and had been based on racial prejudice. Brookins said furthermore that he later formed a strong friendship with Ward and developed a high regard for him as a distinguished judge. Although in earlier times a supporter of segregation, Brookins changed his view dramatically. Unlike Southerners who still do not wish to remember the South's all-encompassing oppression of black citizens, Brookins recalled the subjugation of blacks and "how it was one of the most detrimental things we [whites] could have done. And of course it was detrimental to Horace Ward and all black people."[45]

The deeds and statements of some avowed segregationists, when juxtaposed against actions and expressed views later in their lives, seem an almost amazing phenomenon. Like former Alabama governor George Wallace, Ernest Vandiver later apologized for his attempt to thwart equality for blacks and for his "no, not one" declaration. During an interview with the author, Vandiver said:

> I made a major statement, neither my child or your child will ever go to an integrated school, no, not one. That was a statement

I should not have made . . . My friends and I sat up all night working out a campaign speech on what I should say and what I should not say. About half my friends told me I should not make that statement. The others said, "Well, you got to counteract the fellow (opponent) over here who is giving you hell." I made the wrong decision.[46]

While some political analysts have attributed such apparent reformations to political motives alone, Vandiver's apology came at a time when his political aspirations were in the distant past. Gary Roberts, in a study of Georgia's governorship from the 1940s to the 1980s, noted that the "essentially moderate Vandiver" assumed the leadership of Georgia when the time-honored traditions of Georgia were under siege and after campaign controversy characterizing him as weak on segregation. It was then that Vandiver espoused a vigorous, hardline "no, not one" rhetoric and policies such as the "Vandiver segregation bills." Vandiver, however, showed signs even during his governorship that despite such actions, he was not simply a rabid segregationist. His support of Kennedy in the 1960 election, his work behind the scenes to seek Dr. King's release from jail in 1960, and his decision not to resist the federal court order for the admission of Holmes and Hunter to the University of Georgia reveal contradictions to his strong segregationist image, although these contradictions hardly make him an advocate for social justice.[47]

Whether politics, changing times, or a change of heart accounts for Vandiver's more recent volte-face to avowed liberalism, he and other segregationists who had fought so bitterly to preserve an unjust system now typically admit they were wrong, or make the claim that they based their past actions solely on political realities. Despite such apologies and apparent reformations, however, it is hard to ignore the past. Though many racial demagogues have faded into obscurity, vestiges of their policies and institutions unfortunately linger on today.

The current status of blacks at many of Georgia's colleges and universities reflects a more subtle, but continuing pattern of discrimination. The University of Georgia itself provides a vivid example of the present inequities and underrepresentation of blacks in colleges and universities. While blacks comprised more than 30 percent of the state's population in the year 2000, of eight vice presidents, one is black; of thirteen deans, only one is black; and of the twenty-one associate deans, again only one is black. Among the more than eighty academic department heads, almost amazingly, still again only one is black, and of more than six hundred full professors, blacks number only nine. Since Hollowell, Motley, and Ward won the admission of Holmes and Hunter in 1961, the percentage of black students has grown, but their numbers also remain dismal in comparison to the percentage of blacks in the state. Among 7,602 graduate and professional students, only 434 (5.7 percent) are black, and among more than 25,000 undergraduate students, only 1,413 (5.6 percent) are black.[48] Charlayne Hunter-Gault lamented these disparities during a January 2001 visit to the UGA campus, saying, "If anyone had given Holmes and me a crystal ball into which we could have looked to the future forty years hence and seen only 6 percent students of color in a student body of thirty thousand, I think instead of walking through that arch we might have sat down and cried."[49]

National data also reflect a distressing gap between the educational status of blacks and whites. According to the 1999 edition of the Statistical Abstract of the United States, 25 percent of whites had college degrees, compared with only 14.7 percent of blacks.[50] Reflecting on the present racial inequities in America, eminent historian John Hope Franklin, appointed by President Bill Clinton to chair a presidential commission examining race matters in the United States, posited that much work still needs to be done to achieve racial justice in America. W. E. B. Du Bois prophetically stated as far back as 1903 that the problem of the twentieth century was that of the color line. Commenting on that statement, Franklin concluded that "by any standard of measurement or evaluation the problem has not been solved in the twentieth century, and thus becomes a part of the legacy and burden of the next century."[51]

While the battle to eliminate racial inequities and discrimination is far from over, Ward's hard-fought struggle to enter the public law school in his home state, his civil rights advocacy as a lawyer and legislator, and his pioneering service as a jurist won many rights for blacks and dealt a powerful blow to segregation in the Deep South. His contributions provide an enduring legacy and blueprint for continuing the struggle for social justice. The tactics of Ward and his comrades were complex and built on years of grappling with insurmountable odds, yet the guideposts they erected through their audacious advocacy illuminate the path in the struggle for social justice.[52]

In his book *Born to Rebel*, the legendary Benjamin Mays said, "Sometimes it happens that the man who stands up and fights for his rights fares far better than the man who plays it safe."[53] The track records of Ward and those who defended his cause amply substantiate Mays's thesis. In addition to Ward, three of the LDF attorneys who represented him became federal judges. President Johnson appointed Constance Baker Motley to the United States District Court for the Southern District of New York in 1966; President Richard M. Nixon appointed Robert Carter to the United States District Court for the Southern District of New York in 1972; and President John F. Kennedy appointed Thurgood Marshall to the Second Circuit Court of Appeals in 1961, with President Johnson appointing him Solicitor General of the United States in 1965. In 1967 Marshall earned the singular distinction of becoming the first African American to serve on the U.S. Supreme Court.[54]

In Georgia, Ward's former attorney, mentor, and law partner Donald Hollowell became known as "Mr. Civil Rights" and as such, a primary force in the movement to eliminate racial injustice. Hollowell's brilliance, dedication, and masterful courtroom skills made him Georgia's foremost civil rights attorney during the 1950s and 1960s, and subsequently led to his appointment as regional director of the Equal Employment Opportunity Commission—thus becoming the first black regional director of a major federal agency.[55] The so-called "agitators" of the segregationist era had not only won the battle against Jim Crow, but ironically become arbiters of justice—for all. Thurgood Marshall aptly summed up the strength, character, and purpose of such formerly maligned leaders this way: "They call us agitators, but you know what an agitator is. It's the thing in the washing machine that gets the dirt out of the linen, and that's what we're doing, getting out the dirt."[56]

Despite personal character attacks and scurrilous insinuations, these individuals do not bear hostility toward their former racist adversaries. During the author's various interviews with Motley and Hollowell, both of whom were castigated by state officials in the past as agitators, they contended that they harbor no grudges against those who maligned them and denied them or their clients equal justice. They and those who shared their struggles are champions of the human spirit with the strength to forgive their opponents. Rising above the injustices heaped upon them, they have assumed a rightful place as regional and national leaders, esteemed for their contributions to the struggle for social justice.

In an interview with Robert Benham, Chief Justice of the Supreme Court of Georgia and the second black student to graduate from the University of Georgia School of Law, Benham described the importance of Ward's contributions to the struggle for justice and those of civil rights leaders whose earlier efforts also helped pave the path for him to the chair of Chief Justice. Recalling the era when committed African American lawyers worked for unpopular causes and unpopular clients, often for little or no money, Benham declared that although those lawyers had to fight every step of the way, they were resilient and determined to make the American dream a reality for all.[57] Benham further described Ward as a person who had to sacrifice his own dreams and fight for the dreams of the next generation. Though Ward indeed realized many of his dreams later in life, he was forced to delay his legal education for many years and to endure numerous hardships in his quest for personal and societal justice. Although criticized by blacks for "moving too fast" and by whites for moving at all, Ward achieved high distinction among a panoply of movement lawyers and activists dedicated to the fight for social equity.[58]

During his long career as an attorney and judge, Ward has amassed an impressive record of successes in his advocacy for the principle of equal justice in the Deep South, and his actions stand as a model to others who face adversity in the struggle for justice. Neither impoverishment nor discrimination dissuaded Ward as he sought to educate and prepare himself for a constructive life and an exemplary, trailblazing career. His journey from a humble background in La Grange to the impressive chambers of a federal judge should remind us that wealth, power, and status are not necessarily prerequisites to the highest levels of achievement. The astonishing degree of success attained by this still relatively unsung hero is magnified when one considers that leading officials of the state of Georgia, armed with the power of its treasury, constantly battled against him for so many years. But again, Ward does not choose to nurse past hurt, but to accept it, rise above it, and even dismiss it with humor; for example, in claiming, with tongue no doubt in cheek, that he is one of the best-prepared of lawyers as a result of "spending seven years trying to get into one law school and three years trying to get out of another."[59]

Horace Ward's fight for equal justice under the law changed the course of history in various ways: from his initial lawsuit against the University of Georgia and subsequent role in Holmes and Hunter's historic case; to serving as a civil rights champion, both as an attorney and state senator for many years; to a succession of three precedent-setting judicial appointments that have established beyond question his significant achievement as a jurist. Nevertheless, in an interview with the author, Ward continued to downplay his contributions, noting that he was merely "a spear carrier and armor bearer for the more prominent lawyers."[60] Despite his modesty, his unassailable legacy shows vividly how his sense of mission, courage, and fortitude spanned his life's work and made justice a reality for countless Americans.

Two outstanding Americans whom Ward influenced discussed his impact on them in recent interviews with the author. Mary Frances Early, actually the University of Georgia's first black graduate (Master's in Music Education, 1962) and now an accomplished musician and chair of Clark Atlanta University's music department, summed up Ward's impact on her and the movement he spearheaded to open the doors for equal opportunity at the University of Georgia. "I certainly was inspired by his struggle. Although he did not get in [himself], he certainly cracked the door for others to come."[61] Early said that she had followed the *Ward* trial when she was in high school and remembered the appalling actions of the state and university officials who rejected Ward's application. She recalled Ward's remarkable perseverance against officials' evasiveness and stubbornness in denying him admission. Early emphatically declared that Ward was a main influence on her determination to overcome the obstacles she herself encountered on her way to becoming the first black student to graduate from the University of Georgia.

In 1963, thirteen years after Ward sought to enter the University of Georgia School of Law, another young and brilliant student-activist finally succeeded in integrating the law school—Chester Davenport, Jr. A Morehouse College *cum laude* graduate whose career includes service as a U.S. Justice Department official, an assistant secretary of Transportation for Policy and International Affairs, and who now serves as CEO of Envirotest Systems (the largest emissions testing firm in the United States), Davenport encountered hostility similar to that endured by Ward, with classmates shunning him when he first entered the law school. However, after the class rankings were announced midway through his first term, his standing was so high that other students asked to be his study partners, and the isolation he had experienced began to dissipate.[62] Davenport noted that Ward's example motivated him to continue the struggle that Ward had started: to gain entrance to the still all-white public law school and to complete his law degree in his home state. In an interview with the author, Davenport paid the following tribute to that example:

> He (Ward) was a great inspiration to me. I thank him for what he did in his efforts to enter the University of Georgia. Although some people say to me that I kind of paved the way for them as the first black student to graduate from the law school, Judge Ward paved the way for all of us.[63]

Irrefutably, Ward's entire career has exemplified an unequivocal refusal to accept second-class citizenship. In a speech Ward made at the 1995 Atlanta Urban League Equal Opportunity Day Dinner at which he was honored, he stated:

> I hope that I have played a role in the movement to provide and expand civil rights for all Americans. I would like to think that I have followed in the footsteps of great civil rights lawyers such as Thurgood Marshall, Constance Baker Motley, and Donald Hollowell. I certainly have given my best effort to this task.[64]

His judicial colleagues, lawyers who practiced before him, students he inspired, and countless others who enter doors that he helped open, more than confirm this modest assertion, placing him among a select group of celebrated civil rights lawyers and revered jurists.

At the height of the civil rights struggle in 1965, Dr. Martin Luther King, Jr., remarked upon the impact of activist lawyers in the struggle for freedom. King said, "The road to freedom is now a highway, because lawyers throughout the land, yesterday and today, have helped clear the obstructions, have helped eliminate road blocks by their selfless, courageous espousal of difficult and unpopular causes."[65] Given the record of Ward's selfless and courageous fight against a multitude of legal and racial obstructions, it is clear that he helped to make the road to freedom a highway. Ward's pioneering struggle to enter the University of Georgia, together with his contributions as a lawyer, public servant, and judge confirm his legacy among champions for the cause of human dignity. The contemporary reader can examine Ward's record of service as a blueprint for personal courage, resolve, and excellence in the pursuit of high goals. Those who would stop short of full achievement in the continuing struggle for social justice in America need only heed this blueprint for the ultimate goal—liberty and justice for all.

CHAPTER 8 NOTES

[1]Charles Pou, "Cook Gets Legal Aid in Fight to Keep Schools Segregated: Negro to Renew Effort to Enter University Law Unit," *Atlanta Journal*, July 8, 1955, 1, 16.

[2]The Georgia Judicial Nominating Commission is an advisory body appointed by the governor, composed of both lawyers and lay persons; its charge is to review the qualifications of candidates for gubernatorial judicial appointment and furnish the governor a slate of nominees.

[3]Ward's cases appealed to the Georgia Court of Appeals or the Georgia Supreme Court are reported variously in the following bound volumes, reviewed by the author for the period of Ward's service (including pending appeals not ruled on until as late as 1982) to determine his percentages: *Southeastern Reporter* (Minneapolis: West Publishing Company, 1974-1982); *Georgia Reports,* and *Georgia Appeals Reports* (Atlanta, GA: Harrison Company, State Publisher, 1974-1982).

[4]George Rodrigue and Linda Field, "Ward Historically Has Been in the Right Place at the Right Time," *Atlanta Constitution*, November 4, 1979, A-27.

[5]Ibid.

[6]George Rodrigue and Linda Field, "Horace Ward Confirmed as Federal Judge," *Atlanta Constitution*, December 6, 1979, C-1, 8.

[7]Charles S. Johnson, III, telephone interview with author, March 16, 2001.

[8]John Hope Franklin, *The Color Line: Legacy for the Twenty-first Century* (Columbia: University of Missouri Press, 1993), 9; Jack Greenberg, *Crusaders in the Courts: How a Dedicated Band of Lawyers Fought for the Civil Rights Revolution* (New York: Basic Books, 1994), 90.

[9]Frederick Allen, "Talmadge, Nunn Urge 5 for U.S. Judgeships," *Atlanta Constitution*, December 7, 1978, C-1, 13.

[10]Herman Talmadge, interview with author, Hampton, GA, January 23, 1995.

[11]Horace Ward, interview with author, Atlanta, GA, May 28, 1999.

[12]Ibid.

[13]James F. Cook, *The Governors of Georgia* (Macon, GA: Mercer University Press, 1995), 257.

[14]Talmadge, interview, op. cit.

[15]Roger N. Pajari, "Herman E. Talmadge and the Politics of Power," in *Georgia Governors in an Age of Change*, ed. Harry P. Henderson and Gary L. Roberts (Athens: University of Georgia Press, 1988), 88. Talmadge was able to obtain General Assembly passage of the Voter's Qualification Act in 1949, which required that voters register every four years and that every person seeking registration should correctly answer

thirty questions—a requirement imposed virtually without exception upon black voters, but not often upon whites.

[16]Constance Baker Motley, interview with author, New York, NY, March 30, 1995.

[17]Louise Hollowell and Martin Lehfeldt, *The Sacred Call: A Tribute to Donald Hollowell—Civil Rights Champion* (Winter Park, FL: Four-G Publishers, 1997), 126.

[18]U.S. District Court: Northern District of Georgia, *Oath of Office Ceremony for the Honorable Horace T. Ward,* Atlanta, GA, 1979, 27.

[19]Donald Hollowell, interview with author, Athens, GA, July 27, 1993.

[20]U.S. District Court, *Oath of Office Ceremony,* op. cit., 19-20.

[21]Library and archival sources contain several references on the civil rights efforts of Rev. Martin Luther King, Sr., and Dr. Martin Luther King, Jr. Among the rich sources are Martin Luther King, Sr., *Daddy King: An Autobiography* (New York: William Morrow, 1980); Martin Luther King, Jr., Collected Papers, Mugar Memorial Library, Boston University; David Garrow, *Bearing the Cross: Martin Luther King, Jr., and the Southern Christian Leadership Conference* (New York: William Morrow, 1986); Taylor Branch, *Pillar of Fire: America in the King Years 1963-1965* (New York: Simon and Schuster, 1998); and Clayborne Carson, *The Papers of Martin Luther King, Jr.,* 4 vols. (Berkeley: University of California Press, 1992-1997).

[22]Coretta Scott King, *The Words of Martin Luther King, Jr.* (New York: Newmarket Press, 1983), 57.

[23]U.S. District Court, *Oath of Office Ceremony,* op. cit., 12. The testimonials quoted here and above are among the most significant of many similar appreciations during the ceremony by representatives of various local, state, and national bar associations.

[24]*Georgia Association of Retarded Citizens v. McDaniel,* 511 F. Supp. 1263 (N. D. Ga. 1981); 716 F. 2d 1565 (5th Cir. 1983); 721 F. 2d 822 (5th Cir. 1983); 104 S. Ct. 3581 (1984); 740 F. 2d 902 (5th Cir. 1984); 105 S. Ct. 1228 (1985).

[25]Horace Ward, interview with author, Atlanta, GA, May 28, 1999.

[26]*United States v. Rivera;* 884 F. 2d 544 (11th Cir. 1989).

[27]*United States v. Evans,* 910 F. 2d 790 (11th Cir. 1990); 504 U.S. 255, 112 S. Ct. 1881 (1992).

[28]*Kemp v. Ervin* , 651 F. Supp., 496-499 (N.D. Ga. 1986).

[29]Ibid.

[30]Ibid., 500, 505.

[31]David Lundy, "UGA Boosters Rally in Atlanta," *Macon Telegraph and News,* April 25, 1986, A-8.

[32]Ibid.

[33]Bill Shipp, "A Questionable Defense Loses to an Award Winning Offense," *Atlanta Constitution,* February 14, 1986, A-19.

[34]Ibid.

[35]Michael J. Bowers, "Clarifications on the Kemp Trial," Letter to the Editor, *Atlanta Constitution,* February 25, 1986, A-14.

[36] Ann Woolner and David K. Secrest, "Kemp Award Cut to $680,000," *Atlanta Constitution*, April 23, 1986, A-1; for a chronology of events in the *Jan Kemp* case, see Diane K. Roberts, *The Jan Kemp Controversy: An Index to Media Coverage* (Athens, GA: University Archives, University of Georgia Libraries, 1987), iv-v.

[37] Marc Rice, "Davison Quits as UGA Chief," *Macon Telegraph and News*, March 14, 1986, A-1, A-10; John A. Crowl, "Davison Resigns as Univ. of Georgia President after Regents Again Fail to Reappoint Him," *Chronicle of Higher Education*, March 19, 1986, 37.

[38] John A. Crowl, "Ga. Defendants Lose Some Duties," *Chronicle of Higher Education*, March 26, 1986, 36; Jane O. Hansen, "UGA's Ervin Meets with Investigators of Remedial Program," *Atlanta Journal*, March 21, 1986, A-19; "Trotter, Ervin Questioned UGA Policies in '80," *Atlanta Journal and Constitution*, April 26, 1986, A-1, A-8. Despite Trotter and Ervin's assertion that they fired Jan Kemp because she caused dissension and conducted inadequate scholarly research, they did acknowledge policy violations in the developmental studies program and expressed to University System of Georgia auditors that they tried for years to limit special treatment of athletes, but failed because of pressure from the president's office and the athletic department.

[39] Horace Ward, interview with author, Atlanta, GA, August 22, 1994.

[40] Sam Heys, "Judge Horace Ward Has Made His Point in the Law," *Atlanta Constitution*, May 2, 1986, C-1. In the article Ward declined to comment on the survey other than remarking to Heys that "I was disappointed and did not think it was fully justified."

[41] According to survey results obtained by the author from the Atlanta Bar Association, Atlanta, Georgia, the 1992 survey of attorneys included 11,518 questionnaires mailed to attorneys of which 1,119 were returned. For a published report of the survey, see Liza Kaufman, *Fulton County Daily Report*, July 16, 1992, vol. 103, no. 38.

[42] U.S. District Court: Northern District of Georgia, *Ceremony Commemorating Senior Status and Portrait Presentation for the Honorable Horace T. Ward Senior Judge, United States District Court*, Atlanta, GA, 1994, 13-14.

[43] Heys, op. cit.; it may be noted that the 1986 criticisms for slowness were also offset by this kind of high praise.

[44] E. Freeman Leverett, interview with author, Elberton, GA, December 8, 1995.

[45] Earnest Brookins, interview with author, Atlanta, GA, May 16, 1995.

[46] Ernest Vandiver, interview with author, Sky Valley, GA, August 14, 1996.

[47] Gary L. Roberts, "Tradition and Consensus: An Introduction to Gubernatorial Leadership in Georgia, 1943-1983," *Georgia Governors in an Age of Change*, ed. Harry P. Henderson and Gary Roberts (Athens: University of Georgia Press, 1988), 9-10.

[48] Integrated Post Secondary Education Data System, "University of Georgia Fall Staff Survey, 2000," University of Georgia, Athens, GA; "Fall 2000: University of Georgia Enrollment Report," University of Georgia Office of Admissions. The numbers of

black senior faculty and administrators are also confirmed by the author's personal knowledge as a member of the UGA faculty.

[49]Erin McClam, "Hunter-Gault Returns to University," *Associated Press*, January 10, 2001.

[50]Christina Duff, "Racial College Degree Gap is Still Wide," *Wall Street Journal*, June 29, 1998, A-2, A-6; U.S. Census Bureau, Statistical Abstract of the United States: 1999 (119th edition) Washington, D. C.

[51]Franklin, op. cit., 5; see also William G. Bowen and Derek Bok, *The Shape of the River: Long-Term Consequences of Considering Race in College and University Admissions* (Princeton, NJ: Princeton University Press, 1998), xxii. The well-known, prophetic assertion by W. E. B. Du Bois that the global problem of the twentieth century was, and would continue to be, the "problem of the color line" may be found in his *The Souls of Black Folk* (New York: Dover Books, 1903), 9.

[52]Donald L. Hollowell, interview with author, Atlanta, GA, July 27, 1993.

[53]Benjamin E. Mays, *Benjamin E. Mays: Born to Rebel—An Autobiography* (New York: Charles Scribner's Sons, 1971), 207.

[54]Carl T. Rowan, *Dream Makers, Dream Breakers: The World of Justice Thurgood Marshall* (Boston: Little, Brown and Company, 1993), 279-286, 288-297, 298-308; Constance Baker Motley, *Equal Justice under Law: An Autobiography of Constance Baker Motley* (Union Square West, NY: Farrar, Strauss & Giroux, 1998), 212-214.

[55]Hollowell and Lehfeldt, op. cit., 210-213.

[56]Ibid., 124.

[57]Chief Justice Robert Benham, interview with author, Atlanta, GA, July 27, 1995.

[58]In addition to those whose contributions have already been highlighted, such as Thurgood Marshall, Constance Baker Motley, Donald L. Hollowell, and Austin Thomas Walden, many other civil rights lawyers could be mentioned who demonstrated inspiring personal commitment and sacrifices in the struggle for social justice. For a comprehensive discussion of these activists, see Greenberg, op. cit., and Motley, op. cit., whose books chronicle their individual contributions in detail.

[59]*Foot Soldier for Equal Justice: Horace T. Ward and the Desegregation of the University of Georgia*, ex. prod. Maurice C. Daniels and prod. Janice Reaves, for the University of Georgia Center for Continuing Education, videocassette. Horace Ward and Donald Hollowell also made helpful remarks to the author following the initial screening of this documentary, February 22, 2000.

[60]Horace Ward, interview with author, Atlanta, GA, June 29, 1994.

[61]Mary Frances Early, interview with author, Atlanta, GA, February 19, 1997.

[62]Gwen Y. Wood, *A Unique and Fortuitous Combination: An Administrative History of the University of Georgia School of Law* (Athens: University of Georgia Press, 1998), 103-104.

[63]Chester Davenport, Jr., interview with author, Atlanta, GA, August 28, 1995.

[64]Horace Ward, "My Georgia Journey," *The Atlanta Urban League's 34th Equal Opportu-*

nity Day Dinner, Atlanta, GA, November 18, 1995, 5.

[65]See Genna R. McNeil, *Groundwork: Charles Hamilton Houston and the Struggle for Civil Rights* (Philadelphia: University of Pennsylvania Press, 1983); Dr. Martin Luther King, Jr.'s quotation is from a speech to the Bar Association of the City of New York cited by McNeil in her preface, xv.

Bibliography

Books

Adair, Alvis V. *Desegregation: The Illusion of Black Progress*. New York: University Press of America, 1984.

Adell, Sandra. *Dictionary of Twentieth Century Culture: African American Culture*. Detroit, MI: Gale Research, 1996.

Anderson, Eric, and Alfred A. Moss, Jr. *Dangerous Donations: Northern Philanthropy and Southern Black Education, 1920-1930*. Columbia: University of Missouri Press, 1999.

Anderson, James D. *The Education of Blacks in the South, 1860-1935*. Chapel Hill: University of North Carolina Press, 1988.

Angelou, Maya, et al. *Essence: 25 Years of Celebrating Black Women*. New York: Harry N. Abrams, 1995.

Aptheker, Herbert, ed. *The Correspondence of W. E. B. Du Bois: Vol. I Selections, 1877-1934*. Amherst: University of Massachusetts Press, 1934.

Bartley, Numan V. *The Rise of Massive Resistance: Race and Politics in the South During the 1950s*. Baton Rouge: Louisiana State University Press, 1969.

Bass, Jack. *Unlikely Heroes: The Dramatic Story of the Southern Judges of the Fifth Circuit Who Translated the Supreme Court's Brown Decision into a Revolution for Equality*. New York: Simon and Schuster, 1981.

Bennett, Lerone, Jr. *Forced into Glory: Abraham Lincoln's White Dream*. Chicago: Johnson Publishing Company, 1999.

Berry, Mary Frances, and John Blassingame. *Long Memory: The Black Experience in America*. New York: Oxford University Press, 1982.

Bigelow, Barbara Carlisle, et al. "Julian Bond, Civil Rights Activist, Politician." In *Contemporary Black Biography*. Detroit, MI: Gale Research International, 1992.

Bowen, William G., and Derek Bok. *The Shape of the River: Long-Term Consequences of Considering Race in College and University Admissions*. Princeton, NJ: Princeton University Press, 1998.

Branch, Taylor. *Parting the Waters: America in the King Years, 1954-1963.* New York: Simon and Schuster, 1988.

_____. *Pillar of Fire: America in the King Years, 1963-1965.* New York: Simon and Schuster, 1998.

Brisbane, Robert H. *The Black Vanguard: Origins of the Negro Social Revolution, 1900-1960.* Valley Forge, PA: Judson Press, 1970.

Broderick, Francis L., and August Meier. *Negro Protest Thought in the Twentieth Century.* Indianapolis, IN: Bobbs-Merrill, 1965.

Carmichael, Stokely, and Charles V. Hamilton. *Black Power: The Politics of Liberation in America.* New York: Random House, 1967.

Carson, Clayborne. *Papers of Martin Luther King, Jr.* 4 vols. Berkeley: University of California Press, 1992-1997.

_____. *In Struggle: SNCC and the Black Awakening of the 1960s.* Cambridge, MA: Harvard University Press, 1981.

Cook, James F. *The Governors of Georgia, 1754-1995.* Macon, GA: Mercer University Press, 1995.

Du Bois, William Edward. *The Autobiography of W. E. B. Du Bois: A Soliloquy on Viewing My Life from the Decade of Its First Century.* New York: International Publishers, 1968.

_____. *The Souls of Black Folk.* New York: Dover Publishing, 1903.

Dickerson, Dennis. *Militant Mediator: Whitney M. Young, Jr.* Lexington: University Press of Kentucky, 1998.

Dyer, Thomas. *The University of Georgia: A Bicentennial History, 1785-1985.* Athens: University of Georgia Press, 1985.

English, T. H. *Emory University, 1915-1965: A Semi-Centennial History.* Atlanta, GA: Higgins-McArthur Company, 1966.

Fairclough, Adam. *Race and Democracy: The Civil Rights Struggle in Louisiana, 1915-1972.* Athens: University of Georgia Press, 1995.

Franklin, John Hope, and Alfred Moss, Jr. *From Slavery to Freedom: A History of Negro Americans.* New York: McGraw-Hill, 1988.

_____. *The Color Line: Legacy for the Twenty-first Century.* Columbia: University of Missouri Press. 1933.

Freyer, Tony. *The Little Rock Crisis.* Greenwich, CT: Greenwood Press, 1984.

Garrow, David. *Bearing the Cross: Martin Luther King, Jr., and the Southern Christian Leadership Conference.* New York: William Morrow, 1986.

Goodman, James. *Stories of Scottsboro.* New York: Pantheon Books, 1994.

Greenberg, Jack. *Crusaders in the Courts: How a Dedicated Band of Lawyers Fought for the Civil Rights Revolution.* New York: Basic Books, 1994.

Griessman, Benjamin, Sarah Jackson, and Annibel Jenkins. *Images and Memories of GA Tech: 1885-1985.* Atlanta: Georgia Institute of Technology Foundation, 1985.

Gurr, Charles S. *The Personal Equation: A Biography of Steadman Vincent Sanford.* Athens: University of Georgia Press, 1999.

Henderson, Harold Paulk. *The Politics of Change in Georgia: A Political Biography of Ellis Arnall.* Athens: University of Georgia Press, 1991.

Higginbotham, Leon, Jr. *Shades of Freedom: Racial Politics and Presumptions of the American Legal Process.* New York: Oxford University Press, 1996.

Hollowell, Louise, and Martin C. Lehfeldt. *The Sacred Call: A Tribute to Donald Hollowell—Civil Rights Champion.* Winter Park, FL: Four-G Publishers, 1997.

Horwitz, Morton J. *The Warren Court and the Pursuit of Justice.* New York: Hill and Wang, 1998.

Hunter-Gault, Charlayne. *In My Place.* New York: First Vintage Books Edition, 1993.

King, Coretta Scott. *The Words of Martin Luther King, Jr.* New York: Newmarket Press, 1983.

King, Martin Luther, Sr. *Daddy King: An Autobiography.* New York: William Morrow, 1980.

Lee, Chana Kai. *For Freedom's Sake: The Life of Fannie Lou Hamer.* Chicago: University of Illinois Press, 1999.

Kluger, Richard. *Simple Justice: The History of Brown v. Board of Education and Black America's Struggle for Equality.* New York: Alfred A. Knopf, 1976.

Lentz, Richard. *Symbols, the News Magazines, and Martin Luther King.* Baton Rouge: Louisiana State University Press, 1990.

Lewis, David L. *W. E. B. Du Bois: Biography of a Race, 1868-1919.* New York: Henry Holt and Company, 1993.

Litwack, Leon F. *Trouble in Mind: Black Southerners in the Age of Jim Crow.* New York: Alfred A. Knopf, 1998.

Logue, Calvin McLeod. *Ralph McGill: Editor and Publisher.* Durham, NC: Moore Publishing Company, 1969.

Martin, Waldo E., Jr. *Brown v. Board of Education: A Brief History with Documents.* Boston: Bedford Books, 1998.

Mays, Benjamin E. *Benjamin E. Mays: Born to Rebel—An Autobiography.* New York: Charles Scribner's Sons, 1971.

McKerns, Joseph P. *Biographical Dictionary of American Journalism.* Greenwich, CT: Greenwood Press, 1989.

McNeil, Genna R. *Groundwork: Charles Hamilton Houston and the Struggle for Civil Rights.* Philadelphia: University of Pennsylvania Press, 1983.

Metcalf, George R. *Up from Within: Today's New Black Leaders.* New York: McGraw-Hill Book Company, 1971.

Meyers, Samuel L. *Desegregation in Higher Education.* New York: University Press of America, 1989.

Miller, Zell. *Great Georgians.* Franklin Springs, GA: Advocate Press, 1983.

Motley, Constance Baker. *Equal Justice Under Law: An Autobiography of Constance Baker Motley.* New York: Farrar, Straus & Giroux, 1998.

Neary, John. *Julian Bond: Black Rebel.* New York: William Morrow and Company, 1971.

Pajari, Roger N. "Herman E. Talmadge and the Politics of Power." In *Georgia Governors in an Age of Change,* ed. Harry P. Henderson and Gary L. Roberts. Athens: University of Georgia Press, 1988.

Powledge, Fred. *Free At Last? The Civil Rights Movement and the People Who Made It.* Boston: Little, Brown and Company, 1991.

Raines, Howell. *My Soul is Rested: Movement Days in the Deep South Remembered.* New York: G. P. Putnam's Sons, 1977.

Roberts, Diane K. *The Jan Kemp Controversy: An Index to Media Coverage.* Athens: University Archives, University of Georgia Libraries, 1987.

Roberts, Gary L. "Tradition and Consensus: An Introduction to Gubernatorial Leadership in Georgia, 1943-1983." In *Georgia Governors in an Age of Change*, ed. Harry P. Henderson and Gary L. Roberts. Athens: University of Georgia Press, 1988.

Ross, Barbara Joyce. *J. E. Spingarn and the Rise of the NAACP, 1911-1939*. New York: Atheneum, 1972.

Rowan, Carl T. *Dream Makers, Dream Breakers: The World of Justice Thurgood Marshall*. Boston: Little, Brown and Company, 1993.

Rudwick, Elliott. *W. E. B. Du Bois: A Study in Minority Group Leadership*. Philadelphia: University of Pennsylvania Press, 1960.

Savage, Barbara Dianne. *Broadcasting Freedom: Radio War and the Politics of Race, 1938-1948*. Chapel Hill: University of North Carolina Press, 1999.

Shipp, Bill. *Murder at Broad River Bridge*. Atlanta, GA: Peachtree Publishers, 1981.

Spalding, Phinizy. *The History of the Medical College of Georgia*. Athens: University of Georgia Press, 1987.

Spalding, Phinizy, and Charles Epps, Jr. "First African-American Graduates of U.S. Medical School." In *African-American Medical Pioneers*, ed. Charles Epps, Jr., Gilman Johnson, and Audrey Vaughan. Rockville, MD: Betz Publishing, 1994.

Talmadge, Herman. *You and Segregation*. Birmingham, AL: Vulcan Press, 1955.

Thirty Years of Lynching in the United States, 1889-1918. New York: National Association for the Advancement of Colored People, 1919.

Trillin, Calvin. *An Education in Georgia: Charlayne Hunter, Hamilton Holmes, and the Integration of the University of Georgia*. Athens: University of Georgia Press, 1991.

Tushnet, Mark V. *Making Civil Rights Law: Thurgood Marshall and the Supreme Court, 1936-1961*. New York: Oxford University Press, 1994.

_____. *The NAACP's Legal Strategy Against Segregated Education, 1925-1950*. Chapel Hill: University of North Carolina Press, 1987.

Weltner, Charles Longstreet. *Southerner*. Philadelphia, PA: J. B. Lippincott, 1966.

White, Walter. *A Man Called White: The Autobiography of Walter White.* New York: Viking Press, 1948.

Williams, Juan. *Eyes on the Prize: America's Civil Rights Years, 1954-1965.* New York: Penguin Books, 1988.

_____. *Thurgood Marshall: American Revolutionary.* New York: Random House, 1998.

Williams, Roger M. *The Bonds: An American Family.* New York: Atheneum, 1971.

Wood, Gwen Y. *A Unique and Fortuitous Combination: An Administrative History of the University of Georgia School of Law.* Athens: University of Georgia Press, 1998.

Zangrando, Robert L. *The NAACP Crusade Against Lynching, 1909-1950.* Philadelphia: Temple University Press, 1980.

Articles from Journals and Periodicals

"A Conversation with Roy Harris and Julian Bond." *Atlanta Magazine,* April 1969, 49-55, 74.

Adams, Charles R., III. "An Oral Interview with Judge W. A. Bootle." *Journal of Southern Legal History* 7 (1999): 115-201.

Cohen, Robert. "G-men in Georgia: The FBI and the Segregationist Riot at the University of Georgia, 1961." *Georgia Historical Quarterly* 83 (1999): 508-538.

_____. "Two, Four, Six, Eight, We Don't Want To Integrate: White Student Attitudes Toward the University of Georgia's Desegregation." *Georgia Historical Quarterly* 80 (1996): 616-645.

Cleghorn, Reese. "The Segs: Perez, Harris, Shelton, Maddox, Simmons: The Five Most Influential Men in the Southern Resistance Tell You Exactly What They Think." *Esquire,* January 1964, 72-76, 133-136.

Crowl, John A. "Davison Resigns as Univ. of Georgia President After Regents Again Fail to Reappoint Him." *Chronicle of Higher Education,* March 19, 1986, 37.

_____. "Ga. Defendants Lose Some Duties." *Chronicle of Higher Education,* March 26, 1986, 36.

DeMarco, Joseph. "The Rationale and Foundation of Du Bois's Theory of Economic Cooperation." *Phylon* 35 (March 1974): 5-15.

Du Bois, William Edward. "Does the Negro Need Separate Schools?" *Journal of Negro Education* 4 (July 1935): 328-335.

_____. "Post script by W. E. B. Du Bois." *The Crisis* 41, no. 1 (January 1934): 20-21; no. 2 (February 1934): 52-53; no. 5 (May 1934): 147-149; no. 6 (June 1934): 182-184.

_____. "Segregation—A Symposium: J. E. Spingarn, David H. Pierce, Leslie Pinckney Hill, and others." *The Crisis* 41, no. 3 (March 1934): 79-82.

Emanuel, Anne S. "Turning the Tide in the Civil Rights Revolution: Elbert Tuttle and the Desegregation of the University of Georgia." *Michigan Journal of Race and Law* 5 (fall 1999): 1-30.

"Excerpts on Segregation Decision." *Georgia Journal*, May 29, 1954, 5.

"Georgia Students 'Burn' Their Governor in Protest of His Academic Meddling." *Life,* October 1941, 43.

Gillis, Lori V. "Insuring Access: Redistricting and Representation." *National Bar Association Magazine*, November/December 1994, 6-8.

Hornsby, Alton, Jr. "Black Public Education in Atlanta, Georgia, 1954-1973: From Segregation to Segregation." *Journal of Negro History* 76 (fall 1991): 21-47.

"Juvenile Damn Foolery." *Time*, December 7, 1953, 56.

Kaufman, Liza. *Fulton County Daily Report*, July 16, 1992 vol. 103, no. 38.

Kuebler, Edward J. "The Desegregation of the University of Maryland." *Maryland Historical Magazine* 71 (spring 1976): 37-49.

Lenoir, Lora D., and James Lenoir. "Compulsory Legal Segregation in the Public Schools with Special Reference to Georgia." *Mercer Law Review* 5 (1954): 211-241.

"Lynching," *The Crisis* 9, no. 5 (March 1915): 225-228.

Motley, Constance Baker. "Remarks on Holmes-Hunter Lecture." *Harvard Blackletter Journal* 5 (spring 1988): 1-11.

Martin, Charles. "Racial Change and 'Big Time' College Football in

Georgia: The Age of Segregation, 1892-1957." *Georgia Historical Quarterly* 80 (1996): 532-562.

Robinson, William H. "Desegregation in Higher Education in the South." *School and Society* 7 (May 1960): 234-239.

Seawright, Sally. "Desegregation at Maryland: The NAACP and the Murray Case in the 1930's." *Maryland Historian* 1 (spring 1970): 59-73.

Shannon, Margaret. "Justice at Last for Horace Ward." *Atlanta Journal and Constitution Magazine*, March 13, 1977, 8, 9.

Southern Negro Youth Congress News Bulletin, October 1946, 1-4.

Turner, Renee. "Remembering the Young King." *Ebony*, January 1988, 40-46.

Willis, Alan Scot. "A Baptist's Dilemma: Christianity, Discrimination and the Desegregation of Mercer University." *Georgia Historical Quarterly* 80 (1996): 595-615.

Newspaper Articles

Associated Press, January 10, 2001.

Athens Banner Herald, November 17, 1953.

Atlanta Constitution, June 24, 1952; November 2, 1952; December 16, 1952; December 5, 1953; November 2, 1964; May 4, 1974; January 25, 1977; December 7, 1978; December 6, 1979; January 16, 1985; February 14, 1986; February 25, 1986; April 23, 1986; May 2, 1986; June 25, 1986; May 5, 1993.

Atlanta Daily World, April 29, 1950; May 9, 1950; June 5, 1950; June 6, 1950; June 11, 1950; June 12, 1951; April 18, 1951; December 14, 1952; December 16, 1952; September 22, 1953; April 9, 1953; March 24, 1956; December 7, 1958; December 9, 1958; August 18, 1964; October 25, 1964; January 12, 1965; March 19, 1976; December 30, 1979.

Atlanta Inquirer, December 17, 1960; June 23, 1962; August 22, 1964; September 12, 1964; September 19, 1964; October 23, 1964; October 24, 1964; November 7, 1964; March 20, 1976.

Atlanta Journal, July 8, 1955; February 10, 1956; January 3, 1957; January 4, 1957; January 21, 1957; February 13, 1957; March 20, 1957; October 13, 1958; May 14, 1959; October 23, 1960; October 24, 1960; October 25, 1960; October 26, 1960; October 28, 1960; August 17, 1961; March 24, 1976; August 19, 1976; November 4, 1979; October 27, 1980; October 5, 1982; March 21, 1986.

Atlanta Journal and Constitution, April 26, 1986.

Augusta Courier, October 2, 1950; October 9, 1950; November 23, 1953; December 14, 1953.

Georgia State Signal, October 5, 1956.

Macon Telegraph/Macon News, December 9, 1953; March 24, 1956; March 14, 1986; April 25, 1986.

New York Times, November 27, 1953.

Red and Black, February 22, 1952; October 8, 1953; October 20, 1953; November 5, 1953; November 12, 1953.

Wall Street Journal, June 29, 1998.

Interviews

Most of the interviews were conducted in person and video recorded in conjunction with producer Janice Reaves and the Georgia Center for Continuing Education. On rare occasions, the interviews were conducted by telephone, noted by the letter (T) below.

Benham, Robert. Atlanta, GA, July 27, 1995.

Bootle, William. Macon, GA, June 14, 2000.

Brisbane, Robert. Atlanta, GA, January 19, 1995.

Brookins, Earnest. Atlanta, GA, May 15, 1995.

Davenport, Chester, Jr. Atlanta, GA, August 28, 1995.

Davis, Priscilla Arnold. Atlanta, GA, May 11, 1995.

Early, Mary Frances. Atlanta, GA, February 19, 1997.

Gloster, Hugh. Atlanta, GA, January 19, 1995.

Hale, Phale. Atlanta, GA, January 19, 1995.

Hill, Jesse, Atlanta, GA, December 17, 1996.

Hollowell, Donald. Atlanta, GA, July 27, 1993; August 22, 1994.

Holmes, Hamilton E. Atlanta, GA, February 24, 1995.

Johnson, Charles S. III. Atlanta, GA, March 16, 2001 (T).

Johnson, Leroy. Atlanta, GA, December 17, 1996.

Jordan, Vernon. Washington, D.C., February 28, 1997.

Killian, Alfred. Athens, GA, July 9, 1997.

Killian, Archibald. Athens, GA, July 9, 1997.

Killian, Darlene. Athens, GA, July 9, 1997.

Leverett, E. Freeman. Elberton, GA, December 8, 1995.

Lundy, Walter A. Atlanta, GA, September 1, 1995.

Mapp, Betty. Atlanta, GA, December 17, 1996.

Malone, Van J. Macon, GA. May 1, 2001 (T).

McCracken, William. Augusta, GA, January 13, 1997.

McIntyre, Edward. Augusta, GA, January 13, 1997.

Motley, Constance Baker. New York, NY, March 30, 1995.

Phelps, Morris. Athens, GA, August 7, 1996.

Pickett, Albert. Augusta, GA, January 13, 1997.

Shipp, Bill. Atlanta, GA, January 23, 1995.

Talmadge, Herman. Hampton, GA, January 23, 1995.

Vandiver, Ernest. Sky Valley, GA, August 14, 1996.

Ward, Horace T. Atlanta, GA, June 29, 1994; August 22, 1994; November 3, 1995 (T); April 15, 1996; November 30, 1998 (T); May 28, 1999; October 29, 2000; February 13, 2001; March 3, 2001 (T).

Ware, Ray. Athens, GA, May 19, 2001. (T)

Papers and Archival Collections

Aderhold, O. C. Papers. Hargrett Rare Book and Manuscript Library/ University of Georgia Libraries, Athens, GA.

Bloch, Charles J. File. Georgiana Collection, Hargrett Rare Book and Manuscript Library/University of Georgia Libraries, Athens, GA.

Boyd, William Madison. Papers (Private Collection of Betty Boyd

Mapp). Atlanta, GA; Special Collections, Atlanta University Robert W. Woodruff Library, Atlanta, GA.

Caldwell, Harmon. Papers. Hargrett Rare Book and Manuscript Library/University of Georgia Libraries, Athens, GA.

Danner, Walter N. Subject File. University of Georgia Hargrett Rare Book and Manuscript Library/University of Georgia Libraries, Athens, GA.

Harris, Roy V. Papers. Richard B. Russell Library for Political Research and Studies/University of Georgia Libraries, Athens, GA.

Hosch, J. Alton. Papers. Hargrett Rare Book and Manuscript Library/University of Georgia Libraries, Athens, GA.

King, Martin Luther, Jr. Collected Papers. Mugar Memorial Library, Boston University, Boston MA.

King, Primus. Papers. Columbus State University Simon Schwob Memorial Library, Columbus, GA.

Lenoir, James J. Papers. Tucson, AZ.

Lundy, Walter A. Collection. Richard B. Russell Library for Political Research and Studies/University of Georgia Libraries, Athens, GA.

Papers of the NAACP. The Campaign for Educational Equality: Legal Department and Central Office Records, 1913-1950, 1951-1955, 1956-1965. The Papers of the NAACP Collection are located at the Library of Congress, Washington, D.C. Reproduced copies of the 1913-1950 and 1951-1955 records are located in the University of Georgia Libraries, Athens, GA; 1956-1965 records are located at the Emory University Robert Woodruff Library, Atlanta, GA.

Sparks, George M. Collection. Georgia State University Special Collections, Georgia State University, Atlanta, GA: Griffin Bell, interview with Clifford Kuhn and William L. Bost, June 12, 1990; Ernest Vandiver, interview with Dr. Charles Pyles, March 20 and July 28, 1986.

Ward, Horace T. Collection. Archives and Special Collections, Robert W. Woodruff Library, Atlanta University Center, Atlanta, GA.

Ward, Horace T. Personal Papers. *Ten Significant Litigated Matters,* unpublished manuscript, 1998; *Politics and the State Senate,* unpublished manuscript, 1998; Governor James Earl Carter taped remarks at the swearing-in ceremony of Horace T. Ward as Fulton County Civil Court Judge; U. S. District Court: Northern District of Georgia, *Oath of Office Ceremony for the Honorable Horace T. Ward* transcript, Atlanta, GA, 1979; U.S. District Court: Northern District of Georgia, *Ceremony Commemorating Senior Status and Portrait Presentation for the Honorable Horace T. Ward, Senior Judge,* United States District Court transcript, Atlanta, GA, 1994.

Court Cases

Alexander v. Bibb Transit Company, C. A. no. 1822 (M.D. Ga. 1962).

Bell et al v. Fulton/DeKalb Hospital Authority, et al., Civil Action #7966 (1964).

Bell v. Georgia Dental Association, 231 F. Supp. 299 (N.D. Ga. 1964).

Brown v. Board of Education, 347 U.S. 483, 74 S. Ct. 686 (1954).

Buchanan v. Warley, 245 U.S. 60 (1917).

Cobb v. Balkom, 339 F. 2d 95 (5th Cir. 1964).

Cobb v. State, 126 S.E. 2d 231, 233, 239 (Ga. 1962).

Cobb v. State, 133 S. E. 2d 596, 601 (Ga. 1963) (denying extraordinary motion for new trial).

Cobb v. State, 222 Ga. 733 (1966).

Cobb v. State, 389 S. Ct. 12 (1967), Relying on *Whitus v. State of Georgia,* 385 U.S. 545 (1967).

Cooper v. Aaron, 358 U.S. 1, 16, 78 S. Ct. 1401, 1409 (1958).

Emory University v. Nash, 218 Ga. 317, 127 S.E. 2d 798 (1962).

Flanigan v. Preferred Development Corporation, 226 Ga. 267 (1970).

Gaines v. Canada, 305 U.S. 337, 352, 59 S. Ct. 232, 238 (1938).

Georgia Association of Retarded Citizens v. McDaniel, 511 F. Supp. 1263 (N.D. Ga. 1981); 716 F. 2d 1565 5th Cir. (1983); 721 F. 2d 822 5th Cir. (1983); 104 S. Ct. 3581 (1984); 740 F. 2d 902 5th Cir. (1984); 105 S. Ct. 1228 (1985).

Guinn v. United States, 238 U.S. 347 (1915).

Harris v. Gibson, 322 F. 2d 780 (5ᵗʰ Cir. 1963).

Holmes v. City of Atlanta, 223 F. 2d 93 (5ᵗʰ Cir. 1955), 350 U.S. 879 (1956).

Holmes v. Danner, 191 F. Supp. 394, 398, 407 (M.D. Ga. 1961).

Hunt v. Arnold, 172 F. Supp. 847 (N.D. Ga. 1959).

Johnson v. Georgia State Board for Vocational Education, Civil Action No. 1523 (N.D. Ga., Rome Division, 1964).

Kemp v. Ervin, 651 F. Supp. 495–499 (N.D. Ga. 1986).

King v. Chapman, 62 F. Supp. 639 (M.D. Ga. 1945).

King v. Chapman, 154 F. 2d 460 (5ᵗʰ Cir. 1946).

King v. State, 119 S.E. 2d 77, 79, 81 (Ga. App. 1961).

Lucy v. Adams, 134 F. Supp. 235 (D.C. N.D. Ala. 1955); *Lucy v. Adams*, 350 U.S. 1, 76 S. Ct. 33 (1955).

McLaurin v. Oklahoma, 339 U.S. 637–642 (1950).

McNeese v. Board of Education, 373 U. S. 688 (1963).

Meredith v. Fair, 306 F. 2d 374 (1962).

Moore v. Dempsey, 261 U.S. 86 (1923).

Nixon v. Herndon, 273 U.S. 536 (1927).

Norris v. State of Alabama, 294 U.S. 587 (1934).

Pearson et al. v. Murray, Court of Appeals of Maryland 592 (1936).

Plessy v. Ferguson, 163 U.S. 537 (1896).

Sipuel v. Board of Regents of University of Oklahoma, 332 U.S. 631, 68 S. Ct. 299 (1948).

Stell v. Savannah-Chatham County Board of Education, 333 F. 2d 55 (5ᵗʰ Cir. 1964).

Smith v. Allwright, 321 U.S. 665 (1944).

Sweatt v. Painter, 339 U.S. 629 (1950).

Taylor v. City of Augusta, Civil Action No. 972 (S. D. Ga. 1962).

United States v. Evans, 910 F. 2d 790 (11ᵗʰ Cir. 1990); 504 U.S. 255, 112 S. Ct. 1881 (1992).

United States v. Rivera; 884 F. 2d 544 (11ᵗʰ Cir. 1989).

Ward v. Regents, 191 F. Supp. 491 (N.D. Ga. 1957).

Public Documents

City Charter. City of Atlanta, Adopted by General Assembly and Approved by Governor, March 16, 1973, City of Atlanta Charter Commission.

City of Atlanta Election, October 2, 1973, and City of Atlanta Runoff Election, October 16, 1973, Summary Reports.

Code of Alabama, Section 181 (Recompiled 1958), Amend. 55 (Ratified 1946).

"Fall 2000: University of Georgia Enrollment Report." University of Georgia Office of Admissions, Athens, Georgia.

General Acts and Resolutions, vol. 1. Georgia Laws 1953, Nov.-Dec. Sess., no. 97 (House Resolution 232-743r).

General Appropriations Act. Secs. 8, 9, Ga. Laws 1951, 425.

General Appropriations Act. Secs. 8, 9, Ga. Laws Jan.-Feb. Sess. 1953, 154.

General Appropriations Act. Secs. 8, 9, Ga. Laws 1956, 762.

Georgia Appeals Reports. Atlanta, GA: Harrison Company, State Publisher, 1974-1982.

Georgia House of Representatives. HR1013 (1998). State of Georgia Government Documents, Atlanta.

Georgia Laws. 1973 Session, City of Atlanta, Atlanta Board of Education reorganized, etc., no. 52 (Senate Bill 49).

Georgia Reports. Atlanta, GA: Harrison Company, State Publisher, 1974–1982.

Griffin, Marvin. "Interposition Is An Appeal to Reason." *Interposition Address of Governor Marvin Griffin*. Atlanta, Georgia Commission on Education, 1956.

Hamilton E. Holmes et al. v. Walter N. Danner et al. Civil Action no. 450 (December 1960), National Archives-Southeast Region, Federal Records Center, East Point, GA.

Hunt v. Arnold. Civil Action no. 5781 (December 1958), National Archives-Southeast Region, Federal Records Center, East Point, GA.

Integrated Post Secondary Education Data System. "University of Georgia Fall Staff Survey, 2000." University of Georgia, Athens, GA.

Journal of the House of Representatives of the State of Georgia, January 12, 1953-December 16, 1953, Atlanta, GA.

Journal of the Senate of the State of Georgia at Regular Session, January 11-March 12, 1965; January 12-February 21, 1970, Atlanta, GA.

Journal of the Senate of the State of Georgia at the Extraordinary Session, September 24-October 8, 1971, Atlanta, GA.

Radio and Television Remarks Upon Signing the Civil Rights Bill, July 2, 1964, National Archives and Records Administration, Lyndon B. Johnson Library and Museum, Austin, TX.

Remarks in the Capitol Rotunda at the Signing of the Voting Rights Act, August 6, 1965, National Archives and Records Administration, Lyndon B. Johnson Library and Museum, Austin, TX.

Senate Bill 40. Georgia Laws 1955 Session, I Gen. Acts and Res. (1955).

Senate Bill 3. Georgia Laws 1959 Session, I Gen. Acts and Res. (1959).

Senate Capital Punishment Committee Report (1966). State Senate, Atlanta, GA.

Southeastern Reporter. Minneapolis: West Publishing Company, 1974-1982.

State Flag, Senate Bill 98. Georgia Laws, 1956 Session. General Acts and Resolutions, vol. 1.

The Southern Manifesto, 102nd Congressional Record 4515-16, 1956.

University System of Georgia Board of Regents Minutes. April 23, 1943; August 11, 1943; July 12, 1950; June 11, 1952; April 10, 1957. Atlanta, GA.

U.S. Statutes at Large, 78. Public Laws 24th Amendment to the Constitution, *Civil Rights Act of 1964,* July 2, 1964, Public Law 88-352, 78, Stat. 241.

U S. Statutes at Large, 79. Public Laws, Public Law 89-110, *Voting Rights Act of 1965*, August 6, 1965.

Horace T. Ward v. Regents of the University System of Georgia. Civil Action no. 4355 (1956), National Archives-Southeast Region, Federal Records Center, East Point, GA.

Television Transcripts/Radio Presentations

Boyd, William Madison. WERD Radio Taped Presentations, 1954, 1955. Atlanta, Georgia.

Foot Soldier for Equal Justice: Horace T. Ward and the Desegregation of the University of Georgia. Georgia Public Television Broadcast, 2000, 2001, Maurice C. Daniels, ex. prod., Janice Reaves, prod., George Rodrigues, co-prod., Derrick Alridge, academic adviser, University of Georgia Center for Continuing Education. Video Documentary.

Index

243

250